The Thriving Pastor is a must-read for every pastor who desires not just to survive ministry but to flourish in it. With honesty and clarity, Richard Black addresses the issues many of us feel but rarely articulate, areas we often overlook or avoid. He speaks with the wisdom of experience and the heart of a shepherd, offering insight that is both deeply personal and profoundly practical. This book is timely, necessary, and deeply strengthening. I highly recommend it to pastors at every stage of their journey.

— **Boyd Ratnaraja**
National Leader, Elim Church of New Zealand

It's not easy to write a book that is both optimistic about local church ministry and brutally honest about the current challenges pastors face. Richard Black is deeply aware of the factors that undermine effective church leadership, and he's got a plan to help pastors thrive, not just survive. If you're yearning for a healthier sense of self, a clearer calling to ministry, and stronger alignment in your church work, read this book.

— **Dr Michael Frost**
Morling College, Sydney

I have known Richard for many years in his capacity as a consultant, coach, and counsellor to our church. This book is timely and much needed. My background in business and church leadership, and pastoral training, leads me to conclude that the role of the pastor in the contemporary church is too often not working. Richard illustrates that the root cause will not be addressed by just trying to make pastors more resilient. Issues of role definition and the organizational system need to be questioned. The role definition is often flawed, expectations unachievable, and church systems failing our pastors, too often leading to a spiritual and mental health crisis. My hope is that Richard's book will be a catalyst, not just for pastors but for our churches, denominations and ministry training institutions, to rethink our whole approach to church leadership.

— **Mark Powell**
Former CEO, Warehouse Group
Team Leader, Whangaparaoa Baptist Church

Richard Black has written a timely and deeply researched book that names what so many pastors feel but struggle to articulate. The evidence he presents on the emotional intelligence of clergy is sobering, and his analysis of how the pastoral role itself contributes to psychological harm deserves serious attention from every denomination and training institution. What makes this book so valuable is the way Black integrates rigorous research with pastoral sensitivity, offering a clear framework for realigning identity, calling, and role. I recommend this book to every pastor, denominational leader, and theological educator who cares about the health and fruitfulness of those who lead our churches.

— **Graham Joseph Hill OAM PhD**

Assoc Professor, Charles Sturt University

Author of more than thirty books, including *World Christianity*

Richard Black's *The Thriving Pastor* is a timely and deeply insightful contribution to the ongoing conversation about pastoral wellbeing and sustainable ministry. Drawing on research, theological reflection, and practical wisdom, Richard writes from a place of deep compassion and lived experience. Having benefited from attending Richard's workshops, I am consistently impressed by his integrity, clarity, and pastoral heart. In his book, he addresses the hidden pressures that shape pastoral identity, calling and effectiveness, offering both honest diagnosis and hopeful pathways for realignment. This is an invaluable resource for pastors, church leaders, and those involved in ministry formation. I warmly recommend *The Thriving Pastor* to anyone in ministry who longs not just to survive, but to thrive in their calling.

— **Dr Francine Bennett**

Former Principal of Pathways Bible College

Senior Lecturer in Education, Laidlaw College

I've long trusted Richard Black—he brings a researcher's rigour and a pastor's heart to everything he does, and this book is no exception. *The Thriving Pastor* is one of the most honest and hopeful books I've read on pastoral ministry in years. Richard names what too many leaders quietly know: something is stuck, and the story needs to change. What alarmed me most was the research showing that emotional intelligence in clergy actually decreases the longer they serve—but Richard's gift is making confronting realities like this simple and—crucially—changeable. In a city like Auckland, where 250,000 people attend a church gathering at least monthly, books like this call us to see ourselves as one team, clarify what success actually looks like, and pursue healthy, fruitful mission together. This should be at the top of the list for every pastor and leadership team to read—especially together.

— **Jonathan Dove**
Senior Pastor, Gracecity Church
Executive Chair, Auckland Church Network

I can't wait for this book to be published so I can recommend it to all the pastors I know! Richard deals carefully with the issues that plague church ministers, and he does so with kindness and deep insight gained from many hours of listening to their hearts. More than that, this is also a book to be read by those who know a pastor and want to help him or her thrive. It paints a convincing and hopeful picture of how a pastor and a church can fulfil God's call, and maybe even have fun doing so.

— **Rev Canon Simon Martin**
Bishop's Chaplain in the Nelson Anglican Diocese

Richard's genuine concern and passion for pastors' wellbeing shines brightly throughout his book. He highlights one of the key pitfalls of ministry, namely when a pastor's identity becomes fused with the role. To address this issue, he offers a healthy distinction between identity, calling, and role, and practical exercises to help pastors distinguish and align these three key areas in their lives. The book is also full of personal stories and examples from Richard's work with pastors that will resonate with anyone in pastoral ministry. I believe this book will be a valuable resource to help pastors I work with across Aotearoa to thrive in ministry.

— **Dr. Glenn Melville**
Director, Carey Centre for Lifelong Learning

In the church in New Zealand, where I get to lead, we are at a moment of crisis of leadership. We don't have enough leaders to sustain existing churches, and we need more thriving gospel-centred churches for those who don't yet know Jesus. It means we need to help existing leaders to lead more healthily and sustainably. It means we need to raise up a new generation of leaders who can do the same. *The Thriving Pastor* is a timely and vital contribution to this work. I am so grateful to Richard for his expertise and investment in my leadership over the past decade. I hope this book is read widely, reflected upon deeply and applied relentlessly.

— **Simon Gill**
Senior Pastor, The Street Church

Richard Black offers something really refreshing for anyone in pastoral ministry. He has a way of holding up a mirror that brings clarity and insight to what's really going on beneath the surface. His writing feels honest, practical, and full of hope, pointing to down to earth ways to grow in health, resilience, and genuine fulfilment. This book will help church leaders feel seen, supported, and encouraged in every aspect of the world they navigate each day. I know I'll be picking this book up again, and I recommend it without hesitation to anyone who's walking the day to day realities of ministry.

— **Major Kylie Tong**
The Salvation Army, Wellington

The Thriving Pastor brims with Richard's trademark pithy wisdom and insight, and his heartfelt passion for pastors, churches, and the kingdom of God. I found it to be necessary reading - thought-provoking, challenging, and bravely asking important questions that we might be too busy or nervous to ask. Not only are questions asked, but practical and doable solutions are offered, and, as sons and daughters and stewards of God's church, we would do well to read this, consider its wisdom carefully, and boldly make some changes to safeguard and champion the church and its ministers for a thriving future.

— **Tessa Cameron**
Te Kāinga C3 Church

THE THRIVING PASTOR

**TORN CURTAIN PUBLISHING**
Auckland, New Zealand
www.torncurtainpublishing.com

ISBN Softcover 978-1-991299-93-2
ISBN EPub 978-1-991299-94-9

Unless otherwise noted, all scripture is taken from the New International Version®, NIV®. Copyright © 1973, 1978, 1984, 2011 by Biblica, Inc.™ Used by permission of Zondervan. All rights reserved worldwide.

Scripture quotations marked ESV are from The Holy Bible, English Standard Version®, copyright © 2001 by Crossway, a publishing ministry of Good News Publishers. Used by permission. All rights reserved.

Scripture quotations marked AMP are taken from the Amplified® Bible (AMPC), Copyright © 1954, 1958, 1962, 1964, 1965, 1987 by The Lockman Foundation. Used by permission. www.lockman.org.

Scripture quotations marked TPT are from The Passion Translation®. Copyright © 2017, 2018 by Passion & Fire Ministries, Inc. Used by permission. All rights reserved. ThePassionTranslation.com.

Scripture quotations marked NRSV are from the Revised Standard Version of the Bible, Copyright © 1946, 1952, and 1971 the Division of Christian Education of the National Council of the Churches of Christ in the United States of America. Used by permission. All rights reserved.

Typeset in Raleway, Minion Pro, Myriad Pro, Brittanic Bold

Cataloguing in Publishing Data
Title: The Thriving Pastor: Realigning Ministry so Leaders Excel and Churches Flourish
Author: Richard Black
Subjects: Christian ministry, pastoral issues, leadership wellbeing, organisational psychology, counseling (for pastoral care), education (for leadership training), models of ministry.

A copy of this title is held at the National Library of New Zealand.

THE THRIVING PASTOR

REALIGNING MINISTRY SO LEADERS EXCEL AND CHURCHES FLOURISH

RICHARD BLACK

*To Jennifer, my beloved wife, companion, and greatest
cheerleader. Thank you for your unwavering support and belief.
To my children, Ellena, Brontë and Elliot, and Leo. Thank you
for the deep joy you bring me simply by existing.
To Jesus, my Lord, Saviour, and friend. It is all about
You. May Your Kingdom come, Your leaders thrive,
and Your Church transform this world by the power of
the Holy Spirit and for the glory of the Father.*

FOREWORD

Every generation of the church faces the same question: how do we sustain vibrant, life-giving leadership in communities that easily drift toward maintenance and institutional gravity? Pastors frequently enter ministry with a deep sense of vocation. Over time that vocation can become entangled in expectations, structures, and inherited assumptions about what a pastor must do in order for the church to function. The result becomes a gradual loss of alignment between the leader's calling and the actual practice of ministry.

My old friend and colleague Richard Black addresses this challenge with wisdom and pastoral realism. *The Thriving Pastor* helps leaders rediscover the centre from which all authentic Christian leadership flows—identity in Jesus and participation in the mission of God. In language that pastors will immediately recognise, Black exposes the subtle ways pastoral vocation becomes absorbed into the machinery of church life. His image of the "jammed rudder" captures a dynamic that many leaders experience: activity continues, programs run, yet the deeper orientation of the church quietly drifts away from the original apostolic impulse.

What makes this book so valuable lies in its recovery of calling. In my own work I have often described the church's missional vitality through reactivating the essential elements embedded in the life of the early Jesus movement. When those elements come alive again, leadership becomes generative, discipleship becomes catalytic, and communities begin to embody the life of Jesus in fresh ways. Black's work contributes to this recovery by helping pastors realign identity, vocation, and role around the mission of God.

This realignment matters deeply. When leaders rediscover their God-given calling, the church gains new imagination for its participation in God's redemptive purposes in the world. Energy flows again through the body of Christ. Pastoral leadership becomes less about sustaining an institution and more about cultivating a community of disciples caught up in the adventure of the kingdom.

Richard Black writes as a seasoned practitioner who understands the pressures of ministry from the inside. His insights will resonate with pastors who sense that something in the ecology of leadership requires renewal. *The Thriving Pastor* offers a hopeful and practical guide for that journey. I gladly commend it to those who long to see local church leadership flourish again in service of the mission of Jesus.

— **Alan Hirsch**
Award-winning author of numerous books
on missional leadership, organization, and spirituality.
Founder of Forge Missional Training Network,
100 Movements, and the 5Q Collective.

CONTENTS

Prologue: Dear Pastor . . . Some Good News   1

Introduction: "Houston, We Have a Problem!"   3

PART ONE   MISALIGNED MINISTRY   13

Chapter 1   The Jammed Rudder   15

Chapter 2   Ministry in Reverse   41

Chapter 3   Identity: Sourced in the Wrong Master   46

Chapter 4   Calling: Sleeping in the Wrong Bed   59

Chapter 5   Role: Succeeding in the Wrong Jungle   71

Chapter 6   Blinded to Dysfunction, Blinded by Success   81

Chapter 7   The Wider Church System   93

Chapter 8   How Do You Turn a Super Tanker?   101

A Biblical Interlude: Overcoming the Impossible   107

PART TWO   FREE-FLOWING MINISTRY   111

Chapter 9   The Pastor's Identity: Keys for Differentiation   113

Chapter 10   The Gravitational Pull of Counterfeits   124

Chapter 11   Sourced in the Right Master   132

Chapter 12   Centred in Jesus   147

Chapter 13   The Pastor's Calling   155

Chapter 14   Clarifying Your Macro Call   163

Chapter 15   Sleeping in the Right Bed   177

Chapter 16   Succeeding in the Right Jungle   192

Chapter 17   Clarifying Kingdom Outcomes   203

Chapter 18   The Importance of Aaron and Hur 221

To the Pastor . . . A Vision for the Future 229

About the Author 232

About Thriving Churches HQ 234

Your Next Steps in the Thriving Pastor Journey 235

A Final Word 236

Endnotes 237

PROLOGUE

DEAR PASTOR . . . SOME GOOD NEWS

I want to start with some good news. We need it. We all know how tough ministry can be, and I want you to thrive in ministry. Not just survive, get by, or even do a good job—but genuinely excel! I want you to be who God created you, gifted you, and called you to be. That's what this book is all about.

I deeply care about you—and every church leader—and the life and ministry you are leading. Because it is not only about you. When leaders are flourishing, they release Kingdom power and potential in the church they are leading and enable that church to make a greater Kingdom impact in their community. This is what I want to see and be a part of: transformed churches transforming their communities. It is something we all want but do not always see.

Each pastor is at a different place in their flourishing. Some of you reading this are going through mental health challenges. Some of you came into ministry already struggling in certain areas, while others may have developed those mental health difficulties during your ministry or even as a result of your ministry.

Many of you are stuck. You feel like you are treading water or experiencing another Groundhog Day in ministry. Others will be doing well. You are enjoying your ministry—and praise God for that!

Wherever you are in your ministry journey and whatever you might be experiencing, I want to give you some good news, some very good news.

Your ministry life can be decidedly better than it is right now. This is not just some inspirational message or wishful thinking, but the result of many years of ministry, research, and clinical work supervising and coaching pastors.

Although ministry can be hard—no one said it would be easy—there are dynamics occurring that make it harder than it needs to be. There are, in fact, several factors that are needlessly sabotaging pastors in the Western Church, whether they are pastoring within a mainline denomination or an independent Pentecostal church, whether their church is small and stagnant or large and growing. Yet when these factors are addressed, and healthier alternatives are put in place, both the wellbeing and effectiveness of pastors show improvement.

Whatever your story, situation, or success, I want you to be healthy, whole, equipped, released, and thriving. When you fully understand who God has created you to be and what He has called you to do, everyone benefits, and God's Kingdom comes more and more.

A NOTE ABOUT THE TERM 'PASTOR'

Throughout the book, the general term 'pastor' is used to describe all those leading a local church community. Even though different denominations use terms like 'minister', 'priest', 'vicar', 'clergy', or 'officer', I want you to know that the terminology I have chosen includes you all.

INTRODUCTION

"HOUSTON, WE HAVE A PROBLEM!"

So now the bad news. You knew it was coming.

Ministry is in crisis.

You may not realise there is a crisis on any given Sunday. Church services are still occurring, people are still attending, and sermons are still being preached. Some of you may be sceptical about this. You know ministry is not easy, but is it really in crisis?

As we step back and look at patterns across the Western Church, we see a disturbing picture emerge that relates to the wellbeing of pastors and the effectiveness of churches within an increasingly secular culture.

Here are the highlights of those lowlights.

- Church leaders continue to report mental health challenges at a higher level than the general public.[1]
- The role of the pastor is negatively impacting the emotional intelligence of those in the role.[2]
- We have seen the fall of high-profile church leaders, who many looked to as heroes and mentors, and whose churches were considered models to follow.
- Most denominations are experiencing decline and have been for decades, especially the mainstream churches.[3]
- Many denominations are reporting a worrying lack of new leaders entering training for ministry.[4]

- Most churches' confidence in their ability to evangelise effectively is alarmingly low.[5]
- The relevance, purpose, and potency of the Church are increasingly being questioned.

As one commentator put it:

> "One of the more interesting public conversations has been about whether churches are essential to a society. Are we dispensers of goods and services? Are we optional gatherings like concerts and sporting events? Are worship services leisure activities or sacred duties? . . . there is no ignoring it: Christianity's influence in society has been receding . . . Christians are seen as irrelevant at best, dangerous at worst."[6]

If we take a closer look at the personal experience of pastors, the reports are quite concerning. Certainly, the challenges of pastoral ministry are well recognised, and it is commonly understood to be an emotionally demanding role. Then again, so are many professions. So, it would be fair to ask: Is it really that bad? Is the personal impact of the role of a pastor any worse than other demanding jobs? Is this not simply the reality of this type of work and lifestyle? When we delve into the research, the answers to these questions are not just bleak but staggering and alarming. In fact, just by taking a cursory look, it is evident that the role of pastoring is impacting church leaders detrimentally in several ways.

THE IMPACT ON PASTORS' WELLBEING AND MENTAL HEALTH

Across the Western world, pastors continue to show moderate to high levels of mental and emotional distress.[7] This shows up in a litany of negative and detrimental outcomes, including but not limited to the following:

- Loneliness
- Isolation
- Feelings of inadequacy

- Serious conflict
- Anxiety
- Depression
- Stress
- Psychological distress
- Emotional exhaustion
- Repression of emotions
- Burnout
- Sexual misconduct
- Reduced emotional intelligence
- Non-constructive forms of stress relief
- Non-mutually beneficial forms of resolving conflict
- Spiritual dryness or numbness
- Doubting one's calling
- High turnover (leaving the role)[8]

Even though these detrimental outcomes have been evident for decades, and the mental health and wellbeing of pastors is now at an all-time low, it is both heartbreaking and intensely frustrating to see that very little has changed about the role.[9] In fact, Rae Jean Proeschold-Bell and Jason Byassee recently documented the results of a decade-long study in the United States that outlined the negative psychological impact on pastors, showing them to have a higher rate of mental health challenges than the general public.[10] The United States is not alone in this, as research from other countries reflects similar results. Another author summarised the research in this area by saying,

> "There is evidentiary consensus that clergy experience physical, social, and emotional harm to a greater degree than other helping professions and the general population."[11]

With these types of outcomes, it is surprising anyone wants to work as a pastor.

THE IMPACT ON PASTORS' EMOTIONAL INTELLIGENCE

One of the most staggering outcomes concerns the impact of the role on a pastor's emotional intelligence (EI). Emotional intelligence refers to our ability to manage emotions—our own and others. It is our emotional skillset. The term 'emotional intelligence' was first coined by psychologists Mayer and Salovey, who defined it as:

> "The ability to perceive accurately, appraise, and express emotion; the ability to access and/or generate feelings when they facilitate thought; the ability to understand emotion and emotional knowledge; and the ability to regulate emotions to promote emotional and intellectual growth."[12]

The American psychologist and author, Daniel Goleman, has popularised the notion of emotional intelligence, famously stating that it matters more than IQ.[13] He later refined his definition as:

> "The capacity for recognizing our own feelings and those of others, for motivating ourselves, and for managing emotions well in ourselves and in our relationships."[14]

Since it is measurable, EI is often used as a concrete way to evaluate the more intangible concept of emotional health. It is also a key factor in our emotional resilience and our ability to establish and maintain healthy relationships, including working through conflict constructively.[15] These two crucial skills underpin our wellbeing and people-ability, and as such, are essential for pastoral ministry. More than that, high EI is considered a crucial quality in leadership, and the key difference separating higher performing, productive, effective and seemingly gifted leaders from others.[16] We must, therefore, take measures of EI seriously as we seek to understand and determine the wellbeing and effectiveness of pastors.

Understandably, it is often assumed that pastors will exhibit higher emotional intelligence and possess superior emotional resources to enhance their resilience because they operate in a role that is rich with relational and emotional components.[17] Pizarro and Salovey went so far as to say that:

> "Religious organizations are often inherently 'emotionally intelligent' organizations. These organizations efficiently impart emotional skills to the believer and thus maintain the believer's psychological and physical well-being."[18]

If you live, breathe and work in a highly relational environment, it makes sense to assume that you will grow in emotional intelligence and people skills. Surprisingly, however, research shows that not only is this not the case for pastors, but the opposite is true.[19]

Using different assessment tools in different countries across different denominations, pastors consistently demonstrated lower EI than the general public.[20] Wow! This is staggering. Now, is this because the Church attracts people with lower EI to the role, or does the role itself lower their EI? The answer—drumroll please—is the latter. Let that sink in for a moment. There is something about the role of the pastor that is detrimental to the emotional intelligence of our pastors.

Let us look at what a sample of the research reveals about the impact of the role on pastors' emotional intelligence. A pioneering, fourteen-year longitudinal study that investigated the EI of Anglican clergy in England and Wales showed clergy to have a lower EI than almost any other group that had used the assessment tool. It concluded, "It may be that the clergy role shrinks the EI [emotional intelligence] of the clergy."[21]

Another piece of research exploring the emotional intelligence of pastors predominantly from the Baptist denomination in the southern United States found that instead of EI increasing the longer a person was in ministry, the opposite was the case.[22] Those with fewer years in ministry had higher emotional intelligence than those who had been in ministry for longer.

In a third study, investigating the EI of Irish clergy, clergy members were found to have a significantly lower EI score than therapists, a slightly lower score than a group of prisoners, and a score similar to those in a substance abuse recovery programme.[23]

We need to pause here for a moment and do a shout-out to female pastors, who repeatedly scored higher in their emotional intelligence than their male counterparts across different countries, denominations, and assessment tools. To be fair, their emotional intelligence was still not great, but they did fare better than their male counterparts.[24]

Clearly, this is a massively disturbing trend, and it is critically important for anyone involved in ministry or the training and oversight of pastors to acknowledge it, investigate it, and create strategies to rectify this outcome. We cannot, with any good conscience, leave our pastors to experience the same detrimental effects over and over.

THE IMPACT ON PASTORS' CONFLICT RESOLUTION ABILITY

Another indicator that the role itself has a detrimental effect on pastors is evident in the second study I mentioned, which also explored pastors' methods of resolving conflict or conflict management style (CMS). There are five commonly used methods for managing conflict.

- Accommodating (I lose/you win)
- Avoiding (We both lose)
- Competing (I win/you lose)
- Compromising (We both win and lose)
- Collaborating (We both win)

The last two, 'compromising' and 'collaborating', are generally seen as the two most constructive forms of managing and resolving conflict, with 'collaborating' considered the best. High levels of emotional intelligence are generally an asset when it comes to resolving conflict, and there is a strong correlation between the two. Studies have repeatedly shown that people in the general public or in secular leadership who have higher emotional intelligence will use constructive conflict management strategies.[25] Surprisingly, however, this was not the case for pastors in Christopher Gambill's study, which showed *no* correlation between EI and CMS.

> "No significant correlations between the two were found . . . conflict management style and emotional intelligence seemed [to] be unrelated constructs. Knowing an individual's emotional intelligence score could not be used to predict which conflict management style that individual might prefer. In the same way, knowing someone's preferred conflict management style could not be used to predict that person's relative level of emotional intelligence."[26]

This research indicates that something about the role itself is preventing pastors from effectively accessing and applying their emotional skillset when managing conflict.

STUCK IN UNHEALTHY EXPECTATIONS

The reduced wellbeing and emotional intelligence of pastors is clearly a problem. Yet, these unhealthy patterns have not been addressed, at least not in any substantial way, to improve these detrimental outcomes.

This is evident in my clinical work. For many pastors, the role and the demands of ministry are taking a serious toll. Some are feeling depressed, others are despondent or frustrated. Some are struggling but will not leave for fear of failing, letting key people down, or never being welcomed back into a pastoral role. Others feel the pressure to achieve and become fixated on growing the church to the point where they churn through staff or are too demanding of their people.

Why do we, year after year, continue to recruit, train and release men and women into a ministry environment that is producing such unhealthy and damaging results? This is not happening intentionally, but it should raise some questions. What is occurring, why is it occurring, and why have we not addressed it before now?

The answer, in part, is that we have not been aware of the true extent of the problem. We know that some pastors are struggling, but we view them as the exception, not the rule. We may also just assume that the detrimental outcomes we see in the lives of pastors are a normal but unfortunate byproduct of the role. Ministry is a calling and a sacrifice, after all, so we surely shouldn't expect it to be easy!

Before we go any further and look more closely at the hidden saboteurs in ministry, I do need to clarify something. While the role of a pastor is not intrinsically damaging to a person's health and wellbeing, it appears to be inherently so. This is an important distinction. What this means is that the role is not toxic in and of itself (intrinsic), but rather, there are significant elements embedded in the role which could potentially have a detrimental impact (inherent). In other words, it is our expectations and execution of the role (the way we do the role), rather than the role itself, that is proving harmful.

Another reason we are stuck in this unhealthy pattern is that we are so invested in the current model of church ministry that we either do not know how to change or do not want to. The church, the denomination, and the ministerial training institutions (MTIs), which comprise the wider church system surrounding the pastor, are all unintentionally contributing to the negative outcomes we are seeing. The focus within this church system has simply been on how to do 'church' better, how to tweak the model, or how to make pastors more resilient within the role.

There is almost a sense that our current model of ministry, including the job description of a pastor, was established by Jesus Himself, rather than being constructed by humans over the centuries as a means of fulfilling what Jesus has commanded us. It does not necessarily mean that what we are doing is intrinsically wrong, nor does it mean that the way we are doing it now is how we always have to do it. We need to step back, assess, pray, and re-evaluate what ministry looks like from Jesus' perspective, then explore healthy and constructive ways to fulfil that. The danger comes when we confuse our own investment in the model of ministry with Jesus' plans and purposes for the Church.

It is important, then, that we not only look at the hidden saboteurs impacting pastors and how to overcome them, but also consider the unhelpful influence of the wider church system and what needs to be done to realign it. We cannot effectively address the former without also addressing the latter. If we do not change the wider system, then any change the pastor applies to their own life and ministry will likely be short-lived. Systems are powered and empowered to maintain the status quo. As such, our journey to help pastors overcome these hidden saboteurs will focus on both the pastor and the wider church system. To that end, the book is split into two sections:

Section One explores the problem, what I refer to as 'the pastor's jammed rudder'. We will first explore the factors that put pressure on pastors and reveal the unhealthy ministry model most pastors are caught in that undermines their wellbeing and limits their effectiveness. Following that, we will do a deep dive into the three components of this unhealthy model of ministry: identity, calling, and role. The final two chapters of part one zoom out to include the wider church system and the force it is exerting to maintain this unhealthy model of ministry. I demonstrate how key stakeholders unintentionally contribute to reinforcing this unhealthy system and what an alternative, healthier system could look like.

Section Two offers a solution for unjamming the pastor's rudder. We will start by outlining how to bring a pastor's identity, calling and role into a healthy realignment. Then our focus will shift to how the wider church system can support this healthy realignment by redefining and realigning the markers of success with Kingdom outcomes. I offer specific recommendations to the key stakeholders on how they can support a healthier ministry model and end with a call to revolutionise ministry by releasing pastors to excel and churches to flourish.

The good news is that the bad news no longer has to be the norm. There is hope. To reach that new normal, however, and understand what is occurring and why, we need to take a closer look below the surface.

PART ONE

MISALIGNED MINISTRY

1

THE JAMMED RUDDER

Kerry Spackman is a sports psychologist. He works with the top echelon of athletes, including Formula One racing drivers, the New Zealand All Blacks rugby team, and high-performance units. Kerry tells the story of when he challenged Steve Ferguson, a champion kayaker, to a race on the water over 100m.[1] I imagine the conversation going something like this:

"Hey Steve, how about you and I have a race?"

"What! Oh, Kerry, I would blitz you. It wouldn't even be a competition. Don't embarrass yourself."

"Nah, come on. Give it a go."

"Okay, okay, it's your funeral."

The race is set. People gather around to watch this mismatched race between a champion kayaker and a sports psychologist. Steve and Kerry get into their respective boats, they steady themselves, and the gun goes off. Kerry starts paddling as fast as his arms will allow, churning up the water as he goes. Steve, however, being the consummate professional that he is, takes long, rhythmic, powerful strokes—that is, until he finds his boat pulling in the wrong direction. The onlookers watch as Kerry pulls out in front of Steve. Bemused by this, Steve digs deeper and paddles harder; however, it is Kerry who ultimately wins. I can imagine Steve getting out of his boat, wandering over to Kerry, and saying, "Okay, fair enough, you won. But you've got to tell me how you did it!"

"Oh, it was quite simple," Kerry replies, "I got down here before anyone else showed up, and I jammed your rudder to the right. It didn't matter how hard you paddled; you were going nowhere fast."

This is a brilliant analogy for what is occurring in ministry. Many pastors are busting their guts trying to serve their Lord and lead His people. They are working tirelessly. They are dedicated, called, and faithful, but they do not seem to be making the progress they hoped for. What they do not realise is that deep below the surface, below their conscious awareness, their rudder has been jammed. The harder they work, the more weary, exhausted, disappointed, and disillusioned they become. Nobody wants this. Nobody intends for this to happen. Most of the time, pastors are not even aware that it is occurring, although they often have a hunch that *something* is not right.

Since we are not aware of the problem, we have not seen it, and if we cannot see it, we cannot address it. What can keep us blind to the problem is our tendency to spiritualise or internalise the issue. We may use internal language like:

> "Well, God never said ministry would be easy. This is just part of the sacrifice of serving."

> "I feel called here, so this must be what God wants for me. I just need to submit myself to how things are."

> "I will just do what I can do, and I'll leave the rest to God."

> "God knows if my ministry flourished, I might become proud, so He is using this to keep me humble and refine me."

Whatever language we use, the outcome is the same. There can be a spiritual resignation, which leads to tiredness, loneliness, disappointment, and lack of progress. This is completely understandable, because, after all, what else can you do when you sense that God has called you to the ministry and the church you are in? It may be that God is refining you—or maybe deep below the surface, your rudder is jammed.

Equally, we may say that ministry is spiritual warfare. The enemy is obviously attacking us. Now it might indeed be the case that spiritual warfare is going on—or it may just be that your rudder is jammed.

Alternatively, pastors may internalise the experience. They conclude that ministry is hard, and they doubt whether they are really cut out for it. They doubt their abilities, their giftedness, and even their calling. They will often compare themselves with other leaders whose ministry seems 'successful' and be left with a profound sense of inadequacy and failure. Despondency sets in. They may consider leaving ministry, but often will stay, finding ways to quiet but never remove the nagging sense of their own inadequacy and failure. I have sat with countless pastors who experience this daily.

Please do not mishear me: many factors make ministry and leadership difficult. I am not saying that it should all be plain sailing. What I am saying is that many pastors are experiencing the effects of a jammed rudder, and we need to straighten them out before we can more effectively address other issues in ministry. Church leadership is not easy, but the current model of ministry and the inherent role of the pastor are not only making it harder for them but are also proving to be psychologically and spiritually harmful.

What is this jammed rudder in ministry? It is an unhealthy model of ministry that is steering most pastors. It is the way we have shaped the role of the pastor, the mindset pastors put on when they step into that role, and the way they practically outwork their life and ministry in that role. The rudder is the model of ministry in which pastors live and work. I will clarify this as we go on, but let me first outline five factors that are sabotaging pastors, their ministry, and their wellbeing. These five saboteurs are jamming the rudder of the pastor.

FIVE SABOTEURS IN MINISTRY

When I was in pastoral ministry, I certainly felt various pressures, but if you had asked me at the time what they were, I would not have been able to answer you specifically. Instead, I would have given a more general answer about how hard it is to make it all work. Trying to balance being a husband and father with pastoring. Trying to lead the church to health and growth. Trying to manage people well and manage the limited resources we had. If I were being honest, I would have also told you about the weight of the expectations placed on me by myself and others, and the ever-present question: *Was I any good at leading a church?*

In my clinical work, I have had the privilege of journeying with numerous pastors and have seen, firsthand, the pressure that so many of them are under. If I were to ask them what was causing this pressure, they might point to such things as: conflict with staff or a church member, the demands in the role and the time-consuming nature of it all (having to do sermon preparation on Saturday night, for example), or disappointment at the lack of volunteers or attendance on Sunday. In some situations, they may even internalise the issue as being their fault—they were clearly not good enough, failing, or just not cut out for pastoral ministry.

When I left pastoring and was retraining as a counsellor, I was keen to explore this question further. What is causing this high level of pressure and mental health challenges we are seeing in pastors? Is it an accumulation of circumstantial events, or is something else going on? As a result of my master's research, I was able to identify five factors that are sabotaging the wellbeing and effectiveness of pastors:

1. Over-identification with the role
2. Misdirected calling
3. Pull to perfectionism
4. Isolation
5. Misdirected spirituality

As we will see, these five saboteurs exist within the inner world of the pastor but are also shaped and perpetuated by the system and culture around them. All five factors overlap and influence one another. The first two pertain to identity and overall ministry purpose, and are the most significant, while the following two are concerned with how pastors live and minister as a result of the first two. The final factor is about how pastoral leaders relate to God. Together, these five saboteurs have the potential to make pastors more psychologically vulnerable and restrain their effectiveness in the role. Let's take a closer look at them now.

1. Over-identification With the Role

Of all the saboteurs, this one is probably the most powerful and foundational, yet it is also the most obscure. It is the one pastors find most difficult to acknowledge and identify in their own lives because it is like asking a fish to describe water. When I explain it to pastors, their initial response is often, "I can see how that would be an issue for others." It is not until we take a closer look at the symptoms that we discover that far from this being an extraordinary issue that *others go through*, it is, in fact, an issue commonly affecting those in leadership.

Over-identification with the role occurs when the role transitions from simply being a job that pastors are doing, to becoming a key part of their identity. According to *Role Identity Theory*, people may internalise their social and vocational roles in ways that profoundly shape their understanding of self, worth, and sense of purpose.[2] This isn't just about a person associating with a specific role, occupation, or job; rather, it is an enmeshment or fusion of their identity with the role—the role becomes *who they are.*

Pastors are especially susceptible to this 'enmeshment' because their work is typically viewed as a calling or a vocation, where their service to God and their community is an expression of their faith. It encapsulates so much of their life. It is who they are. Even as you read this, you may be thinking, *But being a pastor isn't just what I do; being a pastor is who I am.* While it is totally understandable for pastors to think this way, let me explain why this is such an issue.

When a pastor's identity becomes fused with their role, it unconsciously determines their sense of worth, significance, and adequacy. Subsequently, they can become psychologically vulnerable to the feedback they receive about the role and their performance in it. This can create a state of vigilance within pastors to perform in ways that protect them from negative feedback or lead to increasing states of distress when they are unable to do this. This explains why so many pastors live or die by what happens on Sunday. If attendance is good and the service goes well, they feel good inside, but if attendance is low or stuff-ups occur, they feel awful.

When I explain this idea to pastors, I often say, "If you want to know whether your identity has become fused with the outcomes of your role, here is a simple litmus test: How many of you take what happens on a Sunday personally?" They usually tilt their heads, look at me with incredulity, and say, "How do you not?!"

When the difficulties, mistakes, or attendance numbers of a Sunday feel personal to you, it is a common indicator that your identity has become enmeshed with your role.

For many pastors, Monday blues are an all-too-common reality. I will speak with pastors who tell me they will feel the emotional aftermath on Sunday afternoon, then start to feel better as the week progresses, only to feel increasing pressure as they get closer to Sunday again. It is Groundhog Day, a never-ending, weekly cycle of self-examination—not of their work, but their *worth*. No wonder over-identification with the role has been shown to have a strong correlation with burnout, emotional exhaustion, and negative psychological wellbeing.[3]

Some pastors may not get the Monday blues or feel down about attendance size. They may feel great because their numbers are great. However, if their identity is fused with their role, the pressure is still there; it is just not revealed. For them, the detrimental effects of over-identification with the role are not seen in the performance outcomes themselves, but in what is needed to maintain those successful outcomes. This is why pastors become overly driven or turn into bullies, because they desperately need to keep achieving positive results. This can even be viewed positively by others as a form of 'culture shaping' or strong leadership. The results justify the means, and the means may well be what other successful pastors are doing.

The detrimental effects of over-identification with the role may also be evident in the amount of time pastors spend away from their family, their attitude and behaviour towards their family, staff, or volunteers, or the unhealthy pressure they put on others to perform and deliver results. Success may also create an unhealthy sense of self-importance in pastors, who become dismissive or judgemental about 'ordinary' pastors or unimportant people in their congregation.

The impact of the role on a pastor's identity is immense and yet often under-realised. Research in this area shows how over-identification with the role explains the presence of many common, unhealthy factors in pastors' lives, such as lack of self-care, lack of clear boundaries, failure to identify their need for help, failure to seek help, undesirable responses to conflict, tendency towards isolation, and few friendships.[4]

2. Misdirected Calling

When I run leadership training, or I am having a one-on-one session with pastors, I will often ask them questions like:

- Why did you get into ministry?
- Why did you get into church leadership?
- What was it that you wanted to do or achieve with God?
- What did you feel especially called to do?

These are also the types of questions that are asked of people in ministerial training to gauge their motivation and vision for entering pastoral ministry. Answers vary but commonly include such things as:

- To see people come to faith
- To train disciples
- To make a difference in our communities
- To help the marginalised, disempowered, and disenfranchised experience justice
- To help people experience the unconditional love of God
- To grow a redemptive community

Although there are differences in their answers, we can categorise all these heartfelt expressions of purpose under their spiritual calling and their desire to be a spiritual leader. When a person enters local ministry, however, they experience pressure from concrete realities and measurements in ministry, which subsequently redirects their focus and involvement. These pressures include: how Sunday attendance is tracking, what the income level looks like, if enough people are serving in the children's ministry, how to combat the need for more small group leaders, if the health and safety policy is up to date, and how the new building project is going. Such pressing issues redirect the person from being a spiritual leader to an organisational leader, whose focus is now primarily on fulfilling the organisational outcomes listed above.

For some pastors, this happens almost immediately when they enter pastoral ministry and are loaded with the weight of these powerful organisational expectations and measurements. They experience a jarring shift, a type of culture shock, which can leave them reeling and despondent. For others, it can be a more subtle process, though the result is the same. Either way, they transition from serving and fulfilling their spiritual calling to serving and fulfilling organisational outcomes set by others.

Now, do not get me wrong, organisational aspects will always be a part of pastoral ministry. For many pastors, however, it becomes the proverbial tail that wags the dog. The issue is not that there are organisational components that need to be managed and attended to, but that the organisational components and outcomes usurp or even masquerade as the pastor's spiritual calling. When pastors veer off course in this way—fulfilling the organisational needs and the KPIs of the church instead of their personal purpose and priorities—their calling becomes misdirected. It's no wonder that pastors experience a high level of disconnection between their sense of calling and the daily requirements of their role.

In one study, eighty-three per cent of pastors saw their role as a 'calling' that entailed being a spiritual leader, yet ninety-one per cent felt that being a minister was more like a job than a calling. Seventy-seven per cent said they felt more like a CEO than a pastor, and eighty-three per cent said they believed their church preferred them to be a CEO rather than a pastor.[5]

These results are not isolated to one study. Pastor and author Glenn Packiam reported that the pastors in his focus group experienced similar levels of frustration with the amount of administration and organisational requirements of the role.[6] A New Zealand study by Dr. Glenn Melville into the emotional state of Baptist pastors currently in ministry, reveals evidence of misdirected calling. [7] Many lamented a sense of unfulfilled calling as the role requirements consumed their time and attention.

> One expressed a desire to help people grow in their relationship with Christ, but laments that their role is "ninety per cent administration."

> One wants to see 'souls saved' but is occupied with the needs of a declining church.

> One has a heart for pastoral care but finds themselves needing to delegate this to others.

> One wants to preach, teach, and be hands-on in the pastoral care of people, but feels the need to act like a CEO, strategising, and vision casting.[8]

These individuals are experiencing a strong mismatch between their perceived calling and the reality of their role as a pastor. They are not alone. Interestingly, even though they and many others feel frustrated, stuck, or disappointed, they will often resign themselves to the restrictive and even detrimental aspects of their role rather than seeking to change, challenge, or even leave it altogether. They continue to find new and creative ways to accept and cope with the pain of the mismatch they experience.

I have had pastors express to me that they feel like a failure or are despondent because the requirements of the role are not what they are gifted in or ultimately what they feel called to do. They see the issues as being with them—they are simply not good enough to fulfil the role with its restrictive requirements and limited resources. Some feel trapped because their denomination has placed them there because of a need, with little consideration to their spiritual calling or giftedness, or the reality of the task they are being asked to fulfil.

Some pastors who contacted me felt trapped but believed they needed to submit to their denominational or senior leaders because that was the humble and godly thing to do. Others believed they were just in a 'stretch' season to build their capacity and had to stay to prove that they could make it work. Many felt that by leaving or trying to change the role, they would be letting God and the congregation down, so the only option was to remain.

Dr. Glenn Melville's interviews highlight how pastors respond to the sense of disconnection between their calling and their role:

> "I just accept that this is the reality."[9]

> "It goes up and down, and while He has called me here, I'll do what I can . . ."[10]

> "I hold it a lot more lightly . . . I do my bit and then God does his bit."[11]

One of the pastors interviewed knows that the role is not a good fit for him so focuses on "seeing the good in things." As Melville notes, "He sought to let go of his expectations of the role and hold things a lot more lightly."[12]

While Melville sees these responses primarily as positive expressions of acceptance, I hear a range of ways pastors resign themselves to this disconnection. It is a common emphasis within discussions on pastoral wellbeing to focus on how pastors respond to the pressures associated with expectations, role demands, and ministry structures, rather than on whether those realities need to be fundamentally addressed, challenged, or changed. This can create a sense that the only way to survive the unhealthy or ill-fitting aspects of the role is to submit to them. In these situations, this is not an expression of healthy resilience, but a form of unhealthy resignation.

I find it sad that, for many participants in this study, the confines of the role were seen as an inevitability over which they were powerless to change. This is primarily because of their understanding that this is what God has called them to, so this is how God must want it. If we follow that thinking through to its natural conclusion, however, we reason that God must want them to experience the limitations and detrimental effects of the role. This may sound ludicrous, but consider the consequences of this belief system. We have many pastors whose callings, gifts, strengths and passions are being neutralised in ill-fitting roles. We have pastors who are suffering mentally and emotionally in the misguided sense that they are serving God. If that is you, I want to tell you that there is a way through this or out of it. Unless God has clearly told you to endure the specific detrimental aspects of the role, staying put is not honouring Him or the specific call He has given you.

Hold on, you might say, *hasn't God called them to that role, that church, or that context? And if God has called them to that role, it makes sense that they would need to submit to His leading. Being a pastor is not just about doing what you want or what you like. They need to be obedient to Him.*

All of those are very good points, and they also underpin the confusion that keeps so many pastors limited, stuck, and ineffective.

I am going to explore this in more detail later, but let me clarify here where the difference lies between a person's calling and the role they are in. The concrete role or job a person is fulfilling is not their *calling*. At least, it is not their macro call or their capital 'C' calling; rather, it is the context in which they are currently fulfilling their calling. God may, in fact, have called them to a specific role, but this is their micro or little 'c' calling.

Let me explain.

The previous saboteur we explored looked at how easy and common it is for pastors to fuse their identity with the role. There is a similar dynamic that occurs with calling. Pastors will commonly fuse and confuse their calling with their role. It is not just pastors who do this; other Christians and denominations do it too. The default way we perceive *calling* is a common misconception, and it's easy to see why.

When a church needs to fill the position of a pastor, they will put out a 'call', and when a person applies for the role of pastor at a specific church, it is often described as responding to or accepting 'the call'. We also see the fusing and confusing of the role with calling in the language used in mainstream Christian thinking and denominations.

According to the *Baptist Churches of New Zealand Administration Manual:*

> "A true call to a pastorate is a call of the Holy Spirit. It is heard through the fellowship of believers and is ratified by the Pastor's conviction that this call is indeed God's will. A call to a pastorate involves the relationship between a minister and a congregation based on a call of the Holy Spirit."[13]

The *Presbyterian Church of New Zealand* website states:

> "The terms of call refers to the documented relationship between a parish and a minister. It covers such things as:
>
> - The size of the charge (full-time/part-time).
> - The start date and length of the call.
> - Stipend, expenses, leave.
> - Any other additional points the parish and minister may have agreed on."[14]

A mainstream Christian publication, *Christianity Today,* stated:

> "The term *call* now has a specific definition and use in some church denominations. In these circles, a call is generally understood as an invitation to pastor a church. A 'called position' requires a personal sense of 'call' by the minister, a confirmation of that individual's call by the denominational governing body, and an actual 'call' (or invitation) by the congregation to a specific position within that church."[15]

Terming the role or job position as a calling creates the sense that God has called you to all the requirements of that specific role. This makes it extremely difficult for those who have pledged their lives to follow God to challenge or seek to change the role, even though it is ultimately restraining or suffocating their ability to fulfil what they have been called to do.

Now, there may well be a 'called' aspect to accepting a given role, but it is crucial to understand that this is a micro call, not the person's macro call. The role itself is not synonymous with *the* Call. This is where so many are getting stuck. This is why so many pastors are being restrained and their gifts limited.

Even though there is little consensus at an academic level about the definition of calling, those in ministry usually associate it with a sense of being called or guided by God. It therefore carries a profound, spiritual meaning for them.[16] If one's calling is perceived as being synonymous with a specific local role, it is understandable for a pastor to have difficulty challenging its expectations or requirements, or even consider leaving, without also feeling the guilt of abandoning one's call or opposing God.

As researcher, Randy Cook, points out,

> "The profundity of the Call eliminates or minimizes an individual's freedom to say, 'I don't like this work; I will choose something else,' which is available to other professions . . . This dynamic could potentially result in 'a loss of autonomy for ministers caught between their pain and their Call.'"[17]

When a pastor views their role as *their calling,* their purpose, their relationship with God and their submission to Him become entangled with their understanding and response to their role. As researchers Kreiner, Hollensbe, and Sheep highlight,

> "A high degree of calling often pushes individuals towards a high degree of overlap between their personal and occupational identities."[18]

Believing that the role or job *is* the call can result in pastors unintentionally submitting to detrimental outcomes under the incorrect assumption that this is what God wants for them. After all, ministry involves sacrifice, and many pastors assume the pressure and pain they are experiencing in the role is simply part of the sacrifice they signed up for and the death to themselves that they are required to die.

I remember when Mark[19] came into my office. He was caught up in this confusion and close to burnout. What I heard from him, I had heard many times before from other pastors. He loved God, he felt called, he wanted to serve God wholeheartedly, and he knew ministry was not supposed to be easy. Mark told me he felt called to the church he was in and to be a pastor. He believed he needed to surrender himself, his needs and his preferences to God, and do whatever the role required of him. Despite this, he was severely struggling and at a loss to know what to do. "I can't leave," he said. "This is where God wants me. I don't want to be another statistic, another leader who has failed God. I know that if God has called me here, He will empower me and sustain me." There was a long pause as Mark reflected on what he had just said. Then he added, "Although He had better come through soon because I don't know how much more I can take."

I explained the difference between Mark's calling and his role, between his macro call and micro call. I also shared something I have needed to say to many pastors, "If the enemy can get you to believe that this role is your calling (macro) and submitting to the requirements of the role is submitting to God and what He wants from you, then he can get you to minister yourself into an early grave. He can get you to passionately serve yourself into burnout, ill health, resignation, or ineffectiveness."

The confusion comes because it makes logical sense. Most pastors' reason, *If I am required to sacrifice and die to myself, and in this role I am experiencing sacrifice and a type of death, this must be what God wants for me. Therefore, I must be in the right place.*

As Peter Scazzero from *Emotionally Healthy Discipleship* puts it, we are "dying to the wrong things."[20] Ministry in church leadership does involve sacrifice and obedience. It is not always easy or pleasant. It does not always look the way you want it to. But that does not mean that the opposite is true either. Just because it is hard, unpleasant, and involves sacrifice does not mean this is the experience God has called you to and wants for you. Coming back to our analogy of the kayaker, competitive kayaking may involve muscle strain and exhaustion, but it is made a whole lot harder with a jammed rudder. Pastors not only need to untangle their identity from their role, but they also need to straighten out their understanding of calling versus role.

3. The Pull to Perfectionism

The third saboteur in ministry is the pull to perfectionism. This is not about the requirement for pastors to do everything perfectly but the pressure on them to appear as though they are.[21] Like living in a fish bowl, many pastors feel that their lives are constantly on display, being scrutinised and assessed by others. Their marriage, parenting, purchases and emotional responses are all in the public domain and open for critique.

One study revealed that seventy-eight per cent of Canadian pastors believed their position as a minister demanded 'perfection'.[22] The study also showed that sixty-two per cent acknowledged that they maintained an outward appearance of happiness and contentment while they were, in fact, emotionally distressed, seventy-five per cent acknowledged that they were afraid to let parishioners know how they really felt, and fifty per cent acknowledged that they were not consistent in presenting their true identity to others. I have also seen this reflected in the conversations I have had with pastors, whether in a session or in a casual conversation over coffee at a conference.

The role of a pastor is often referred to as a high calling, and comes with idealised expectations they feel they have to live up to. Pastors carry with them an often-unconscious set of rules about how they are to present themselves, which are known as 'display rules'. As a result, they may never feel able to show they are struggling or express any issues they have. Unless, of course, they have overcome those struggles and can use them as great sermon illustrations!

One of the privileges I have is to be a safe place and a confidant to pastors. Many tell me this is the only place where they can be fully honest. They will confess that they are drinking too much, comfort eating, looking at porn, feeling depressed, distressed, or bitter towards their elders, struggling with aspects of their marriage, attracted to someone in their congregation, struggling emotionally with one of their children, feeling shamed as one of their children is not following Jesus, or struggling with abuse they have experienced. On top of facing these challenges, they are also often shaming, condemning, criticising or punishing themselves in some way. It is a double-whammy, and it is heartbreaking.

The pull to perfection is not simply about appearing to be perfect, but rather not showing any area of lack. It includes both the perception of how a pastor should *behave* and how a pastor is supposed to *be*. These idealised expectations might include always being calm, responding empathetically, never having an issue with one's spouse or children, never upsetting anyone, having a spiritual life that is always rich and character-forming, and never struggling with any unwanted activities such as comfort eating, drinking too much, or viewing porn. It also might look like being a strong, forthright leader who is always in charge and in control.

To understand the impact of this on the wellbeing of pastors, we need to understand a dynamic called 'emotional labour'. Anyone who has ever been involved in customer service will get it immediately. When a customer comes to you complaining about something, you respond, "I am really sorry, sir/madam. Let me see how we can put this right for you." Inside, however, you are annoyed, thinking, *You plonker, I don't get paid enough to put up with people like you!* When there is a gap between what you are really thinking or feeling and how you choose to behave, it requires more emotional energy.

Emotional labour refers to the additional emotional energy required to maintain an outward appearance that aligns with expected display rules. The greater the gap between your external appearance and your internal emotional state, the greater the amount of emotional energy you will need to expend. When your actions and emotions are congruent with display rules, little or no emotional labour is needed, but when you are required to act in ways that differ from how you genuinely feel, more emotional labour is required. Now, I am not suggesting that you should just let everyone know what you are really thinking about them all of the time. However, if pastors believe they need to constantly appear perfect according to their display rules, it will require an ongoing high level of emotional expenditure to maintain this appearance.

If we take a closer look at emotional labour, there are two ways a person demonstrates behaviour in keeping with their display rules: surface acting or deep acting.[23] Surface acting is when a person's emotional response differs from what is required, so additional energy is expended to give the expected response. Essentially, they are knowingly pretending or faking it, or to put it more positively, they are attempting to maintain their professionalism despite their feelings.

Deep acting is when a person seeks to fundamentally change their internal response to better match the one expected of them. They are often critical and judge themself for having the wrong internal response in the first place. Pastors may even dismiss their thoughts or feelings as being ungodly or unbecoming. This is not so much about the refinement of one's character or conforming to the likeness of Christ, but rather involves the ongoing suppression of one's own emotions and needs. As Frederick et al. put it, "Deep acting may lead to self-alienation as one loses touch with one's authentic self."[24] It causes the pastor to create and live behind a well-developed mask to maintain what they perceive to be the required Christian appearance.

If many pastors feel the pressure to appear perfect, then consider the high levels of additional emotional energy they are expending to continually appear this way, every day, every week, every month, and every year! Is it any wonder that so many feel exhausted or experience burnout?[25] Whether they are surface acting or deep acting, it is draining and potentially dehumanising.

This is not the abundant life Jesus called us to, nor does it reflect the scriptural truth of Matthew 11:30: "My yoke is easy and my burden is light."

Interestingly, pastors who refuse to buy into these idealised expectations and choose a 'take me as you find me' approach show greater resilience and experience reduced stress.[26] In other words, those who allow their humanity to show within the context of their pastoral role are healthier overall. They still desire to improve themselves and pursue conformity to Christ, but their starting point is an authentic expression of who they are. Part of the antidote here is to rehumanise the role and allow our leaders to be humans in their role.

This pull to perfectionism may explain the unexpected emotional intelligence results evident in pastors. We saw earlier in Gambill's study that those with higher levels of emotional intelligence tend to use constructive forms of conflict management (CMS), such as collaborating; however, there was no such correlation for pastors.[27] Pastors did, however, demonstrate an order of preference in their CMS strategies regardless of their level of emotional intelligence:

- Compromising
- Accommodating
- Avoiding
- Collaborating
- Competing

Compromising and accommodating were the two most preferred management styles of pastors seeking to resolve conflict, with collaborating and competing the least preferred. While compromising and accommodating focus on facilitating the other person's needs and wants, collaborating and competing are strategies that advocate for one's own needs and wants, with varying degrees of prioritising the other person's needs and wants. This makes sense when you consider the stereotypical expectation that pastors are to be selfless and gentle, putting the needs of others before their own. In other words, they are expected to adhere to the display rules set for them.

This order of preference does not demonstrate selflessness but rather minimises the pastor's individual needs. If the pastor's motivation was genuinely selfless and healthy, then the obvious response would be to collaborate. This is the strategy commonly used by those with higher levels of emotional intelligence. It involves working with the other person to get them what they need, without minimising one's own needs. Collaboration also makes biblical sense since this approach allows us to love our neighbour *as* ourselves—not more than ourselves or less than ourselves (Matthew 22:39). However, rather than collaboration being one of the preferred options for pastors, especially by those with high EI, it is one of the least preferred.

Why do the display rules influence pastors to the point where they offset the benefits of having a high EI? It all relates to the first saboteur: over-identification with the role. We can understand the power here when we realise that for most pastors, fulfilling those display rules is fused with their sense of identity, success, and worthiness. This makes it a psychological imperative, more than just a social expectation, to demonstrate those required expectations. To act otherwise would impact a pastor mentally and emotionally. It is not that pastors consciously think like this; they simply feel the pressure to behave in this way. Their jammed rudder is directing their behaviour, ministry and life towards ways of being that are detrimental to their wellbeing and effectiveness.

4. Isolation

It is often said that church leadership is a lonely job. This may be true, but the three saboteurs above can cause leaders to further isolate themselves emotionally. If you are feeling the pull to perfectionism, then it makes sense that the only safe place to be is by yourself. Research by Barna revealed that seventy-three per cent of pastors sometimes or frequently felt isolated from others, and sixty per cent said they sometimes or frequently felt lonely that year.[28] Many pastors do not believe they have people with whom they can be honest and vulnerable, whether it's congregants, denominational leaders, or other pastors.[29] These three categories of people are often viewed as some form of threat to the pastor, in terms of how they might perceive them and their ability to succeed in the role.

Congregants

Pastors usually do not feel they can open up to members of their congregation about difficulties they are experiencing because they cannot trust that what is shared would not be leaked to others. They may also fear that what they share might be used against them, damaging their reputation or decreasing the respect that the congregation has for them. If they are to be successful leaders, they need their congregation to trust and follow them, and this might be negatively impacted if the pastor's struggles and difficulties are made known to those they lead. Pastors are also understandably uncertain how to navigate the dual roles of being a pastor and a friend who receives care and support. I often find that many pastors are not even aware of what dual roles are, let alone that they have multiple ones occurring in their lives and ministries.

Boundary lines around these roles are often blurred. When someone is wearing multiple hats, there will always be one hat that trumps them all. Unconsciously, we all have a hierarchy to our hats, and other people will also place a hierarchy on the hats we wear. You can imagine the difficulty when there is no agreed consensus on which role or hat trumps the others. Whether you are hanging out watching the game, listening to someone, or sharing your own struggles, it can be hard for people to view a pastor as anything other than 'the pastor'. As one pastor put it, "It is very difficult for people not to see you with that title."[30] It is not that it is impossible to find genuine friends in the congregation, and some do, but it can be hard and fraught with difficulties.

Denominational Leaders

The dual roles held by denominational leaders mean these leaders are also not always a safe source of support for pastors. Different denominations have different levels of authority over their pastors. As some denominational leaders are also their pastors' employers, they can directly impact their employment status and threaten their job security. Some denominational leaders have the power to intervene in a church; others are more like network facilitators. Either way, it may feel precarious to share vulnerably with someone who also holds power over your job security and autonomy in the role.

Pastors may also feel emotionally vulnerable when they feel scrutinised by denominational leaders and believe their value as a person is based on how their performance compares to that of other pastors. The perception for many is that denominational leaders are primarily interested in you to the degree that your church is succeeding. As one Baptist pastor put it, "You are valued by the size and perception of your church."[31] One former Salvation Army officer said she felt the continual pressure to perform in ways consistent with being an officer, even if this was at odds with her identity or her mental health.[32]

I remember speaking with Simon, who told me he had given up trying to talk to his denominational leaders about the difficulties he was facing in the role. He had been sent to a small church that had claimed they were keen to grow, but when he arrived, he discovered they had no interest in changing. "When I raised this with my denominational leaders," he said, "the message I got back was I just had to make it work. I was given the impression that there must be something wrong with me as a leader because my peers were managing to grow their churches. It was then I realised they weren't interested in me or my wellbeing; they were just interested in growth. I just feel so stuck. What can I do?"

The issue is a multifaceted one. This conflict can arise as a result of a denominational leader's interpersonal skills or a clash of personality types with the pastor. It may be related to the denominational leader's priorities, which may be focused on the success of the church or denomination as a whole rather than the pastor's wellbeing. It could be because of the power they hold over the pastor, making them hesitant to share anything vulnerable. Finally, the pastor's perception of what is expected of them by the denominational leader can lead to difficulty being fully transparent.

I do not want you to mishear me here. I have had the privilege of spending time with many wonderful denominational leaders who deeply care for and support the pastors they oversee. Yet for many, despite their best intentions, their dual roles make it difficult for them to be an effective source of support to whom pastors can turn.

Fellow Pastors

The difficulty with opening up to other pastors is that they are often seen as competitors rather than a source of support. In Irvine's study of clergy wellbeing, eighty per cent of pastors reported feeling jealous of the success of other leaders.[33] This is certainly not the case for everyone; in fact, it has been a joy in my travels to see pastors' groups being genuinely authentic and supportive of each other. Sadly, however, the pressures of the role can turn colleagues into competitors, further reducing avenues of available support. This may result in pastors relying solely on their spouse for deeper support or 'spiritualising' their needs in the sense that: *All I really need is Jesus.* While spousal support and spiritual practices can be helpful, they can also be insufficient and unhealthy coping strategies that avoid addressing the issues pastors are facing. This can leave pastors in the terrible predicament of ministering from a place of accumulated stress, unresolved tensions, unaddressed depression, anxiety, hurt, grief, and the list goes on. As the internal pressure builds, pastors are more likely to use questionable means of coping, which compounds the burdens they are carrying.[34]

Establishing trusted, healthy and supportive relationships is key for pastors' overall wellbeing and longevity in the role. When the influence of role identity has been addressed, fewer people will be seen as a threat to a pastor's success, and more avenues of support will become available. As with any role, we need to wisely discern the people with whom we choose to be vulnerable, but when role performance is separated from our worth, and shame is removed from our imperfect struggles, there are more options for support. In other words, the more we rehumanise the role of the pastor, the more sources of support become available to the pastor.

One of the avenues that pastors have available to them is the professional support of external supervision. With increasing awareness of the mental and emotional health of pastors, many denominations are making supervision mandatory. This is a great step forward; however, there is confusion at all levels about what this supervision should look like. Many pastors do not see the need for supervision and prefer to receive mentoring from others who can help them advance their role success. Some pastors even view the addition of supervision as 'pathologising' ministry.

At the other end of the spectrum, denominations and external agencies may view supervision as a type of cure-all, as though its very existence will keep pastors healthy and congregations safe. Unfortunately, it is not. Professional pastoral supervisors are not line managers who are familiar with pastors' day-to-day interactions, nor are they in a position of authority over them and able to hold them fully accountable. They are an external, professional resource to support the pastor, and as such, they have limited time with them and are at the mercy of what they choose to share.

Whether it is referred to as 'supervision' or is given another name, pastors need to have a safe space with a skilled professional where they can process pressures, conflict, unwanted behaviours and reactions, workload, and relationships. The role of the pastor is multifaceted, and the world in which they minister is becoming *increasingly* complex. As such, it is important they have someone who can competently help them unpack, process, and navigate all of this so they can continue to minister in healthy and effective ways.

One of the reasons I enjoy supervising pastors so much is that I have the privilege of journeying with them as they seek to fulfil God's call. My aim is to create an intensely safe space where pastors can share anything. During the course of my work with pastors, I have had the privilege of helping them navigate the highs and lows, the daily struggles, and the crises they experience. It is wonderful to bear witness to breakthroughs, growth, personal change, moves of God, and all manner of situations worth celebrating.

It is equally a privilege to offer support, strength and strategies when life is far from rosy. This may include:

- The daily grind and struggles of ministry
- Difficulty with key people
- Church splits and conflict
- Questioning whether they are good enough
- Struggles with alcohol, comfort eating, and pornography
- Weariness, frustration, stress, and burnout
- Compassion fatigue
- Grief
- Secondary trauma
- Overworking
- Leadership dilemmas
- Leading staff and people through uncertainty
- Ethical dilemmas
- Responding to unrealistic expectations
- Clarifying their calling and flourishing in their role

Pastors will often tell me there is nowhere else they can share these issues. It is a privilege to be able to provide that support, but I hope that as we rehumanise the role of the pastor and realign the pastor's rudder, they will gather more trusted, supportive people in their lives.

5. Misdirected Spirituality

The link between spirituality and wellbeing has been researched for some time now, with results continuing to show a strong positive correlation between the two. Research has also shown that those who consider themselves to be spiritual people are less likely to suffer from anxiety, depression, burnout, and substance abuse.[35]

This is good news since, as Christians and pastors, spirituality is our zone. We are spiritual beings whose whole lives revolve around the spiritual expression of following Jesus. Pastors, then, should naturally experience the positive effects of their spirituality; however—and it is another big however—there is another significant variable that determines whether pastors can gain these benefits.

I was fascinated to discover that the orientation of a pastor's spirituality determines whether their mental and emotional health is enhanced or diminished.[36] If the pastor's spirituality is orientated 'intrinsically', it means they are focused primarily on God for the relationship's sake. Pastors with an intrinsic spirituality read their Bible because they want to hear from God, they pray because they want to pour their heart out to Him and speak with Him, they worship because they love Him, they have a devotional time because they enjoy spending time with Him, and they practice other disciplines like silence and solitude because they want to remove other distractions and have Him all to themselves. In other words, intrinsic spirituality is being internally motivated to connect with God and foster a relationship with Him. Intrinsic spirituality provides pastors with mental and emotional protection and resilience—a kind of spiritual immune system, if you will. Much like how a physical immune system operates, having an intrinsic spirituality does not make you impervious to illness, but rather supports your mental and emotional wellbeing and aids your recovery if you do become unwell.

Spirituality is extrinsically orientated when one's spiritual expression and relationship with God is centred on external purposes. Pastors with an extrinsic spirituality read their Bible because they need to prepare a sermon for Sunday or materials for small group, they pray in groups or for others because that is just part of the job, their prayers are focused on external things such as wanting the church to grow or difficult people to be removed, and they have a devotional time or engage in spiritual activities because they feel they should and would otherwise feel a sense of guilt that they were a 'bad pastor'.

The startling reality is that when spirituality becomes extrinsic, it removes this spiritual immune system, leaving pastors with a greater likelihood of experiencing burnout and emotional distress. They are also more likely to utilise unhealthy forms of coping and have lower emotional intelligence.

This is certainly what we see when we examine different research in different countries, exploring different forms of Christian ministry and different aspects of Christian spirituality.[37]

In one sense, it is not surprising. Another way of saying your spirituality has become extrinsic is that you have 'lost your first love', or you have become spiritually dry. Similarly, intrinsic spirituality can be described in the sense that you are remaining in Jesus and in His love. Pastors and Christians are likely very familiar with these phrases, yet they also align with a profound psychological reality. Ultimately, the substance of our love relationship with God impacts our psychological wellbeing. When our spirituality becomes misdirected, it can cause us to become mentally and emotionally vulnerable. Our busyness, pragmatism and material culture can all play a role in orientating us towards an extrinsic spirituality.

When we consider these five saboteurs, we can see how they each build pressure on the pastor, moving them from having a wellbeing-supportive intrinsic spirituality to a detrimental extrinsic spirituality. It is no wonder that pastors often find the role emotionally taxing and can experience ongoing mental health challenges and frustrations.

2

MINISTRY IN REVERSE

All five saboteurs take their toll on pastors. The two most significant saboteurs, however, are over-identification with the role and misdirected calling. In many ways, they are producing, or at least fuelling, the other three. They have gone unseen and unrecognised and, therefore, unaddressed. Unfortunately, they have also shaped a model of ministry that traps pastors in an unhealthy dynamic, damages their wellbeing, and limits their effectiveness.

The influence of these five saboteurs has caused the reversal of a healthy model of ministry. What makes this worse is that we have tended to normalise it. In fact, we have even begun to view this unhealthy model of ministry as 'normal ministry'. We will try to justify any detrimental dynamics as the realities of the role or the high calling of leadership. Yet, this is not the ministry Jesus set up, nor is it the leadership role Jesus is calling us to.

We need to shine a light on what is occurring, so we can provide a substantive response that unjams pastors' rudders and releases their ministry potential. To do this, let us pull the threads together and look at how an unhealthy model of ministry is masquerading as normal ministry. Let us see just how profoundly jammed the rudder is.

MODEL OF MINISTRY: HEALTHY AND UNHEALTHY

When we examine the model of ministry more closely, we find it is composed of three distinct parts: a pastor's identity, calling, and role. Together, they form the rudder. Within a *healthy* model of ministry, these components are ordered in a specific way; there is a healthy hierarchy to them. In these cases, the rudder is unjammed, and the pastor can flourish. Sadly, most pastors operate within an *unhealthy* ministry model in which these factors are not aligned correctly. When this happens, it makes ministry harder, reducing the effectiveness of pastors and heightening their psychological vulnerability. This is the effect of the jammed rudder.

DIAGRAM 1. *Three Components of Ministry*

In supervision or in workshops, I will often explain the dynamic to pastors like this:

> "There are three distinct parts to ministry: identity, calling, and role. The identity part is who you are, the essential 'me'. If you are operating from a healthy position, your identity is in Christ. This comes from the fact that God created you on purpose for Himself: 'For we are God's handiwork, created in Christ . . .' (Ephesians 2:10a). He loves you, redeems you, forgives you, restores you, and wants you. Your sole purpose is to allow God to love you and to love Him back. Full stop.
>
> Because God loves you, He has also given you a calling. There is something He has placed in your heart that you long to do. The Bible tells us that, 'It is God who works in you to will and to act in order to fulfil his good purpose' (Philippians 2:13).

We are 'to do good works, which God prepared in advance for us to do' (Ephesians 2:10b). Tied to this are your gifts and strengths. Your calling is the big purpose—the macro purpose—that you desire to fulfil for Him.

The third area is your role. This is the concrete expression of your calling, and hopefully, a wonderful fit with your calling. It is your calling fully expressed in a specific context. Whether you are the Senior Pastor of Mt. Albert Baptist Church, the Senior Leader of Richmond AOG, the Vicar at All Saints, Kelburn, or an Officer at Heston Salvation Army, every role has distinct requirements and expectations associated with it.

Even if your role turned to custard or you got fired (if that is possible in your denomination), your calling remains the same, and who you are in Christ never alters. A healthy model of ministry occurs when you minister out of your identity in Christ, you minister towards fulfilling your calling, and you minister in accordance with your role. Your role serves and facilitates your calling as you serve, submit to and draw your sense of self from Jesus."

DIAGRAM 2. Healthy Ministry: healthy hierarchy

The difficulty for most pastors is that their identity, calling, and role become fused or misaligned. When they feel they are fulfilling the requirements of the role, they feel good in themselves and about themselves. If, however, they are not achieving whatever they believe the role requires of them, they feel horrible, inadequate, a failure, tense, stressed, despondent, angry, or experience any number of massively unpleasant feelings. Their lack of achievement is felt personally and deeply, since it unconsciously reflects their adequacy and worth.

The rudder for most pastors has been unwittingly jammed in the opposite direction. Their role and its outcomes determine everything else, creating a hierarchical ascendency—organisationally and psychologically— that is difficult to break free from. In addition to this, the role itself is often confused with and referred to as 'the call'. As such, if the role falls apart or pastors fail in the role, others may assume that they are not, in fact, called or have failed their call. The role becomes the defining and determining factor of a pastor's understanding of call and identity.

This is the unhealthy model of ministry. The role, and the pastor's performance within it, now has the power to determine a pastor's identity, worth, and sense of self. It also has the power to subsume a pastor's calling, leading them to believe that the context in which they are serving is *the call* of their life, and must be submitted to, despite how detrimental it may be to their wellbeing or the extent to which it limits their original call.

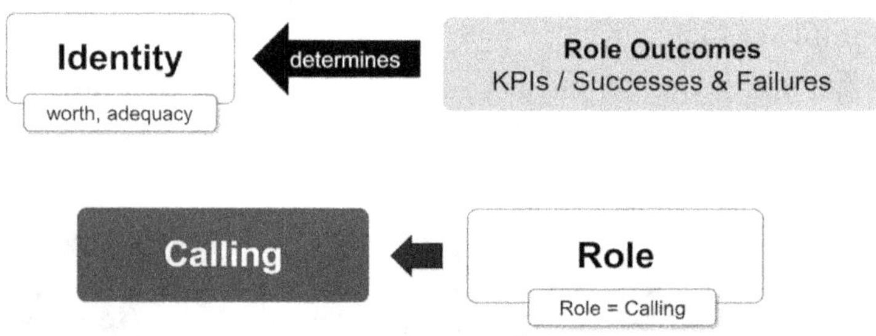

DIAGRAM 3. Unhealthy Ministry: fusion and order reversal

When the rudder is jammed, and the healthy ordering of identity, call and role is reversed, pastors can't avoid being vulnerable to their performance metrics in the role. They remain susceptible to anything that potentially threatens their success or sense of achievement. It can feel like a wound that remains open and never heals. It is like leaving the door constantly open for the enemy to come in and "steal and kill and destroy" (John 10:10).

To improve a pastor's spiritual and psychological health and realign their rudder, these three areas—identity, calling, and role—have to be separated and experienced distinctly. Pastors need to differentiate themselves from the role, sourcing who they are in Jesus. They also need to differentiate their macro calling from the role they are fulfilling. This gives greater psychological objectivity to the role and role outcomes. It also enables the pastor to better assess the degree to which the role is a suitable fit for their calling.

To get to the heart of what is going on and explore ways to unjam the rudder, let's go on a deep dive into the areas of identity, calling, and role. We will also examine the wider church system, because it unwittingly contributes to the jammed rudder and keeps pastors trapped in an unhealthy model of ministry.

3

IDENTITY: SOURCED IN THE WRONG MASTER

We say Jesus is our Master, we want Jesus to be our Master, but unfortunately, whatever we tie our worth to will end up mastering us. This is what over-identification with the role will do. As we read in 2 Peter 2:19, "People are slaves to whatever has mastered them."

OVER-IDENTIFICATION WITH THE ROLE

Over-identification with the role can happen to anyone in any role. When we take a closer look at this dynamic, however, we will better understand why it is so prolific among pastors and why it has such a profound impact on their psychological wellbeing.

Role identity is more than a person's association or affiliation with a specific role, occupation, or job. It is about the meaning they draw from the role and the significant influence it has on their sense of identity, self, and self-esteem.[1] More specifically, it impacts a person's:

1. Self-efficacy: sense of competency.
2. Self-worth: sense of being worthy and valuable.
3. Self-authenticity: sense of congruence between actions and perceived self.[2]

As you might imagine, anything that has the potential to define your competency, worth and authenticity will have enormous power in your life, commanding your attention and allegiance. The more your identity is sourced in, enmeshed with, or fused with your role, the greater the degree of potential psychological vulnerability when there is a perceived failure in fulfilling the expected behaviour or outcomes related to that role. Pastors will be left in a state of vigilance to perform in a way that protects them from unwanted messages of failure or inadequacy in the role. They will experience increasing states of distress if they are unable to perform in ways that keep these negative consequences at bay. Furthermore, when pastors are not performing well in their role, this can create a self-reinforcing feedback loop. For instance, a person with a low sense of adequacy or competency is less likely to perform well, thereby reinforcing the sense that they are not good enough and, in turn, increasing their distress.

This dynamic has a depersonalising, even dehumanising, effect. In a ministry context, it can cause pastors to unconsciously lose touch with their true, God-given self. Without even realising it, we begin to see ourselves not as beloved sons or daughters, but as indistinguishable from the role we carry out. We keep performing the expectations of the role in the hope that it will affirm our worth, prove our value, and secure our sense of belonging.[3] Before long, the line between who we are and what we do becomes blurred. We become the role, and the role becomes us.

In his seminal book, *The Fifth Discipline*, Peter Senge gives an example of what happens when a person's identity becomes fused with their role. He describes a situation where steelworkers were made redundant and were unable to accept offers to retrain because of the identity crisis they experienced. They had internalised the role, believing, *I am my position*, and were unable to perceive ever doing anything different. "I am a lathe operator," said a worker. "How can I do anything else?"[4] When a person's identity is so fused with their role, they are unable to perceive themselves as being anything other than what they do. Yet, any role, occupation, career or job can only describe *what* you do; it can never truly define *who* you are.

The role will hopefully be a wonderful outworking of who you are without informing who you are. This is the critical distinction that is often missed.

Within the context of role identity, there is a double dynamic that occurs, amplifying the impact. Role identity includes both a 'state' and a 'process'. A person can draw a sense of meaning from desirable associations with a role (state). For example, when someone becomes a pastor, they may appreciate being affiliated with favourable associations like spiritual leader, godly person, or someone worthy of respect. The very fact that they are a pastor communicates something to them that is dignity-enhancing. Of course, there can be other associations with the role that are less desirable, and these will, equally, have an impact.

The 'process' dynamic is concerned with how well a pastor is managing to fulfil the requirements of the role. This comes from their own self-assessment, their subjective comparison with other pastors, and feedback from congregants, governance, and denominational leaders. Feedback may come in the form of direct communication from someone or indirectly from the pastor's inability to motivate a team or volunteers in the way they had hoped. It may look like direct criticism of their performance by a congregant, or be expressed indirectly by congregants not attending services, by people being unwilling to serve or participate in a church project, or from the lack of growth they observe in someone they are working with. Many pastors feel like they are under the continual scrutiny of others, which increases the pressure to be perfect or avoid revealing their authentic selves.[5]

PERVASIVENESS OF ROLE IDENTITY:
PLAGUING PASTORS GLOBALLY

If you thought it was just you, it is not. The impact of role identity is not just happening to a few pastors or those from certain denominations or countries; it is global. I see it in my work with pastors from New Zealand, Australia, the United Kingdom, Europe, and the United States. I see it in mainstream churches, including Presbyterian, Methodist, Anglican,

Brethren, and Baptist denominations; I see it in the Pentecostal and independent churches; and I see it in the Salvation Army.

We also see the dynamic of role identity clearly evident in global research. One senior pastor of a large church in the United States commented, "It's not the things in ministry that kill you, it's the things you don't get done . . . every night you leave knowing that there's another twelve people you should call, another three books you should read, another eight people that you need to visit in hospital."[6]

Research into Episcopalian clergy reveals the significant impact of role identity on their lives. One priest commented, "The human Tom and the priest Tom are so intertwined generally that I cannot separate them."[7] Another made the statement, "You have human beings, and you have *priests*" (italics original).[8]

We also see the impact of role performance on identity in the words of three New Zealand pastors from Melville's study. They have been given the pseudonyms Deborah, Samuel, and Aaron. Deborah said: "I had known for years, and I've always had a struggle with success and failure, just this huge fear of failure, and because it was all tied to my core identity, because if I failed at something, then I was a failure . . ."[9] Samuel commented, "What people think of me matters, even though I know that it doesn't need to matter."[10] His concern significantly interfered with his ability to lead the church well, as he worried that taking certain actions might be perceived negatively by others. Aaron said, "If I have performed and it's still not good enough, what does that say about me as a person?"[11]

What I find fascinating is that even if pastors have a high degree of self-awareness of what is going on, this does not help lessen the profoundly negative experience of failing to fulfil the requirements of the role. Other pastors, however, have no awareness of the fusion between their identity and their role. That is, in part, because their awareness is being obscured by the manner in which unhealthy expectations are created, affirmed, and enforced by the congregations and denominations in which they are serving.[12] When the external environment affirms that those unhealthy expectations are normal, reasonable, and required, it is hard to perceive that the problem is external; instead, one carries a sense that the problem is you.

This is understandable since, as people, we do not form our identity in isolation. We come to understand who we are through the feedback we receive from those around us. In this way, there is an element of our identity being socially constructed. When ministry is not going well, or there is some difficulty, it is easy to internalise this.[13] And if pastors believe they are the problem, then the only solution is to change themselves to better fit the expectations of the role or the people they serve.

We will look at this type of feedback loop in more detail later when we explore the wider systemic forces influencing pastors.

IF IT'S THAT BAD, WHY NOT LEAVE?

If pastors are experiencing distress or ongoing mental health challenges, it would be understandable to think, *Why don't they just leave and get a different job?* Certainly, many pastors contemplate leaving, and this was especially the case during the COVID-19 pandemic. In his book, *The Resilient Pastor*, Glenn Packiam highlights Barna's 2021 research, which revealed that approximately thirty per cent of pastors had seriously considered leaving ministry during those Covid years.[14]

When I was pastoring, I certainly remember daydreaming about becoming a barista. In my mind, that meant spending my days making great coffee and talking with people, without all the pressures of leading a church. It seemed like a dream job. However, as we will see, leaving ministry roles is not that simple. The dynamics of role identity make it incredibly difficult to break free, often trapping pastors in the role despite their distress.

To explain why this is, we need to understand feedback loops. You have probably heard the awful sound that occurs when you hold a microphone to a speaker. This is known as a feedback loop or a reinforcing loop, where the sound gets caught in a never-ending, always-increasing loop. In the same way, pastors are getting caught in an awful feedback loop, where they remain in a never-ending, potentially increasing state of distress. However, while we might assume their distress would force them to leave the role, it actually forces them to stay.

You see, when pastors over-identify with their role—when they *are* that role—how can they safely leave it? To leave will seem like losing themselves. It will feel like losing who they are. They may feel like a failure with no opportunity to redeem themselves. A pastor, therefore, will remain in their distress and endure all the negative experiences in the role because to consider leaving the role or the profession would be emotionally debilitating.[15]

In other words, when your identity and sense of competency, worth and authenticity are all fused with a role, you are likely to persist in that role despite the level of distress you are experiencing because the thought of leaving the role feels like a greater psychological threat. When a pastor is trapped within such a loop, they will understandably experience a continual erosion of their wellbeing and mental health.

This is more than theory; it is exactly what is happening for many pastors. Despite all the evidence that pastors are experiencing burnout, mental health challenges, and considering leaving, they are generally hanging in there. Allison Hamm and David Eagle from Duke University recently published their review of the research on clergy leaving congregational ministry in the United States. They found that the number leaving either Protestant or Catholic ministry was actually quite low, at around one to two per cent per year.[16] So, despite the distress pastors are experiencing in their role, they are choosing to stay and 'survive' instead by finding unhealthy coping mechanisms. These are what Counselling Psychologist Dr. Kathryn Kissel describes as "a last-ditch cry to escape ministerial pressure."[17]

The profound, psychological pressure pastors experience from over-identification with the role was brought home to me a few years back at a conference where Carey Nieuwhof was speaking. He told the story of catching up with a friend who had been a pastor but had to leave the ministry after it was revealed he had been having an affair. This was sad enough to hear, but it was even more staggering to hear that he justified the affair as a 'valid' way of getting out of ministry.[18] Wait, what?!

Pause for a second and consider that. How much pressure would a pastor have to be under for them to think it was preferable to have an affair, causing pain to significant people in their life and being disqualified from ministry, rather than simply resigning? I find that utterly astounding. For some reason, this person believed having an affair was a better or safer reason for leaving their ministry than being viewed as a failure or unable to 'cut it'. As bizarre as this seems, I often encounter this type of thinking in a lesser way with students who do not turn up for their exam. In their mind, it is better not to sit the exam than to be tested and fail. It makes sense, however, when we understand that they have fused their worth to their performance. This is not just a test of their work but a test of their worth. Any examination of their performance is viewed as a critique of their personal value and significance, but if they choose to simply not turn up for the exam, their worth remains protected.

Thankfully, using an affair as a means to exit ministry is not a common occurrence, although I did come across a similar case when doing my master's research. It does highlight, however, the pressure that many pastors are under because their identity is fused with the role. When this is the case for any of us, it feels impossible to leave without losing ourselves in the process. As damaging as it may be to stay, the alternative feels worse. The result is pastors remaining trapped in a psychologically detrimental reinforcing loop.

ALL ROADS LEAD TO ~~ROME~~ ROLE

The immense psychological pressure that stems from role identity is taking a devastating toll on pastors. In many ways, pastors are more vulnerable to this than those in other professions. Why? Because the pastoral role often acts like a 'super-source' of identity. It becomes the lens through which every other meaningful part of life is seen and experienced.

We draw our sense of self from many different sources, which have the potential to powerfully shape our sense of reality. The most influential ones are those that are emotionally significant to us, such as our family of origin, our peer group, our ethnicity and social group, our culture and society, our profession, our faith, our values, our beliefs, our spirituality, our gender, our skill set or competencies, our academic or sporting achievements, and our professions. We look to these sources to inform us about who we are and to help us understand: *What makes me, me?* Not only that, but they also tell us what is required of us to be acceptable and successful. They send us messages about what is permissible for someone like us, what is expected of someone like us, or what is possible for someone like us. They provide information about where we rank in terms of significance, worthiness, and lovability.

Someone may source their identity in being a mother, a son, a friend, a climate advocate, a woman, a lawyer, a Christian, heterosexual, a golfer, a business owner, or someone known for their integrity. The more sources someone draws from, the greater the resilience they tend to have. If one area of life is not going well, it is not *everything* about them. For instance, if someone works as an accountant and has been underperforming, they may find it discouraging, but their work does not define them entirely. They can still draw on being a loving husband, a dad, a valued friend, a faithful supporter of World Vision, a squash player, or a church volunteer. These other identity sources act like psychological shock absorbers. The whole of who they are is not wrapped up in how they are doing in one area.

For pastors, however, it is different. The role is so all-encompassing that it can act like a 'super-source' through which other important facets of the pastor's life must pass. Spiritual identity (being a child of God), relational identity (being a spouse or parent), community identity (being part of a denomination or local church) and personal values (like integrity, compassion, or calling) are all filtered through the pastoral role. How they are performing in any of those other areas reflects on their performance as a pastor.[19] In other words, how well they are getting on with their spouse or parenting their children, how effectively they conduct themselves and serve others, and how they behave as a friend to others and a follower of Jesus will all be viewed as a reflection of who they are as a pastor. When they are faltering or failing in any of those areas, it can feel like they are faltering or failing as a pastor. They are not being all they should be, and more specifically, they are not being all that a pastor should be. Their identity is inextricably linked to their role.

We can see an example of this in the experience of one New Zealand pastor, Benjamin, as he reflects on how his relational, vocational and personal domains merge:

> "One of the biggest challenges in ministry is that your relationships get tricky because your work and your community are often one and the same. So, 'normal' people have their work life, and then they have their family life, and then they have other stuff. They might have some overlap, but generally they don't, whereas for pastors, all three get merged, so the family is part of a subset of the church, and I think that is enormously challenging."[20]

For some pastors, it may seem like everything is fine because they are meeting the required expectations. The pressure begins to build; however, the moment they start to feel like they are falling short. Instead of being able to draw from other areas of life for encouragement when one part is not going well, pastors experience a greater psychological burden, since they are expected to perform in every area with the same level of excellence. The result is a constant pressure where failure in one area is experienced as a deficiency in who they are as a person.[21]

Even though most of us draw our identity from several sources, there is usually one that we deem as being of greater importance than the others. One source rules them all. One source becomes the anchor or the lens through which we experience the rest. One source becomes the defining voice, while the others fall in line. Take, for example, a woman who is a mother and a senior academic. She may draw great meaning from being a 'parent' and a 'professor', but both these identities may be subservient to her identity as a woman.[22]

She does not just see herself as a parent; she sees herself as a *mother*. There is a corresponding sense of fulfilment and pressure that flows from that identity. Likewise, her role as a professor communicates significance and dignity to her. She sees herself not simply as a professor but as a woman in a senior academic role, excelling in a space where men have traditionally held the power. Seeing herself primarily through the lens of being a woman, she may feel, on the one hand, like a pioneer for other women in the field. On the other hand, there may also be different rules and expectations for her to succeed and be accepted *because* she is a woman. This is the power our primary identity holds; it shapes how we see and experience everything else.

For church leaders, being a pastor is their dominant identity. One pastor shared how even friendships operate under the domain of his role and identity as a pastor:

> "Inevitably whenever I was interacting with people it would be ministry . . . inevitably [with] your friends, you still would be doing pastoral work . . . ministry is an incredibly lonely role as well . . . we try to be vulnerable and open with people, but when you are wearing a pastoral hat, it changes relationships."[23]

When I was pastoring, I distinctly remember watching the rugby at someone's home with a group from church. Conscious that I was not just one of the boys watching the game, I knew that how I responded and behaved would reflect upon me as a pastor—as *their* pastor. Of all the hats I wore, the pastor hat was always the dominant one. David Pooler puts it this way, "Over time, the role of the pastor becomes not just what one does but who one is."[24] As one Episcopal priest stated, "I feel that who I am as a priest and the role associated with that and who I am are the same."[25]

When a pastor's role acts as the super source, anything that validates their performance will be pursued and protected. In turn, there is a greater vulnerability to psychological distress when they are unable to satisfy the requirements of the role. Since the pastoral role is often idealised, and expectations around it are broad and relentless, most pastors will feel at some point that they are not measuring up. This is where emotional exhaustion, psychological distress and burnout begin to take hold.[26]

The impact on pastors becomes clearer when we recognise that the sources from which we draw our sense of self are deeply connected to our deepest questions:

1. Am I good enough?
2. Am I significant, worthy, and worthwhile?
3. Am I lovable?
4. Am I acceptable?
5. Am I adequate?

When we are not reassured by the answers we receive, this may leave us in a psychologically dark and fearful space of believing, often unconsciously, that the painful opposite is true:

1. I am not good enough
2. I am not significant, worthy, or worthwhile
3. I am unlovable
4. I am unacceptable
5. I am inadequate

Beneath protective layers of professionalism, performance, and personability, a belief that any of these statements was true would be psychologically damaging and exhausting for any individual. Unfortunately, for most pastors, the primary source they draw from for this information is their role, and more critically, how they are performing in that role. Whatever a pastor believes they should be doing or achieving to be 'successful' carries immense weight because it has the power to determine if they are a worthwhile, adequate or acceptable human being. When we understand this, it becomes clear why pastors are more psychologically vulnerable and typically experience increased mental health challenges than the general public.

Of course, this is all occurring below the surface, below their conscious awareness. Pastors do not come to me and say, "I think I am over-identifying with my role and because of this I'm feeling depressed . . . frustrated. . .

anxious . . . despondent . . ." They will pin the cause of their feelings on other things, such as: "I'm just tired, I think I need a holiday, the Sunday attendance has been disappointing, people can be so fickle, I have a lot on my plate at the moment, others just don't get what we are trying to build." Only when we take a closer look can we see there is much more going on. Once we have peeled back a few layers, I will usually hear them say what Chris said to me,

> "Oh, wow. I wouldn't have picked that as the issue when I
> walked in, but now that I look at it, yeah, that's what is going
> on. I am so dependent on how the church is doing."

My hope is that this chapter will bring this unseen issue into the light. Over-identification with the role is not only a significant issue, but also one that is prolific and powerful for pastors. When your sense of self becomes intertwined with the expectations and outcomes of the pastoral role, those outcomes will hold immense power over you. Without even realising it, you will find yourself more yoked to the role than to Jesus Himself.

None of this is intentional, but it makes sense when we understand that this *fusion* has created *confusion* around role expectations and outcomes. When pastors do not meet them, it hits hard, and it is felt not just as a professional setback but as a spiritual failure.

When who you are is fused with what you do, and what you do is fused with what you believe God has called you to and must therefore be obediently submitted to in service of Him, then succeeding at the role (within the confines of the role) will feel like an act of faithfulness to God. Failing, however, will feel like failing God and being inadequate, unusable, and worthless. It can seem hopeless to escape, leaving pastors with a very similar lament to Paul's:

> *"O what a wretched man I am! Who will rescue me from this*
> *body that is subject to death? Thanks be to God, who delivers*
> *me through Jesus Christ our Lord!"*
>
> **Romans 7:24-25**

The good news is that there is freedom. We first need to see what is happening, name it, and understand it. Only then can we begin to untangle ourselves from the messiness of this situation and find a way forward.

4

CALLING: SLEEPING IN THE WRONG BED

In their book, *Reframation*, Hirsch and Nelson tell the story of Procrustes, a character from Greek mythology.

> "Procrustes, whose name means 'he who stretches,' is arguably one of the most intriguing characters in Greek mythology. He was a devious villain who kept a house by the side of the road where he would offer hospitality to passing strangers. The guests were invited in for a pleasant meal and a night's rest in his 'very special bed,' which Procrustes described as having the enchanting property of matching the exact length of anyone who lay on it. What Procrustes left out of the description was the method by which this miracle was achieved. As soon as the guest would fall asleep in the special bed, Procrustes would begin his villainous procedure, stretching the guest on the rack if they were too short for the bed or chopping off their legs if they were too long—a rather unfortunate way of making everyone conform to his one-size-fits-all bed."[1]

THE PROCRUSTEAN ROLE: DISTINGUISHING MACRO AND MICRO CALLINGS

Hirsch and Nelson use the Procrustean myth as an analogy to describe the reductionist approach the Church has taken to most things, including the gospel message. However, I also see it as an uncomfortably accurate analogy of what happens with the role of the pastor. We take leaders—their calling, their gifts, and their strengths—and fit them into a one-size-fits-all role. This begs the question: How many of our leaders are being stretched out of shape or disfigured to fit within this Procrustean role? How many are limiting their evangelistic, prophetic, shepherding, apostolic or teaching callings and gifts in an attempt to fulfil the preset requirements of their job description?

As we briefly mentioned earlier, misdirected calling—one of the most significant saboteurs in ministry—occurs when the macro calling God has given a person is both restricted and redirected to fulfil the organisational markers of success in the role. The reality is that achieving those markers is usually outside the pastor's direct control. And when a pastor's sense of identity, worth and adequacy is tied to those measures, it is no wonder their wellbeing and mental health suffer.

A CALLING TO WHICH YOU HAVE NOT BEEN CALLED

In Ephesians 4:1 (AMP), Paul exhorts us to "live a life worthy of the calling to which you have been called." Expressed here is something so obvious that we can miss it. We are not asked to be worthy of a calling to which we have not been called. Yet many pastors are doing just that. They are trying to fit into a role-shape which was never their calling-shape. They are trying to sleep in a bed that was never designed for them.

If we are to unjam the rudder and move pastors towards greater health and effectiveness, it is not enough to separate their identity from the role; we also need to distinguish their calling from the role. God may have indeed called a pastor to their current church or ministry position, but we need to understand that this is their *micro calling*—a specific expression of the much broader *macro calling.* Your macro calling is the deeper, broader purpose God has placed on your life. It's the unique way you fulfil His purpose, reflect His heart, and serve His Kingdom, wherever you go.

When we confuse the two, it can feel like the validity of our calling is determined by how things are going in our current role. Your calling, however, is not confined to a job description, a season, or even a location. It is something God has entrusted to *you.* When you understand this, it changes everything.

UNDERSTANDING CALLING

We need to take a breath here and unpack the idea of 'calling' because it is an important concept that is often misunderstood. We often think and talk about one type of calling: the specific task or role God has called us to fulfil. When we look to Scripture, however, we do not just see one type of calling; we see three. These three callings relate specifically to the following three areas of ministry:

1. Who we are
2. What we are here for
3. How we should serve

Author and theologian, Os Guinness, helpfully clarifies the first two callings, distinguishing between what he calls our primary and secondary callings.[2] Our primary calling is to Christ. Jesus has called us to Himself, to be with Him and follow Him. We are called to the Kingdom banquet to dine with our King. Our primary call to Christ is *the* source of our identity. Recognising that our primary calling is to Christ is an essential starting point because anything we do for Jesus stems from who we are in Him.

Who we are in Christ precedes anything we do with Him and for Him. We serve Him in response to who He has made us to be, who we are in Him, and who we are because of Him. This is our foundation; He is our foundation. Remaining in Him as the Vine precedes the producing of fruit, and everything else.

Guinness then clarifies that our secondary calling is to a purpose. This is what is commonly understood when we use the term 'calling'. We are called to do or achieve something for Jesus and His Kingdom. The key, Guinness highlights, is to understand that this secondary calling is derived from our primary calling. We discover what we are to do from who we are in Christ. Our primary calling provides the healthy basis for our identity. From here, we discern how God wants us to serve Him. This discernment of purpose and service to God is termed our secondary calling.

As we establish this healthy ordering of our primary and secondary calling, of our identity and purpose, the pastor's role can be viewed appropriately and related to in a much healthier way. This secondary calling is what I also refer to as our macro call.

Os Guinness has offered a helpful foundation in distinguishing between our *primary* and *secondary* callings, but we need to go further. In his framework, the role of a pastor is included under the umbrella of secondary calling, and this is where the confusion often begins. Hopefully, the role of the pastor will be a wonderful, faithful expression of one's secondary calling; however, this is not always the case. Someone's role or job is not automatically the same thing as their secondary calling. That distinction matters.

Scripture invites us to an even more nuanced understanding. It affirms that we can indeed be called to specific contexts, roles, and assignments, but these need to be understood as *tertiary callings*. This third aspect of calling is important and offers further clarity:

> **Primary calling:** to Christ, discovering who we are in Him because of Him.
>
> **Secondary calling:** to a key purpose in participating and fulfilling the great commission.
>
> **Tertiary calling:** the specific role or context in which we are currently fulfilling that purpose.

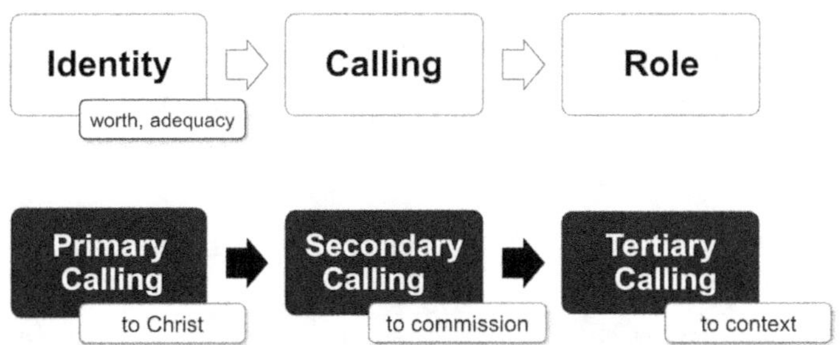

DIAGRAM 4. Three Areas of Ministry: healthy hierarchy

Our primary calling is to Christ, who is the bedrock of our identity. Our primary calling gives rise to and informs our secondary calling as we determine who we are in Christ and the purpose He has called us to. Our secondary calling subsequently gives rise to and informs our tertiary calling. The role or context God specifically calls us to is simply the current means by which we are endeavouring to fulfil our secondary calling. If the work we are doing in that context falls apart, our secondary calling does not change, nor has it been removed. This is why a call to a specific role is tertiary in nature; it serves and is a subset of our secondary calling as we serve and submit to Christ.

The healthy order of these three callings is critical for pastors to understand. A healthy model of ministry is where the role of pastoring (tertiary calling) is a subset of calling (secondary calling), and both are based on and informed by a grounded identity in Christ (primary calling). Living and ministering from this healthy order is life-giving. A jammed rudder occurs when pastors reverse the order of their primary, secondary and tertiary callings and find themselves ministering within an unhealthy framework.

CALLING VERSUS ROLE

Now that we have explored the wider theological framework, let us return to the focus of this chapter, namely, the confusion of calling and role. Since these terms are often used synonymously, we need a more helpful way to clarify the distinction between the two. Theologically, we can describe them as our secondary and tertiary callings; However, when talking with pastors, the terms 'macro calling' and 'micro calling'—in other words, our big 'C' versus our little 'c' calling—often bring greater clarity.

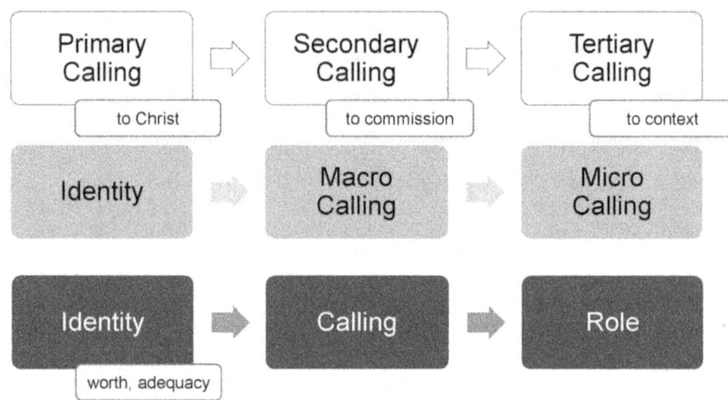

DIAGRAM 5. *Three Areas of Ministry: healthy hierarchy*

The more closely we look, the more obvious the distinction between these two callings becomes. We have just explored it in theological terms, but the distinction also exists in a vocational sense. Someone may have a calling, but that does not mean they will be living out that calling in their specific job. Consider the difference between *having a calling* and *living a calling*, or between *perceiving a calling* and *enacting a calling*.[3] It makes sense, does it not? The role someone is doing may not be a good match for their calling. They may not be able to live or enact their calling in the role, and even when they can, there are varying degrees to which they can express their calling within a role.

In vocational language, it is clear that the role is not the calling. The role is simply a vehicle for the calling. The question is: What is the quality of the vehicle? In other words, how well does the individual's calling fit their role? Interestingly, when an individual is unable to live out or enact their calling, this is often described as having an "unanswered call."[4] We saw this sense of disconnect between calling and role expressed when we introduced the concept of misdirected calling. Pastors have a strong sense of call, but equally, many have a strong sense of grief from not being able to express that calling fully through their role. Many feel the role demands different things from them, and they lament feeling like a CEO or administrator.

It is critically important for the health and effectiveness of the pastor that we clearly differentiate their calling from their role. This distinction will help to straighten out a lot of confusion, as well as empower pastors to better fulfil their God-given calling. It is important to clarify that a sense of call does not necessarily mean a call to be a pastor; there may be a different calling God has for you. Furthermore, receiving the call to be a pastor does not necessarily mean that any church that is seeking a pastor is your calling. Simply because they need a pastor and you feel called to be a pastor does not make this a match made in Heaven.

If you do have a clear sense that God has called you to pastor a specific local church, this needs to be understood as the *context* to which God has called you for the purpose of giving expression to (enacting) your calling in this season. The role itself is not the calling.

A little while ago, I sat with Sarah, a small church pastor in a mainstream denomination, at a minister's conference. We got talking, and it became obvious that she was incredibly frustrated in her role. She sighed several times as we spoke, clearly showing how stuck she felt. The church was nice enough, the people at the church were nice enough, and her denominational leader thought it would be a good fit. Yet she said to me, "I don't know what to do. I feel called, I can't deny that. I guess I just need to keep pressing into God and His strength, and allow Him to lead me and grow me, so I can better lead His people."

I felt for her. Trying to understand her situation better, I asked, "What do you feel called to?" She turned and looked at me oddly as if I had asked her something blindingly obvious. "To ministry," she said emphatically.

"Ministry simply means service," I responded. "We are all called to ministry. What specifically are you called to do or fulfil for your Lord?" She paused, sat back, and reflected.

What followed was a fascinating conversation about calling, service, and God-prompted passion. It turned out that she primarily felt called to work with people who were marginalised, disempowered, and hurting. Sarah deeply desired to see people journey to healing and live empowered lives. They did not need to have a Christian faith; her heart was for anyone facing these challenges. Pastoring a church of predominantly white, middle-class Christians, who were managing life pretty well and had a healthy level of resources, was, unsurprisingly, a poor fit with her calling.

After reading an article of mine, another pastor, Levi, reached out for help. A church had put out a call for a new pastor after their previous one had retired. They had shared with him that they wanted someone to develop the church further and grow it to a new level. Levi definitely felt called to be a pastor and was excited by this vision. Even though it was a smaller church, they seemed to have a big heart and a desire for growth. Yet he told me that the reality of the role had not been what he expected. The people seemed keen for him to carry on with his pastoring work but did not seem keen to participate or be involved in anything new. Levi had shared with them that bringing the type of growth they wanted would mean changing several things, including how they shaped the Sunday service. This had been met with a very cold response. To make matters worse, he had raised his frustrations with his denominational leader and was told that a few of Levi's contemporaries had been able to make it work at small churches. He just needed to try harder.

"Maybe he's right," he said. "Maybe I just need to keep trying. Or maybe I am just not cut out to be a pastor. No one ever said it would be easy. I just didn't think it would be this hard." Levi sighed. "I have thought of leaving, but I can't do that. I feel called to be a pastor. If I leave, I will be letting the congregation down. I will be letting God down. It will mean I have failed, and where do I go then? No," he said more resolutely. "I feel called, so I will trust God to lead me through this."

We subsequently discussed the difference between calling and role, and macro and micro calling. I could see Levi starting to have a lightbulb moment. "You certainly feel called to be a pastor. That's great," I affirmed. "But do you feel called to pastor a church that doesn't want to be led, that doesn't want to change?" That hit him. He shook his head slowly.

"You entered the role of pastoring this church because it sounded like you would be able to be the type of pastor you feel called to be. But then things changed. Whatever happened, whatever their intention, whatever was said, the current reality is that the type of pastor they want and the type of pastor you feel called to be are different. This needs to be resolved; otherwise, you will implode, and there will be tension with the church. You need to get back into true agreement with the church. Amos 3:3 said, 'Do two walk together unless they have agreed to do so?' You need to be in true agreement with them."

With Levi's new awareness of his situation, we discussed how to resolve this and bring true agreement with his church. This included:

- Praying to discern what God was asking of him.
- Considering what would need to change for his calling to better fit his role, and with whom he should discuss this.
- Accepting that if this was not where God specifically wanted him, he would not be letting God down by leaving the role. On the contrary, it would be a step towards better fulfilling what God has called him to. Furthermore, leaving would enable another pastor who was a better fit for the church to be found.
- Redefining failure as refinement. Levi's contemporaries may be doing well in other smaller churches, but each church and situation is different. To make an informed assessment of his situation to determine what role or context would be a better fit for him, he needed to ensure he was comparing 'apples with apples'.

Once you have a clearer sense of your macro call, you can more easily assess if a role will be a good fit with your calling. You can discuss and clarify the expectations of the role before you accept it. And if a role does not seem to be working out, you will be able to make decisions more objectively without personalising the situation or assuming you have failed in your calling.

Even though the process of hiring a pastor works differently within different denominations, the principle holds true. Within denominations where pastors have autonomy to choose their placement and role, this process becomes somewhat easier to navigate. In the second section of this book, we will explore more complex situations where the pastor's church placement is directed by their denominational leadership. In these contexts, it is important to recognise that the denomination or organisation to which pastors belong should be viewed as their tertiary or micro calling, not their secondary or macro calling. I appreciate that may have stunned some of you. Put simply, if you end up needing to leave your denomination, God's calling on your life goes nowhere. He will still use you.

PAUL'S MACRO AND MICRO CALLINGS

We see the difference between macro and micro callings helpfully illustrated in Paul's life and writings. Paul's overarching macro call is to be an apostle with a specific purpose or goal: "Paul, called to be an apostle of Christ Jesus by the will of God…" (1 Corinthians 1:1).

He goes on to say:

> *"… because of the grace God gave me to be a minister of Christ Jesus to the Gentiles. He gave me the priestly duty of proclaiming the gospel of God, so that the Gentiles might become an offering acceptable to God, sanctified by the Holy Spirit"*
>
> **Romans 15:15-16**

Here we see that Paul's macro calling is nuanced. Although he is called to be an apostle, his purpose is more specific than that. Paul reveals that:

- His function is to be an apostle.
- His activity is to involve "proclaiming the gospel."
- His focus is the Gentiles.

- His desired outcome is to see that these Gentiles "become an offering acceptable to God."

While fulfilling this purpose and living out this overarching macro calling, we see another calling at work. Paul receives a specific micro or tertiary call, which occurs through a vision he has of a man from Macedonia standing and begging him:

"'Come over to Macedonia and help us.' After Paul had seen the vision, we got ready at once to leave for Macedonia, concluding that God had called us to preach the gospel to them"

Acts 16:9-10

Paul's call to go to Macedonia can be considered a micro or tertiary calling because it fits within the greater sense of what he has been called to do. In this case, his macro call finds a contextualised expression in a specific time, place, and role. When God directs Paul to Macedonia, it does not displace or supersede his overarching calling to be an apostle to the gentiles. Rather, it is the specific context in which God wants Paul to fulfil his calling at that time.

If Paul's role and experience in Macedonia had not gone well, it would have changed nothing about his macro call to be an apostle to the gentiles. The same needs to be understood for any pastor accepting a call to a local ministry context. A micro call should facilitate, rather than hinder, the individual's macro call. If the role does not go well, it is important to realise that their macro call remains unchanged, and who they are in Christ (their identity and primary calling) has not altered.

This is critically important for pastors to understand and live out. When your identity calling and role are rightly aligned, and your role is viewed as a *micro calling* that flows from and serves your *macro calling,* then you will walk with greater freedom and agency.

Your role must serve your calling, not define it. If it is not helping you fulfil what God has called you to do, I hope this understanding gives you greater agency to challenge its requirements or, if necessary, to leave the role.

Your priority is not the position, but the call of God on your life. The role must serve and submit to your macro calling as you serve and submit to Jesus.

All of our *doing* needs to flow from our *being* with God. It is our relationship with Him that grounds us and empowers us. The role is not the mediator of our relationship with God. Jesus is.

Living from this healthier ordering of identity, calling and role reshapes how pastors view the expectations that come with ministry. It offers the freedom to assess role demands more clearly and respond to them more wisely. We see this affirmed theologically, supported by research, and illustrated beautifully in Paul's life. The good news is that this is not just a theory; it works. When pastors live with this kind of appropriate ordering and healthy distinction of their identity, calling, and role, they thrive![5] We see reduced rates of burnout, increased resilience, and greater enjoyment in pastoring.[6]

Now that we've clarified the difference between a pastor's macro calling and their micro calling, the next step is to help them break free from the organisational markers of success, which are so deeply embedded in their role.

5

ROLE: SUCCEEDING IN THE WRONG JUNGLE

An unintended effect of misdirected calling is that many pastors have transitioned from being spiritual leaders to organisational leaders. Instead of focusing on spiritual outcomes, their primary energy and focus have shifted toward meeting quantitative measures related to the organisational aspects of their role. Since these organisational, quantitative outcomes are often confused with calling, they have not been questioned. We need to ask ourselves, then: *What if our definition of success is not success at all, at least not the kind that truly matters?*

THE MESMERISING MARKERS OF SUCCESS

You are probably familiar with the old saying about being careful when climbing the ladder of success, lest you find it is leaning against the wrong wall. That is the very question we need to consider here: As church leaders, is the ladder we are climbing leaning against the right wall? Are the outcomes we are unconsciously and unquestionably pursuing the ones to which Jesus wants us to dedicate ourselves?

When considering the pursuit of specific organisational success, Stephen Covey employs the metaphor of a jungle rather than a wall. He addresses the different roles managers and leaders play in the success of an organisation:

> "'Management is doing things right; leadership is doing the right things.' Management is efficiency in climbing the ladder of success; leadership determines whether the ladder is leaning against the right wall. You can quickly grasp the important difference between the two if you envision a group of producers cutting their way through the jungle with machetes. They're the producers, the problem solvers. They're cutting through the undergrowth, clearing it out. The managers are behind them, sharpening their machetes, writing policy and procedure manuals, holding muscle development programs, bringing in improved technologies and setting up working schedules and compensation programs for machete wielders. The leader is the one who climbs the tallest tree, surveys the entire situation, and yells, 'Wrong jungle!'"[1]

The indicators are that we have been trying to succeed in the wrong jungle. Using this analogy, success can be viewed as the speed at which we cut through the jungle and the quantity of jungle we have cut through. We have been growing in our ability to more efficiently cut through the undergrowth and take ground. We have found new ways to grow the Church, increasing the size of congregations and becoming more efficient in creating scalable systems. But we have not stopped to consider if we are even in the right jungle.

It would be understandable to say, "Hang on, if a church is growing, how can that be wrong?" Or even, "The Church has been practising ministry and 'doing' church like this for years. If we were climbing a ladder that was leaning against the wrong wall, or cutting through the wrong jungle, we would have noticed by now. Someone would have stepped in to rectify this."

This might normally be true, but it makes perfect sense when we consider the forces at work around the pastor. Since a pastor's sense of worth and identity is tied to their role, and they often fuse or confuse their calling with their current job, the outcome measures attached to this role will hold immense power over them. Achieving success becomes necessary to maintain both their psychological and spiritual wellbeing.

Think about it for a moment. If your worth, identity and sense of God-given calling are all wrapped up in climbing a ladder that happens to be leaning against the wrong wall, these wrong outcomes will look mesmerising, even intoxicating to you. Additionally, when we create a whole system around you that is geared toward maintaining these outcomes, you can begin to understand why it might be difficult for anyone to imagine a different reality, even if they did question it. Anything that has the power to satisfy or threaten your psychological or spiritual wellbeing will be completely captivating. How could it not be?

If Covey is correct in his distinction between management and leadership, this confronts us with a very challenging question: Has our definition of success meant we are not raising a generation of church leaders but a generation of church managers? If we train and inspire our pastors to be skilled at organising, raising teams, and enabling a church to more effectively cut through the jungle without assessing if it is the jungle Jesus would have them cut through, we are mistaking leadership for what is essentially effective management of a church. The ramifications of this are huge.

This is a big call to make, so let us take a closer look. Using Covey's analogy, management success is doing what we have done before with more effectiveness and efficiency. Leadership success is achieving the right things and heading in the right direction. If we zoom in to assess whether we are doing things right as well as doing the right things, there are two key factors we have to consider: reliability and validity.

These are crucial concepts to consider because they reveal the true outcome of our efforts and where we should commit our time and energy to be the most effective. Reliability is concerned with the process that is used to produce the result. If the process is reliable, then anyone could follow the process and produce the same result. Validity, on the other hand, is about assessing whether the result that is produced is the correct one. Let us take an obvious example to clarify this. If you follow a recipe closely and get a perfectly baked cake every time, that recipe is definitely reliable. But if you actually wanted a loaf of bread, then the process may be reliable, but it is not valid.

Reliability is often confused with validity. If something is successfully reliable, it is assumed that it is also valid. When we train people to do what we do, and they do it, we can mistake this for success. We may have reliably transferred our knowledge and skills, but whether we are achieving the necessary outcome requires a different assessment.

You may have heard the old story about a mother who taught her child how to bake a fish in the oven:

> "One afternoon, a mother was preparing a fish for dinner that night. Her son and daughter were watching her, keeping her company. The woman had learned from her mother the art of baking a whole fish. As she prepared it, she cut off the end of the fish before putting it in the oven. She followed her mother's example for years, and every time, she cut off the end of the fish before cooking it in the oven. On this day, one of her children asked, 'Mum, why do you always cut off the end of the fish?'

> 'Oh,' she said, 'I don't know. That is just what I learned to do from my mother.'

> She rang her mother, the children's grandmother, and asked, 'Mum, why do we always cut off the end of the fish before we cook it?'

> Her mother replied with a giggle, 'Oh, my dear, I did that when you were young because our oven was too small to fit the whole fish in.'"

Just because we are successfully repeating what we have always done does not mean we are achieving the right thing. Sometimes we need to question what we are doing and why we are doing it.

RELIABILITY WITHOUT VALIDITY

Now, let us apply our understanding of reliability and validity to our analogy of the jungle. A person discovers that a group of one hundred people with perfectly sharpened machetes, who are able to stop for regular breaks, water, and food, will be able to cut through a kilometre of jungle per day. They let other jungle-cutting communities know this, and when those communities also follow this pattern, they discover they too can cut through a kilometre of jungle per day. The process is reliable. However, after months of doing this, they cut through a portion of the jungle only to discover they were back to where they started. They had been going around in a circle. The process may be reliable, but it is not valid. If they had been attempting to cut through the jungle to get to a village where their relatives lived, only to arrive at the sea and find they had been travelling in the wrong direction, this too would show a lack of validity in the process.

The issue comes when we assume that what we are reliably achieving is what we are supposed to be achieving. If cutting through the jungle at speed becomes the focus of success, then that community of jungle cutters might set up systems to measure their cutting speed and the distance cut. They may organise teams of cutters on rosters, so people can take turns and work sustainably. They may hold meetings about how to use and maintain their machetes.

If things are going really well, they may even hold conferences on the subject, bringing in speakers to share their experience in organising effective communities of jungle cutters and holding electives on different aspects of managing and leading such a community. During break times, delegates may ask each other questions like: How many cutters and managers do you have? They will share how much distance they have been able to cover over the last year and what they are believing for in the year to come. They may also ask each other about where they purchased their latest machetes, and what systems they are using for recruiting and managing their cutters.

All of this may make them faster and better at doing what they have always done, but it does not necessarily make them effective at achieving what is meant to be achieved. This is why it is so important to understand the difference between reliability and validity and not confuse one with the other. Continuing with this analogy, the existence of efficient and effective systems to recruit, train and deploy jungle cutters is critically important. However, we first need to check the validity of how we are using them. We need to check that we are in the right jungle and heading in the right direction.

EMOTIONAL MARKERS OF SUCCESS

Bringing it back to churches, we need to assess whether the outcomes that pastors are pursuing are the ones Jesus would have them fulfil. Have we simply become more efficient or creative at reliably reproducing what we have always done? An important question I ask pastors is, "If Jesus came and sat in your church, how would He define 'success' for this particular church? What would warm His heart to see?" Despite how we might want to answer these questions, I have found that pastors will often prioritise outcomes that are organisational and quantitative in nature. In other words, the numbers. This response is not usually representative of their hearts; rather, it is the result of the jammed rudder. When our calling is misdirected, our focus shifts. Quantitative markers of success become the driving focus, not because pastors do not love Jesus, but because somewhere along the way, their role began to determine their significance, adequacy, and worth. These outcome measures became the spiritual scoreboard that told them whether they were doing well or failing. Success came to be viewed through the lens of organisational growth instead of spiritual leadership.

I typically ask pastors, "What gives you a sense of achievement and success in ministry? Not what you would logically or even theologically call 'success', but rather, what brings a sense of relief or joy within the context of your ministry?" Pastors will often pause, reflect, and then say something along the lines of, "I know what I would like to say. I know how I should answer that question theologically, but if I am being honest, what gives me a sense of success is if my church is growing." Organisational markers of success usually include such things as congregation size, Sunday attendance, and growth in these areas. These markers of success, or KPIs, tend to be quantitative rather than qualitative. They focus on the numbers rather than change, transformation, or Kingdom impact.

Zek was the pastor of a large-ish church. He was probably in his early forties. He wore a new baseball cap and jacket. He had far more style than I ever had. When we were talking in a group one day on the subject of over-identification with the role and misdirected calling, Zek commented, "Yeah, sure. I can see how other pastors get caught in this, but these results don't drive me. The numbers are important, but they don't define me."

I replied, "Oh, that's great." Then, a thought occurred to me.

"If I were to offer you two scenarios, which one appeals to you on an emotional level?

> **Scenario one:** Over the next two years, your church doubles in size, and you have enough staff and the right systems to manage this. But the level of spiritual maturity in the church remains the same. There is no more depth or growth in this area. It is all 'transfer growth', not 'conversion growth'.

> **Scenario two:** Over the next two years, you lose twenty per cent of your congregation, and the church can keep functioning financially. But those who remain grow in their spiritual maturity and discipleship, and people come to faith. In this scenario, the numbers in the church never increase because people join other churches, plant other churches, or go into mission work, all of which are viewed independently from your church. You gain no direct benefit from it.

Which would you choose?"

There was a long pause as he considered this. After a few moments, someone else in the group (not a pastor) said, "I can't believe you are even having to think about this."

Zek replied, "I know. But it isn't that easy. Initially, I was going to say scenario two before you had finished speaking because even though I would lose people, those who remained would be of the calibre that would get our numbers back up and beyond. But when you said the numbers wouldn't increase, and I couldn't gain the benefit of others going to plant churches or going into the mission field, my heart sank. When you mentioned scenario one, I immediately felt a huge sense of relief. A burden was lifted. So, I know the right answer is scenario two, but if I'm honest, I would choose scenario one."

When I have asked other pastors in different settings which scenario they would choose, there has not even been a pause. "One!" they responded immediately. They may also say, "Isn't that bad? But if I'm honest, I would love that."

Whether it sounds bad or not, it makes sense. When a pastor's identity and calling become fused with their role outcomes, they naturally become psychologically dependent on achieving those organisational outcomes. What entrenches this further is the wider church system—denominational structures, congregational expectations, and even ministerial training—which (consciously or unconsciously) puts pressure on pastors to meet those outcomes. The tension faced by many pastors, along with this additional external pressure, creates a powerful dynamic that prioritises only one type of outcome.

OUTCOMES DETERMINING ACCEPTANCE AND VALUE

I have sat with pastors who admitted that their decision whether to attend their denominational gathering each year often depends on how their church numbers have fared. Pastors have made comments to me along the lines of:

> "After all the initial pleasantries have happened, I know I'll
> get asked by someone, 'How's your church going? What are
> you up to these days?' By which they mean, 'What's the size
> of your church?' And if we have had a bad year, if we've lost
> people, then I just feel shame. I hate it. I feel on display as a
> 'bad leader.'"

This experience is echoed by several Baptist pastors in New Zealand in Melville's interviews, who shared the pressure pastors feel to meet the organisational KPI of numerical growth. The Baptist Union, like many denominations, records the numerical outcomes of its different churches in a Yearbook. Collecting numerical data and statistics is common practice for most denominations, however, it can have unintentional outcomes on pastors' psyches. One pastor described their experience of this as "those shame and blame stats."[2] Another pastor's words are quite telling concerning their experience of the focus on numbers:

> "There is an unspoken pressure to do with the size of church
> and growth. If you are a small church and the numbers are
> declining, or if your numbers are declining and not growing,
> then what does that say about you as a pastor … you are valued
> by the size and perception of your church."[3]

A third pastor, Hosea, felt that the value of the pastor is connected to the size of his or her church. Because of this, he said, the self-esteem of pastors of small churches "takes a hammering, especially in our Baptist system."[4]

When Miriam's church experienced a sharp decline in size, it caused her to feel stressed and even distressed. She had a profound sense of inadequacy, and her self-esteem tanked, causing her to conclude, "I suck at being a pastor!"[5]

The pressure pastors feel is not just about the size or growth of the church; it can come from anything they feel is related to fulfilling the KPIs of their role. Daniel described receiving feedback that he had not performed as successfully as he had thought:

"It was an experience on a scale that I've never had to deal with before . . . the emotional resilience I already had was not adequate to deal with this specific set of circumstances; it required another level again."[6]

Unfortunately, this is the experience of so many pastors across different denominations. In my work with pastors, both in clinical settings and in personal conversations, I continue to see the same pattern. Research also confirms that a pastor's sense of wellbeing is profoundly connected to whether the church is a sufficient size or is growing numerically. It is the answer pastors will repeatedly give me when I ask them to complete this sentence, "Emotionally, I feel I am succeeding in my role, when . . ."

It is not that the numbers are not important. Numbers can be a helpful, concrete measure, and I am not suggesting we ignore them. On one level, it makes sense to focus on these numerical outcomes since churches and denominations are both dependent on them. For a church or denomination to be viable (in its current form), it requires those numbers. Both money and personnel are needed to pay the people and keep the system functioning. However, when these organisational KPIs unwittingly become a priority, while qualitative, Kingdom-centred outcomes are lost in their shadow, we have a serious problem in our churches.

No one sets out to prioritise size and Sunday attendance over depth and discipleship, but when a pastor's identity is tied to these quantitative outcomes, we can clearly see why they capture the focus and agenda of our churches and leaders.

6

———

BLINDED TO DYSFUNCTION, BLINDED BY SUCCESS

The numbers can never determine our worth and significance; only Jesus can do that. The numbers are also not always a reliable guide to the health of a church. They can even blind us to signs of ill-health and dysfunction within a congregation.

Bridget was a pastor who had lost confidence in her ability to lead her congregation well, primarily because her church was not growing and had been a similar size for several years.

I asked her, "What do you think Jesus would say success looks like for your church?"

"Hmm," she replied, "That's a good question. I guess, seeing people coming to faith. Seeing people grow spiritually. And seeing people being mobilised into ministry and mission."

"Ok, great. So, let's look at that. Have you seen anyone come to faith?"

"Oh yes. We run Alpha and have found that to be effective. I always want to see more people coming to faith, though."

"Of course, but you have seen people come to faith. What about seeing people growing in their faith?"

"Yes. I could list many people who have grown spiritually over the last year. It is certainly not everyone, but we do have some good small groups doing good work with our people."

"And is anyone moving into ministry work or even stepping onto the mission field?"

"Yes, people do step up and engage in different ministries. And we have had people go overseas on mission. That hurts; they were good people. We have also had some people leave to be a part of a church plant."

"So, you are seeing people come to faith, you are seeing people grow spiritually, and you are seeing people move into ministry and mission. Did it ever occur to you that the reason why your numbers have not changed is that you are doing the very things Jesus would want for your church?"

There was a stunned silence as that settled in. The reason Bridget's church was not growing, at least numerically, was that they were doing all the right things. The church was, in fact, growing in health, influence, and Kingdom impact. People were coming to faith, maturing in their walk, and moving into some form of external ministry or mission group. The church was healthier and more effective than she had realised. The fact that she was feeling discouraged during this time of internal growth within her congregation is a clear sign that pastors are focused on celebrating the wrong outcomes.

I remember a conversation I had with James at a gathering for pastors many years ago. He was a big-hearted leader of a large church. As we sat side by side, eating our lunch together, he expressed that he really felt for pastors of smaller churches and wanted to help them. He commented, "It's hard when you don't have the numbers." Now, he is not wrong. On this occasion, however, our conversation took an interesting and awkward turn.

I do not know if you have ever experienced a moment when the Holy Spirit drops something inside your mind, and then you carelessly share it without thinking. I had one of those moments. "Yes," I replied, "but numbers can be an anaesthetic to dysfunction."

James stopped eating, turned, and looked at me. "What do you mean?" he said.

I kept chewing and prayed fervently. *Yeah, Lord, what do You mean?*

Swallowing a little harder than usual, I said, "Well, you know, we can be so focused on the numbers that we are not looking at other elements of health."

"Like what?"

"Well, people coming to faith, for example." In my efforts to show I was not meaning any of this personally, and in an attempt to reassure him (and me), I added, "I imagine in a church of your size you see people come to faith all the time."

He thought about it briefly and replied, "I'm sure we have had some, but I can't think of anyone in the last year or so."

"Oh," I said. "Well, it could be something like an increase in the spiritual depth of your small groups."

Again, he pondered this briefly and said, "The groups are mainly relationally based, so I'm not sure what growth is occurring in people spiritually."

This conversation was not going well. I could sense he was feeling a little deflated, and I was feeling deflated for him. I tried a different tack. "Perhaps there's been an increase in ministries within the church that are blessing the local community, or the community-focused ministries that are already established within your church are having a greater impact on people's lives."

"I think we have the same ministries we have had for years now. They just tick on. I can't think of anything new or any growth that has occurred."

The conversation ended. It turned out that although the church was a reasonable size, any conversion growth was mostly historical. The church had been maintained by transfer growth from other churches. The Sunday services were well-received and attended. The small groups were enjoyed. The community ministries continued but were making little impact on the lives, needs and spiritual growth of the people they served.

It was certainly an awkward conversation, and it highlighted to me that day how misleading and unhelpful purely focusing on attendance and church size can be. It also demonstrates how we can confuse quantitative, organisational success with what Jesus wants. Jesus didn't give us the directive, "Go forth and grow large Sunday gatherings . . . This is the fruit I desire you to bear, that your churches would be large." Rather, He said, "Go and make disciples of all nations . . . teaching them to obey everything I have commanded you" (Matthew 28:19-20).

MORE IMPORTANT THAN JESUS

I sat with Luke, a pastor who was frustrated over the diminishing attendance in his church, despite his efforts to be a faithful minister of God's Word.

"Here I am preaching the gospel faithfully each week, and we are not growing," he said. "The pastor down the road, on the other hand—you should hear the heresy he's preaching—his church is growing! What's that about?!"

I replied by asking the same sort of question I asked Bridget, "Well, if we step back from that, let me ask you this: What would Jesus say that success looks like for you and your church?" I thought it was a great question and likely to reveal an encouraging and empowering answer. However, the conversation again went in a direction I was not expecting.

"Yeah, yeah, Richard, I get what you're saying. But sometimes I feel like even Jesus gets in the way."

That floored me.

"I am just being honest with you," he added. And he really was.

It made me wonder if he was revealing what many pastors feel but do not even want to admit to themselves. Their priority is not Jesus; it is to see their church grow.

When Jesus is getting in the way of what we are trying to achieve, it shows how far we have shifted from serving Him. As confronting as this revelation is, it shows the gravitational pull pastors experience on a daily basis to serve, first and foremost, the organisational markers of success. It makes sense that this is happening, though. If someone's identity is tied to the fulfilment of these quantitative outcomes, then those outcomes will be their master more than Jesus. A reminder: "People are slaves to whatever has mastered them" (2 Peter 2:19).

Nobody wants this, and nobody intends for this to happen. Unfortunately, the system around the pastor and the church is geared towards maintaining the status quo. Now, there will always be necessary organisational components of leading a church. Those organisational markers give valuable feedback and point to some worthwhile dynamics. Yet, we need to make sure the outcomes we are celebrating also represent Jesus' view of success, not some misaligned version of it.

The answer here is not simply to do the opposite and ignore the numbers. I have spoken with pastors and ministry leaders who feel fortunate that their leaders place no pressure on them regarding attendance or numbers. "That's great," I reply. "So, what are you aiming for or trying to achieve? What are you measuring?"

"Oh," they say. "Ah, no, we're just supposed to do our job and not worry about the numbers."

This sounds more like one of Patrick Lencioni's five dysfunctions of a team. Ignoring the numbers may remove some of the unhelpful pressure off pastors, but it does not help the pastor focus on achieving Kingdom outcomes. As Yogi Berra said, "If you don't know where you are going, you'll end up someplace else."

Numerical data tells a story that we need to hear about operations and organisational viability. Rather than ignoring this, we need to balance it by highlighting, measuring, and celebrating other markers that relate to the spiritual calling of the pastor and Jesus-centred objectives for the church. We need to put Jesus' qualitative, Kingdom outcomes front and centre.

CHAMPIONS OR CHUMPS

The numbers tell an important story; they just do not tell the whole story. The extent to which we focus on numbers can even cause division within the wider church, triggering comparison and competition among pastors.

I once spoke with Sebastian, a pastor who was struggling and felt like a failure. He voiced his sense of inadequacy by saying, "I have just really struggled to grow this church. It's about 200. I see the church down the road here, and it's over 500. And the church on the other side of town is around 1000."

This is the language of comparison and competition.

The numbers themselves may raise important questions around whether the person is in the right place, what their calling is, what their strengths are, and what resources they have and need. These are key conversations to have, but the language expressed by Sebastian reveals how pastors have turned colleagues into competitors and judge themselves in comparison. What we are missing is a Kingdom perspective.

When I hear pastors make these types of comments and lament over the size of their churches, I will often end up having a conversation, as I did with Sebastian that day.

"Tell me, how many people live in your city?"

"Oh, um, about 400,000."

"And of those 400,000, how many are Christians, or at least, how many attend church each week?"

"I guess about ten per cent. So, maybe 40,000."

"Ok, so let's imagine 360,000 people who do not know Jesus and are not following Him are lined up on one side of the city. Lined up on the other side is your church of 200, the other church down the road of 500, the other church on the other side of the city of 1000, and all the other churches with their collective numbers. Tell me, when you see this, what do you notice?"

Other than telling me that the total church numbers are tiny in comparison, he added, "It's a battle; we're in a fight. But we're all in this together. We're all a part of the same team."

I have noticed this to be a huge and vital shift for many pastors. Rather than comparing themselves and their churches with those around them, they realise that collectively they form a Kingdom team. Their church of 200, the church of 500 and the church of 1000 are each taking their place on the frontline of the Kingdom to engage in the massive task of the Great Commission. A competition mindset just keeps us divided. We need everyone on board. As with every team, we are grateful for our teammates. The church of 200 should be grateful for the churches numbering 500 and 1000 rather than feeling inferior because of its size. Likewise, the church of 1000 should be grateful for the church of 200 and 500, and all the others, who collectively make up the other 39,000 Christians in that city. Ultimately, the only comparison we need to make is not about the size of our churches but the number of people who know and are saved by Jesus and those we have yet to reach.

The focus on numbers has created an unhealthy dynamic of comparison and competition, which not only reduces the mental health and self-esteem of so many pastors but also negatively impacts interchurch unity and cooperation. When your worth is fused with the numbers, and you compare your numbers with others, there are two likely outcomes: You will either feel like a chump or a champion. Neither is helpful. We are co-labourers for Christ; we are not competitors.

CHARISMA VERSUS CHARACTER

A focus on numerical outcomes can act as an anaesthetic to dysfunction in the life of the church leader and the wider church culture. In part, it is this focus on quantitative, organisational outcomes that helps explain why high-profile, 'successful' leaders have come to a heartbreaking end. Our fixation on size has caused us to focus on the wrong characteristics in our pastors and pastors-in-training. It makes sense for an organisation to focus on the key attributes they believe will achieve the results they are after. It is only when there is some form of 'train wreck' that those attributes prove to be insufficient.

The fall of high-profile leaders has subsequently revealed a lack of appropriate character traits and healthy boundaries. In fact, some current pastors I know have reported confusion since what was previously praised as 'strong leadership' is now being described as narcissistic, bullying, abusive, and inappropriate. Many churches with this type of strong leadership may have experienced significant growth, but at a high cost. As one senior pastor put it, "Your anointing can take you to places that your character can't keep you."[1] Unfortunately, we have seen this play out all too often.

When the key markers of success focus on quantitative growth, leaders who can achieve these results will be honoured and elevated quickly. As such, some denominations tend to emphasise charisma over character and miss the associated pitfalls. Perhaps they promote the charismatic children's pastor, youth pastor, or associate pastor and miss signs of immaturity. They may appreciate a leader who oozes confidence but fail to recognise their underlying insecurities. Or maybe they celebrate the results achieved by successful senior pastors while missing or excusing signs of inappropriate or bullying behaviour.

In the same way that people incorrectly assume that a growing church must be a healthy church, there is also the assumption that character always goes hand in hand with charisma. It is tempting to become fixated on the 'fruits' of a ministry leader, assuming that this is all a 'God thing' without questioning the methods to get there. In fact, their type of leadership and church culture may even be emulated and reproduced. They will be viewed as having found the hidden formula for growing a church or possessing the required apostolic anointing that should be imparted to others. They will receive invitations to speak at conferences, write books, and be asked to consult or be a spiritual father or mother to emerging leaders.

We know, however, that growth does not mean health, nor does reliability of process mean validity of outcome. So when we elevate charisma over character, the results can be extremely painful for pastors, their families, and those they are leading. Whether the result is a moral failure or a driven, bullying culture, a pathway of pain and devastation is formed that may take years to be fully revealed or healed from.

The solution is not to elevate character and ignore charisma. Denominations that emphasise character formation and theological education are not necessarily demonstrating vibrancy in their churches and ministry with any consistency. In fact, focus on character can cause us to neglect competency. Just as charisma does not necessarily imply character, character does not imply competency.

We may assume that character is integral to the person, while competency in the role can be learned. This is true, in part, but it neglects giftedness and aptitude. It also begs the question that if competency can be learned, why, in so many situations, has it not been? When we look at denominations that emphasise character formation and theological education over charisma, why are we not seeing the health and vibrancy we would hope for in their churches? Is it that there is more to competency that can be taught, or are we simply not teaching the right competencies to help a church flourish?

There needs to be an emphasis and growth in both charisma (giftedness and aptitude) and character. In the same way, a church's focus should not be on health or growth, as if the one will produce the other, but rather on *healthy growth.*

From here, churches can derive the Kingdom-centred outcomes they desire their pastors to produce or facilitate, check the validity of these outcomes, and then consider the competencies, charisma and character needed to produce these outcomes. This will help everyone to be better informed about the type of person and the type of training required in that particular role.

WHY ARE WE FIXATED ON THE NUMBERS?

If these quantitative, organisational outcomes are so detrimental, why are we so fixated on them? This is especially puzzling when most church leaders would answer the question of "What is success?" very differently from a theological perspective.

Understandably, where we find ourselves now is a result of where we have come from. The priority we place on quantitative outcomes makes sense after doing a cursory scan of our history. The rise of the church growth movement in the 1970s and 1980s came as a response to the exponential decline churches and denominations had been experiencing for decades.

Society had been significantly peeling away from the Church, Christian beliefs, and Christian values, in part due to the death of God movement in the 1960s and the inception of postmodernism. Church attendance and adherence to a Christian community with Christian values were no longer a given. Declining churches could no longer support a paid pastor and began to close. Different denominational churches united together to maintain sufficient numbers just for survival. Theological colleges closed. Something needed to be done.

The church growth movement looked for ways to increase attendance and reach an increasingly secular world. It carried with it both the Kingdom purpose of reaching people as well as the organisational necessity of sufficient numbers for survival and, hopefully, expansion. What started as a genuine desire to survive and reposition the Church as an evangelistic agent in the world ultimately became markers, and then badges, of success. If your church was growing, you had 'made it' and were to be admired and emulated.

Again, please do not mishear me. I am not saying that the numbers do not matter, or that there is anything wrong with large churches. Not at all. The numbers *are* useful to monitor and measure viability and movement. The problem arises when the numbers overshadow or supplant the Kingdom-centred outcomes. When that happens, the metrics become the mission, and the truly important things slowly fade from intentional focus.

One story I find so helpful here is the story of the Boston Drill Bit Company. For years, the Boston Drill Bit Company was an industry leader, known for crafting the finest drill bits in the world. Then, their market share plummeted. They hired a new CEO, who gathered all the managers together and asked them a key question: "What are we about here at the Boston Drill Bit Company? What is our main purpose?"

The managers all discussed this and replied confidently, "We are here to make drill bits, but not just any drill bit. We are here to make the finest drill bits in the world."

The CEO paused and then responded, "No. That's not why we are here at all. We are here to make holes."

That one shift in perspective changed everything. It altered their perspective and realigned their purpose. They stopped focusing on what they *produced* and started focusing on their ultimate purpose. They asked themselves a very important follow-up question: "What is the best way to make a hole?" They moved into laser technology and recaptured the market.

When you've been making drill bits for years, and they are all you have been taught to make, it is easy to lose sight of why you are making them in the first place. After all, drill bits still make holes. The managers in the story had become so fixated on doing what they knew to do, on what they had always done, that it had superseded their ultimate purpose of making holes.

It is the same for those of us in ministry. If we think we are here to run services, grow numbers, or manage programmes, we may miss the point entirely. We are here to make disciples and see Kingdom transformation in our communities. The question we each need to consider is this: Are we making holes or are we just making drill bits?

In the context of the church, we can become so fixated on *what* we do that we lose sight of *why* we do it. We can become focused on refining and perfecting our drill bit, but lose sight of the holes we are called to make. We measure such things as Sunday attendance, revenue, number of small groups, and the personnel needed to fulfil tasks, but don't measure factors like: How many people we have mobilised to share their faith? How many people have come to faith in Jesus? How are we discipling people to be more like Jesus? How are our people loving one another well? In what ways are our people growing spiritually or demonstrating greater growth and transformation? What is the extent of the Kingdom impact we are making in our community?

The hole, for any church, is to fulfil the purposes of Jesus and be obedient to Him. The key question for every church to keep coming back to is: What would Jesus say success looks like for our church? In other words, what is our hole? The next question should be: How can we best achieve that? Is it by doing what we have always done, how most churches are doing it, or is there a better way?

What makes this even more complex is the wider church system. Pastors, churches and denominations are often collectively focused on these organisational outcomes—on producing the drill bits. This system unintentionally trains pastors and churches to produce well-made drill bits rather than teaching them the importance of making holes and equipping them to find creative ways of doing that.

When a pastor's focus is misdirected in this way—producing drill bits or remaining in the wrong jungle—they will continue to prioritise the wrong outcomes at the detriment of their mental health and wellbeing. This creates a powerful feedback loop that is difficult to escape from. For most of us, however, it is the only model we have known. It is the proverbial water we are swimming in. As such, our response has tended toward doing more of the same and hoping for a different result—the very definition of insanity.

Let's now take a deep dive into the wider church system and explore just how deep this rabbit hole goes.

7

THE WIDER CHURCH SYSTEM

Never underestimate the power of the status quo. It is hard to paddle when everything is set against you. American business theorist and economist W. Edwards Deming once wrote, "A system is perfectly designed to give you the results you are currently getting." This is a great quote and begs the follow-up question: But are they the results you want?

This discussion is relevant to our exploration of pastors' wellbeing and effectiveness because the wider system surrounding the pastor is a significant contributing factor.

THE GAME IS RIGGED: THE POWER OF THE STATUS QUO

To fully understand how the game is rigged against pastors, keeping them stuck in unhealthy patterns, we need to zoom out and examine the entire system in which they operate. Enhancing the health and effectiveness of pastors is not simply a matter of them realigning their identity, calling, and role, although that will be a big part of it. We also have to take a closer look at the forces that work against this kind of healthy change. Many of these forces are of our own making. Beneath the surface lies a system we have unintentionally created, a system that has taken on a life of its own.

We have not only struggled to change this system, but have often, without realising it, continued to actively reinforce and support it.

The term 'homeostatic forces' is important to understand here. I describe 'homeostasis' as the power of the status quo. If you have ever tried to change something, whether it's your fitness level or a policy at work, you have met with homeostasis. It is a concept from systems thinking, which states that there are forces within any given system that maintain the status quo of how that system functions, whether this occurs within the context of a family, a business, or a church. It does not matter if we love or hate the status quo; it is simply the way things are, and the system is geared to keep it this way.

Every system has a stable, default way of functioning and will continue to maintain this way of functioning through the use of internal feedback mechanisms (homeostatic forces) until such time as an external event applies sufficient force that the system cannot default back, causing the system to change.[1] A new normal then emerges.

Pastors will be able and willing to realign their identity, calling and role more easily when the system surrounding them also allows and facilitates this. We need, then, to be aware of the homeostatic forces within the system that may prevent this.

By way of example, let's step into Susan's daily ministry experience and see these homeostatic forces at work. Susan gains the agreement from her governing board to cease or reduce her pastoral visits to focus on other agreed priorities. When congregational members complain about this, however, it causes the governing board to pressure Susan to resume her pastoral visits. On hearing of their displeasure, Susan may also automatically resume visitations because she hates the feeling of people being upset with her.

Even when the forces in a system are recognised, change is not easy because every system resists change. This is what homeostatic forces do. They maintain the status quo and try to correct any alterations to the status quo. The system surrounding the pastor is no different.

As we zoom out, we can see some of these homeostatic forces at work against the pastor by taking a cursory look at the standard church model.

Western churches tend to follow a standard model that is based around a weekly Sunday morning service and will primarily include a sermon and time of worship. They will usually host weekday home groups and encourage their congregation to serve and give financially to the church. It may vary slightly, but this is the model that members of churches will be most familiar with. It makes sense, then, that congregations will typically look for a church leader to facilitate, maintain and expand the growth of the church on the basis of this model. The role a pastor performs, therefore, also needs to conform to and uphold this model. This default model is a system, and like every system, it will have homeostatic forces working to protect and maintain it.

Revenue is needed to maintain the employment of the pastor and any additional staff. Within this model, revenue is usually derived from the members of the church. Growth or decline in attendance or membership correlates, to a greater or lesser degree, with the amount of revenue that is generated. If the role the pastor performs changes in any way, affecting the style of service or upending the familiar model of what church should look like, this has the potential to cause unhappiness or even distress among the congregation. If communicating their unhappiness (a feedback loop) is not sufficient to return the pastor's performance to the status quo, then people may choose to leave the church. This would likely reduce income, which in turn could reduce the hours people are employed or the viability of the role itself. Anything that has the potential to reduce the number of attendees and givers, with no reassurance of replacing those people, will make it risky and unlikely to be attempted.

Our current model of church is a system with significant homeostatic forces at play that can make any attempts to change to a different model unviable. This goes beyond trial and failure. The very anticipation of detrimental outcomes within the church context can cause people to persevere with and perpetuate the current model. This includes expectations and understanding about the pastor's role and what it involves. Any attempts to change the role of the pastor and/or the model of church would need to secure the agreement of most of the congregation. The wider church system would also need to be reassured of growth or find an alternative revenue source to support the establishment of a new system. None are easy solutions, and the status quo remains.

We may want to move by faith, being faithful to what God requires of us and trusting Him with the outcome. However, these homeostatic forces can lurk below our consciousness, secretly pressurising us to maintain the status quo. To change this, it helps if we can see and name what is occurring so we can better oppose and resolve these forces.

In the default model of the local church, increased attendance is the major and most common marker of success for congregants, pastors, and denominations. The internal pressure felt by most pastors is reinforced by the homeostatic forces in the wider system. We saw this in the comments from pastors earlier, who referred to the significant influence of the denominational system. Some determined whether they would attend pastors' gatherings based on whether their church had performed well or not. One felt the pressure of "those shame and blame stats", and others felt they received such messages as, "You are valued by the size and perception of your church."[2]

When we look at denominations within the wider system, we can see that they, too, face pressure to maintain the status quo. They have their own homeostatic forces to contend with. When you think about it, denominations also tend to track health and growth based on the number of churches, and the attendance, membership and revenue (levies) generated from these churches. These numbers correlate with the viability of the denomination's structures and perceived success. As such, similar feedback loops will be operating at a denominational level to maintain the current model of church, including the role requirements of the pastor.

Hosea, a Baptist pastor, described his experience of homeostatic forces within the denomination system this way:

> "There is a culture within the Baptist movement that larger churches are valued more than smaller churches ... If you are a pastor of a small church, your self-esteem takes a hammering, especially in our Baptist system. National events such as the

Baptist Assembly provide fertile ground for comparison and competition in relation to numerical growth."[3]

This has been a sentiment that I have heard from pastors across many denominations. Equally, if we look at ministerial training institutions within this wider church system, we see they also experience their own set of homeostatic forces. Their viability and perceived success are based, in part, on the number of students enrolled and the revenue generated by these students and other stakeholders. Since churches and denominations are geared toward maintaining the current model, ministerial training institutions understandably position themselves to meet the demand from these sectors to train people in ways that fulfil the role requirements of the pastor within the current model.[4]

When we step back and let all this sink in, we can see how entrenched the pastor's wider support system is in maintaining the status quo, and how this can jam the rudder for both the pastor and the church. Yet, if the system we are experiencing is perfectly designed to give us the results we are currently getting, we now need to stop and prayerfully consider whether these are the results we—and, more importantly, Jesus—actually wants. When I have asked churches I've worked with what outcomes they believe Jesus would desire for their church, their responses include people coming to faith in Jesus, growing deeper in their spiritual formation, conforming to the likeness of Jesus, sharing their faith in a variety of ways, and making a tangible difference in homes, workplaces, and communities. These are qualitative, Kingdom-centred outcomes. I imagine if I asked most denominations and ministerial training institutions the same question, they would give me very similar answers.

If this is the case, then we need to assess how many churches are experiencing these results at the desired level, and how much time, energy, and resources churches, denominations and ministerial training institutions are dedicating specifically to achieving these outcomes. The answer to both questions is: very few. I do not say that to be disparaging or judgemental; it is simply the result of the system at work.

When I ask churches what they would do differently if they were focusing solely on achieving these qualitative outcomes, I usually hear thoughtful and useful ideas. For example:

> "We would mentor people in our church to deepen their passionate spirituality through the spiritual disciplines. We would train people how to share their faith in the workplace and to approach their work with a mission mindset. We would organise groups around these areas to help them grow, and we would establish a mentoring system to help replicate this in more and more people, especially new Christians."

Despite the strength of these ideas, very few churches follow through in any sustained or significant way. The reason is usually not only the time, energy and resources it would take, but the perceived threat to the viability and success of the current model. Pastors are often conditioned to maintain and increase Sunday attendance. Congregations are usually conditioned by familiar expectations to attend, serve, and give. Anything that detracts from the status quo can feel uncertain and risky.

FOUR COMMON RESPONSES

Over the years, I have observed that instead of challenging the system itself, churches and denominations tend to respond to this ongoing difficulty in four common ways.

1. Denial

Some leaders express the view that there is no real problem, or at least not one that applies to *their* church or *their* denomination. They may point to encouraging outliers or to the growth they are experiencing in their own context. However, even when their growth is healthy and genuinely reflects Kingdom outcomes, the saboteurs we discussed earlier remain, undermining the health of the pastor and the long-term sustainability of their ministry.

2. Resilience Training

In some contexts, the negative impact on pastors' wellbeing is minimised or normalised. If a pastor is not coping, the assumption is that *they* are doing something wrong. The solution, then, is framed around strengthening the individual and growing more resilient leaders who can withstand the demands of the role. This may sound constructive; however, it misses a significant point. If a person is in a toxic relationship, the solution is not to teach them how to be more resilient in that relationship. Rather, we should help them name what is unhealthy and begin to change it.

3. Ignoring

Some leaders acknowledge that a problem exists, but view it as too large, too complex, or too deeply embedded to change. The emphasis is on faithfulness—focusing on doing the best one can and praying that change will someday come. While this posture may be sincere, it often leads to passive resignation rather than hope-filled engagement, leaving the deeper systemic issues unaddressed.

4. Coaching

In this approach, the underlying belief is that pastoral leaders are underequipped. Church denominations and ministerial training institutions (MTIs) subsequently focus on coaching pastors to function more effectively within the current model of church ministry. The assumption is that if pastors can lead better—whether in governance, worship services, small groups, or volunteer mobilisation—they will find the right formula for health and growth.

There is much to affirm here. Coaching and equipping pastors is vital. One of the difficulties, however, relates to the focus of this coaching. Too often, denominations, MTIs and other leadership networks focus on helping pastors produce a better 'drill bit' rather than clarifying the 'holes' Jesus is calling them to make and exploring how best to do that in their specific context. Without this shift in focus, the five saboteurs identified earlier remain active and unaddressed. The unhealthy system continues.

Instead of simply helping pastors to become more resilient within an unhealthy system, we need to recognise the range of homeostatic forces at play—forces that are reinforced by various stakeholders across the wider church system. An awareness of these pressures is essential if we truly desire to reshape the system so that it better serves the qualitative outcomes we seek. Ultimately, a healthy alignment of identity, calling and role will only be possible if it is supported by thoughtful and courageous systemic change from those who shape the culture and structures of ministry.

8

—

HOW DO YOU TURN A SUPER TANKER?

The situation is complex, but it is not hopeless. When a system is strongly geared towards maintaining the status quo, there are at least two significant ways to bring about change. The first is to start new operations (new churches) that carry the new DNA. They need to be tended to and cared for so they do not revert to the default model. A second way to change homeostasis is to persistently and consistently operate in the new way until the system expands and adopts it as the new status quo. Due to the complex nature of the wider church system, identifying significant points of leverage known as 'trim tabs' would need to be identified to facilitate change.

Trim tabs are an incredibly helpful concept that Peter Senge describes in his book, *The Fifth Discipline*. Imagine a super tanker or ocean liner sailing through the sea with force and momentum. If it wants to change course, it is not simply a matter of turning the rudder to move the ship in the new direction. There is too much water pressure on the rudder. The rudder is locked into a status quo direction by the homeostatic forces around it. This is where the trim tab comes in. It is a little rudder for the main rudder. It can be moved more easily and redirects the water pressure. As the water pressure around the trim tab slowly builds, it puts greater and greater pressure on the main rudder until it is sufficiently strong to move the rudder in the new direction.[1] The trim tab is a rudder for the rudder.

In the same way, if we want churches to be different, we must identify areas of leverage that are powerful enough to put pressure on the wider church and bring about change over time. Ideally, this would be a multifaceted approach, involving the pastor, the church, the denomination, and the relevant ministerial training institutions.

This is a useful analogy since we are looking at ways to unjam the stuck rudder that most pastors experience. To find our trim tab, or areas of significant leverage, there needs to be a much larger conversation regarding the nature of ministry and the operation of the Church. We need to identify the 'hole' and the part that each stakeholder within the wider Church can play in creating the hole, rather than just producing the drill bit. We need a conversation that includes all the different stakeholders and addresses the homeostatic forces embedded in the system to maintain the way we 'do' church and the outcomes we celebrate as success. Only then can we discover how they may be unintentionally contributing to these detrimental outcomes and limiting the effectiveness of pastors and churches. The system looks something like this:

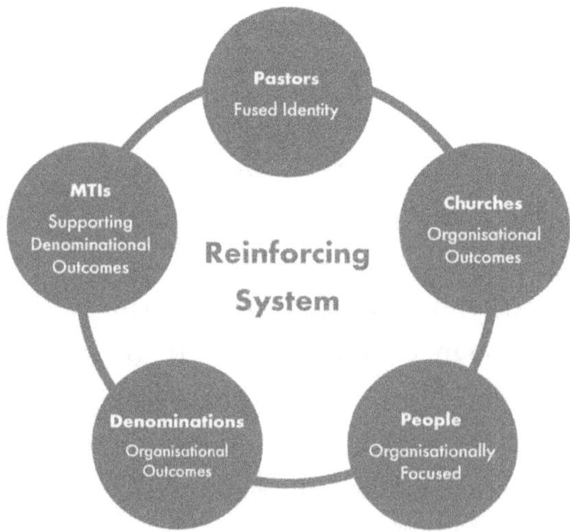

DIAGRAM 6. Unhealthy Reinforcing System

In this unhealthy reinforcing system, the role of the pastor:

- Focuses on quantitative, organisational outcomes.
- Limits the true expression of their calling.
- Determines the identity and sense of worth of the pastor.

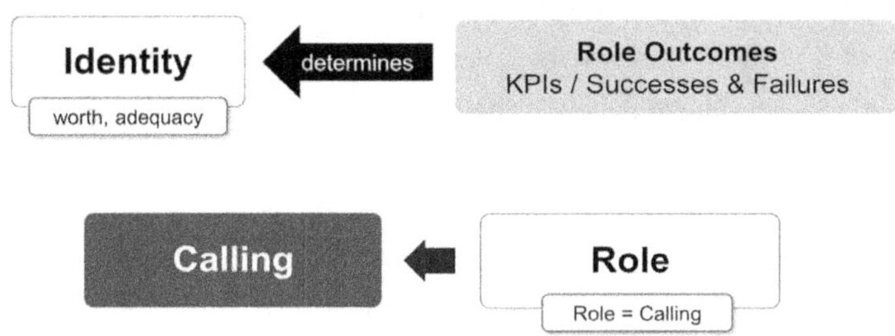

DIAGRAM 7. Unhealthy Ministry: fusion and hierarchy

SYSTEMIC CHANGE: A VIABLE AND COMPELLING ALTERNATIVE

So how do we bring meaningful change when the issue is so systemically complex? We need a compelling and viable alternative, and we need to identify key areas of leverage within the system, where our energy and attention will have the greatest impact.

Within the current system, we can see three such areas that have the potential to become powerful levers for transformation:

1. The Fusion of a Pastor's Identity, Calling, and Role

A pastor's sense of identity and call is often entangled with their role, leaving them vulnerable to role demands.

2. The Fusion of Success with Quantitative Outcomes

Success is frequently measured against organisational markers of success rather than Kingdom outcomes.

3. The Reinforcement of Quantitative Outcomes by the Wider Church System

These markers of success are reinforced and perpetuated by churches, fellow pastors, denominational groups, and ministerial training institutions.

In part two, I will explore the kind of change needed to realign our rudders, both on a personal and systemic level.

We will explore these three leverage points in more detail and discover practical ways to facilitate greater health and change within the system. We will begin by looking at how pastors can unjam the rudder through chapters focused on:

- **Identity:** Cultivating an identity in Christ that is rooted in Him and distinct from the pastoral role.
- **Calling:** Clarifying the pastor's macro calling, differentiated from the role.
- **Role:** Matching and reshaping the role so that it serves the calling, rather than defining it.

Secondly, we will focus on role outcomes, examining how we can realign the markers of success with the Kingdom outcomes Jesus calls us to pursue. Thirdly, we will consider systemic support and how key stakeholders, churches, denominations, and ministerial training institutions can resource and reinforce a healthier model of ministry, which includes:

- **Thriving leaders:** Pastors ministering from a differentiated sense of identity, calling, and role.
- **Kingdom-focused churches:** Churches pursuing and celebrating the qualitative, Kingdom-focused outcomes.
- **Mobilised disciples:** People growing as healthy disciples mobilised in mission and ministry.
- **Releasing denominations:** Denominations focused on supporting thriving leaders and Kingdom-focused churches.

- **Equipping MTIs:** Ministerial training institutions preparing pastors to be thriving leaders who lead Kingdom-focused churches.

Starting with the pastor and then extending to the wider ecosystem of churches, denominations, and ministerial training institutions (MTIs), the aim is to create a new kind of reinforcing system. A healthier one. One that affirms and sustains the proper alignment of identity, calling, and role, and champions Kingdom outcomes over default organisational metrics.

OVERCOMING THE IMPOSSIBLE

There are critical moments in ministry, and in life, when the task in front of us feels impossibly large. The obstacles seem too many and too complex. Your disappointments may feel too deep, and the failures too fresh. Yet the real question is not, "How big is the task?" but rather, "Will I be faithful to the One who has called me?" How we respond in these critical moments depends on the mindset we carry and the perspective we choose to take.

In Exodus fourteen, the Israelites are stuck in a seemingly impossible position, trapped between Pharaoh's advancing army and the Red Sea. We see three distinct perspectives and responses to this desperate situation. From a human perspective, the likely outcome is either slaughter or slavery. Panic grips the people and, in their fear, they turn on Moses. Fear often causes people to seek someone to blame. They deliver what I believe is one of the funniest lines in the Old Testament:

> *"Was it because there were no graves in Egypt that you brought us to the desert to die?"*
>
> **Exodus 14:11**

Their complaining continues:

> *"What have you done to us by bringing us out of Egypt? Didn't we say to you in Egypt, 'Leave us alone; let us serve the Egyptians'? It would have been better for us to serve the Egyptians than to die in the desert!"*
>
> **vv.11-12**

The Israelites have come out of Egypt, but Egypt has yet to come out of them. And so they understandably react from a powerless perspective. Moses, however, is a man of faith. He has seen the power of God firsthand. He speaks from a faith perspective and exhorts the Israelites to stand firm.

> *"Do not be afraid. Stand firm and you will see the deliverance the Lord will bring you today. The Egyptians you see today you will never see again. The Lord will fight for you; you need only to be still"*
>
> **vv.13-14**

Now, you might assume that the faith perspective is the pinnacle, and Moses has nailed it. This is certainly a beautiful declaration of trust. Yet, God is about to take this to a surprising new level.

When God speaks, He asks Moses a seemingly strange question, "Why are you crying out to me?" (v.15). He then gives the baffling directive, "Tell the Israelites to move on."

Moses must have experienced a moment of incredulity, "Um, Lord, how?! We have the Red Sea in front of us and Pharaoh's army pursuing us from behind. We are trapped with a massacre about to occur! Exactly *how* do we move forward?!"

It is a confusing command until you hear the resonance of that Hebrew word *naca*. It does not mean 'leap forward in a single bound', but rather, to move forward in stages. In other words, to move forward one step at a time. The word carries the sense of pulling up your tent pegs.[1] It invites us to loosen the stakes keeping us stuck, so we are ready to move when God says, "Go!" When God is telling us to move forward, we may not know where we are heading or even how we are going to get there. We do what we can do, and leave with God what only He can do.

God gives clear instructions to Moses to do what he can do.

> *"Raise your staff and stretch out your hand over the sea to divide the water so the Israelites can go through the sea on dry ground"*
>
> **v.16**

Moses raises his staff. A small act, humanly speaking, but one which becomes the channel for divine power. Moses cannot part the sea himself, but what he can do is hold up his staff and keep holding it out. What the Israelites can do is pull up their tent pegs, pack up the camp, and get ready to move. A simple act of obedience that makes space for the miracle.

What is interesting here is that, unlike in the movies, the miracle does not happen immediately. As Moses continues to stand there with his arm stretched out, and the Israelites wait, the wind starts to blow, and the waters start to recede "throughout the night" (v.21). It may have seemed impossible, but by dawn, there is a way forward.

The same pattern is true for all of us. As we seek the Kingdom outcomes God has put before us, there will be obstacles, delays, and moments that feel impossible. Our job is not to manufacture the miracle; we simply cannot. Our job is to keep moving forward in faith, persistently doing what we can and are called to do. That is when miracles occur.

Often, it is not that the vision is too big, but rather that our steps are not small enough and our perseverance not steady enough. Our determination can dissipate because it feels easier to stay as we are. It is only when remaining the same becomes unbearable that we find the motivation to move forward. I hope that we've reached that point. If we still need a wake-up call, let the reality of where we are and the trajectory of where we are heading be our motivation.

In faith, let us do what we can, taking small, consistent steps towards what Jesus is calling us to do. This is how transformation happens, even when powerful homeostatic forces pull us towards the comfort of the status quo. Our job is to be faithful with what God has entrusted us with, and to trust the One who has called us. The miracles, we leave to Him.

The call to us is the same as it was to the people at the Red Sea: "Move forward." So, my friends, if you are ready, take up the staff that is in your hand. Gather your courage and creativity, and lift your eyes to the One who calls you. Let us move forward in faith, doing what we can and partnering with Jesus to bring true transformation and see more of His Kingdom on earth as it is in Heaven.

PART TWO

FREE-FLOWING MINISTRY

9

THE PASTOR'S IDENTITY: KEYS FOR DIFFERENTIATION

To effectively unjam the pastor's rudder, we need to begin by realigning their sense of identity, calling, and role, so that they are all pointing in the right direction. This starts by untangling their identity from their role and its outcomes, and grounding it fully in Jesus. Jesus is "the Author and Perfector of faith" (Hebrews 12:2 AMP). He is our beginning and our end. He is the Vine from which we are created and sustained, and from whom we bear fruit. We are to be planted in Jesus, so that everything that grows in us and flows from us comes from Him.

Many of us know this truth logically and theologically, but have not always experienced it on a practical level. The gravitational pull to source our identity in our role is profound, and it continually and imperceptibly works against our best efforts and theological understanding.

In this chapter, I want to introduce an essential tool that will help us separate our identity and sense of worth from what we do and achieve. In the next chapter, we will explore why and how we can practically source our identity in Jesus.

A TOOL FOR REALIGNMENT: DIFFERENTIATION OF SELF

If a pastor's over-identification with the role is the problem, then how do we *not* do that? What is the solution?

The term *differentiation of self*, or DoS, is incredibly important here as we consider how to bring about healthy change. Differentiation of self is, first and foremost, a description of what pastors need to do. By that, I mean that there needs to be a clear distinction and separation of one's identity from the role itself. Secondly, it can be viewed as a measurable quality, with some people having high levels of DoS and others possessing lower levels of it. In other words, DoS is not an either/or; we are all works in progress, and everyone has varying degrees of separation between their identity and role. Thirdly, DoS is a tool that you can learn and be coached in.[1] As you learn and apply the 'how tos', you can enhance the quality of your DoS and become a healthier and more resilient individual.

The concept and language around DoS originated from Bowen family systems theory, where the formation of a person's identity and sense of self enables them to clearly distinguish their values and beliefs from those of others.[2] A higher level of DoS allows people to relate to others and to their work with greater objectivity. The opposite case occurs when a person compromises their own values and beliefs for the sake of fitting in or remaining acceptable to someone else.

Jesus modelled high levels of DoS consistently, and this is highlighted at the beginning of His ministry. His popularity and success could easily have captivated Him, but instead, we see that "Jesus would not entrust himself to them, for he knew all people" (John 2:24).

Jesus' high level of DoS enabled Him to do and say what the Father required of Him, even when it cost Him the equivalent of a 'church split'— losing followers and respect. After Jesus told His followers He was the Bread of Life who had come down from Heaven, John reported that, "From this time many of his disciples turned back and no longer followed him" (John 6:66). This is not a successful ministry by today's standards. Beyond this,

Jesus was willing to be betrayed, deserted, and even crucified to fulfil His calling, because His identity remained hidden in the Father, not in what a successful rabbi should look like.

Differentiation of self is simply the contemporary language used to describe the dynamic we see Jesus embody. It is a useful way to help us understand what we, as Christ followers, also need to display.

The benefit of DoS is that it enables us to respond to challenging situations in healthy and constructive ways. It allows us to speak and act from our values and convictions even in the face of emotional pressure from those around us. We can also allow others to do the same by remaining connected with them throughout the interaction, even when there is tension or disagreement.

Being sufficiently differentiated gives us significant personal and relational resources. Personally, it enables us to regulate our emotions, have greater resilience in the face of negativity, and have a helpful perspective towards the requirements of our role. Relationally, it enables us to respond constructively.[3]

DoS may seem very similar to the concept of emotional intelligence. One difference, though, is that emotional intelligence is focused on emotional awareness and the ability to regulate and work with reactive emotions as they occur. Differentiation of self, on the other hand, helps you remain emotionally healthy by creating a healthy sense of yourself, so you do not get reactive.[4] When you have a high DoS, you typically do not take things to heart, and as such, there is less emotional pressure on you.[5] In other words, emotional intelligence is a tool to enhance resilience and emotional regulation amid distress, whereas DoS helps prevent you from experiencing that distress in the first place.

In recent years, there has been significant research into the extensive benefits pastors experience when they are able to differentiate themselves sufficiently from their role.[6] Some of the highlights include:[7]

- Enhanced self-worth
- Constructive conflict responses
- Maintenance of healthy relationships
- More transformative leadership styles

- Greater resilience
- Greater emotional regulation
- Less psychological distress
- Less burnout

This is quite a staggering list. Distinguishing your identity from your role means that any criticism of your performance or perceived failure is not perceived as a threat. Your levels of emotional reactivity and defensiveness will be lessened, allowing you to perceive and respond to a situation from an emotionally calmer position. How good would that be?

From a calmer position and with a clearer perspective on a difficult or conflicting situation, pastors can respond with better communication skills, utilise constructive conflict resolution styles, set appropriate boundaries, negotiate role expectations, better fulfil their sense of calling, and have a lower intent to leave.[8]

Being more objective, centred, and less reactive reduces the need for emotionally taxing defensive behaviours and reduces the likelihood of emotional exhaustion—a significant factor in burnout. It also reduces stress, anxiety, and depersonalisation.[9]

When we examine all of these benefits, differentiation of self may seem like a superpower. This begs the question, or rather, screams the question: Why is this not an intentional, explicit part of every pastor's training?

If you need more convincing about the importance of this, let us take a closer look at some of those key benefits. Strap yourself in because this gets really good.

First, higher levels of DoS often lead to a more transformative leadership style.[10] Pastors are better equipped to choose their leadership response rather than operating from a reactive or prescribed mindset dictated by their role identity. In other words, pastors are released to actually lead rather than simply reacting to, placating, or avoiding anything that may be difficult or unpopular.

Second, DoS helps to clarify and bolster a pastor's calling, making it essential "for understanding and living out one's sense of call."[11]

Third, it has spiritual benefits for the pastor, including increased spiritual maturity, a sense of spiritual renewal, and a more secure connection with God.[12] Higher levels of DoS can strengthen a pastor's intrinsic spirituality, resulting in a deeper relationship with God and increased wellbeing overall.[13]

Fourth, higher levels of differentiation enable pastors to adopt a far more constructive approach to managing conflict.[14] This is particularly compelling as it addresses an issue I mentioned earlier. Research has shown that higher emotional intelligence levels are generally associated with more constructive conflict resolution styles, except if you are a pastor.[15] For pastors, "conflict management style and emotional intelligence seemed to be unrelated constructs."[16] This raises a crucial question as to whether the real issue here is lower levels of DoS. It appears that differentiation of self is the missing piece of the puzzle. When pastors have higher levels of DoS, they are equipped to access the benefits of their emotional intelligence and use constructive forms of conflict management to resolve the issue.

Fifth, it provides resources for resilience against systemic, homeostatic forces.[17] It is hard to live with freedom, health, and effectiveness when the system around you applies pressure to conform to pre-set role expectations.[18] This could come from congregational or denominational expectations, or discourses embedded in church culture and ministerial training institutions. Any resources that could strengthen a pastor against this would be invaluable.

As we can see, there are powerful benefits from developing a high level of DoS. I told you there would be good news. The great news here is that differentiation can be learned. As one researcher put it, "Bowen systems coaching may offer a valuable pre-emptive clinical intervention that can enhance the ability of clergy to flourish in ministry."[19] In other words, training pastors to differentiate themselves from their role is critically important and can provide significant benefits to their lives and their leadership. But if a person is no longer drawing their sense of identity from their role, from where are they drawing it?

THE SOURCE OF OUR REALIGNMENT

More than simply differentiating our identity from the role itself, the critical factor is *where* we source our identity from. Our identity must be anchored in a source that is real, true, healthy, stable, and unwavering. Jesus is the only One who meets this criterion. Our identity must be anchored in Jesus in a deep, profound, and tangible way. We know this, right? If only it were our lived experience. Often, it is not until the places from where we have been drawing our identity and worth fail that we return to this unshakeable source. It is not until we get to the end of ourselves that we come back to Him.

> *"What happiness comes to you when you feel your spiritual poverty! For yours is the realm of heaven's kingdom"*
> **Matthew 5:3 TPT**

When we discover who we are in Him and because of Him, it is life-giving. Unfortunately, we do not tend to start here; instead, joy and grace await us when we admit defeat and discover that the role can never give us what only Jesus can. Here are four pastors' experiences of just that.

Elijah put it this way:

> "And so, you need to actually have a deep sense of whose you are, and what God has called you to do . . . you're not defined by being a pastor, you're defined as a child of God, which is a bigger thing. So, you've got to find your sense of self-worth outside of the role, otherwise, it's going to unravel for you at some point."[20]

Rebekah realised the importance of sourcing her identity in being a child of God:

> "Just having something so you don't get your identity in just being a pastor, you get your identity in being a child of God.

He's created you with different bents and he wants you to enjoy life."[21]

Isaac encountered greater freedom:

"[I am] just loving what God has given me and not sweating the small stuff, and not thinking that my identity is tied up in my ministry, which is huge for me."[22]

Deborah discovered:

"[The biblical truth that I am a child of God] kind of hit my heart in a way that I actually believed it and kind of felt this sense of freedom, you know, succeed or fail that doesn't change the core of who I am, I'm still God's beloved child, so that was incredibly transformative for me and my thinking."[23]

Deborah's transformation came when she was able to differentiate her identity from her role and source her identity in being "God's beloved child." It was something that she had known previously at a cognitive level, but now she "actually believed it" and experienced its transformative nature.

THE STEPS TOWARDS DIFFERENTIATION IN CHRIST

Learning to differentiate yourself from the role has to involve anchoring your identity in Christ. This is what authors Frederick and Dunbar call *differentiation of self in Christ,* or DifC for short. It entails "basing one's identity in Christ, as adopted into the family of God via Christ's saving work on the cross," and it forms the essential and only appropriate basis of our identity.[24]   They rightly remind us that "Christ's identity becomes the believer's identity."[25]

Rooting our identity in our adoption into God's family through the saving work of Jesus gives us a deep sense of worth and purpose. It provides a secure foundation from which we can more objectively assess the expectations, demands and requirements in ministry, without them threatening our identity, worth, or adequacy.

To help us understand more fully that our identity is in Christ, Frederick and Dunbar use the theological concept of *imago Dei* (image of God). They explain that recognising we are made in the image of God and belong to His family gives us an intrinsic sense of worth and value and empowers us to fulfil God's purposes and directives.[26]

I appreciate this framework; however, there is another theological concept, which I believe may be more helpful for us to consider in this context and which I will discuss in more detail later: *imago Christi* (image of Christ). That said, no matter what theological lens we view ourselves through, Deborah highlights that what truly matters is not merely understanding our identity in Christ cognitively or theologically, but *experiencing* it as a lived reality.

Frederick and Dunbar's explanation of DoC offers a valuable framework for helping pastors disentangle the often-blurred lines between identity, calling, role, and work. They acknowledge the work of Os Guinness, regarding primary calling and secondary calling, which we discussed earlier.[27] Guinness emphasises that we are firstly called to 'Someone' (Christ the Caller) before we are called to something or somewhere.[28]

This call of ours to Someone before anything else is a deep truth in which we must remain sourced and rooted. As authors Cocksworth and Brown put it,

> "Christian identity is fundamentally relational; it is a called
> identity, a vocational identity. This calling into Christ precedes
> what we do for Christ, and even how we live for Christ."[29]

Glenn Packiam puts it simply, "Our first love is our first call. It is not to a purpose, but to a Person—to Christ Jesus himself."[30]

Our primary calling to Christ grounds our identity and becomes the essential starting point for healthy pastoral leadership. It is not only theologically sound, but also psychologically nourishing. It gives us a resource that deepens our wellbeing and strengthens our mental resilience.

Guinness's distinction begins the process of clarifying the blurring of calling and role.[31] What we often refer to as a calling must assume its rightful place as a secondary calling. Although it is important, our calling to Christ is the first and defining one. It gives life to everything else.

This perspective enhances spiritual, theological and psychological differentiation for the pastor by clarifying that it is their primary calling to Christ that gives rise to and informs the work they do. Our secondary calling is an expression of who we are in Him, not the other way around. This ordering is not just good theology; it is essential for pastoral health and resilience.

While Guinness stops at the distinction between primary and secondary callings, I believe there is one further clarification that can strengthen this model for pastoral leaders. Our secondary calling flows from our relationship with Christ and is shaped by finding our identity in Him. Only then does it take on expression in our particular context. In other words, our work is not our secondary calling—it is the *outworking* of it.

This means that what we usually speak of as calling (what Guinness calls our secondary calling) is *derived* from our identity in Christ and subsequently *drives* our job choice.[32] We need to be clear on this healthy order. Of course, this does not negate that a person may also be called to a specific role, but we need to be clear that this is a *tertiary calling*.

One of the challenges that can blur this order is the fact that all three elements—our identity in Christ, our calling to a purpose, and the specific role we have—are a part of every ministry. The issue is not whether you believe your identity is in Christ, whether you feel called, or whether you serve in a specific role. The real issue is how you have ordered them in your heart and mind.

When we understand that there is a healthy hierarchy, we can better examine our lives and realign ourselves where needed. Living out of this healthy order is what produces a healthy and robust differentiation of self. It enables us to embody what Paul prayed for in Ephesians 3:16-19.

> *"I pray that out of his glorious riches he may strengthen you with power through his Spirit in your inner being, so that Christ may dwell in your hearts through faith. And I pray that you,*

*being rooted and established in love, may have power, together
with all the Lord's holy people, to grasp how wide and long and
high and deep is the love of Christ, and to know this love that
surpasses knowledge—that you may be filled to the measure of
all the fullness of God."*

This is the grounding we need, that through the Holy Spirit, we would
be people who experience the vast love of God that is in Christ Jesus. This
experienced love should be the starting point of any ministry that we do
or role that we fulfil. Our ministry is ultimately an overflow of the love we
have received and continue to experience in Jesus.

If we zoom out and look at this model, we see a healthy hierarchy where
our role (tertiary calling) is a subset of our calling (secondary calling), and
both come from and are informed by our identity in Christ (primary calling).

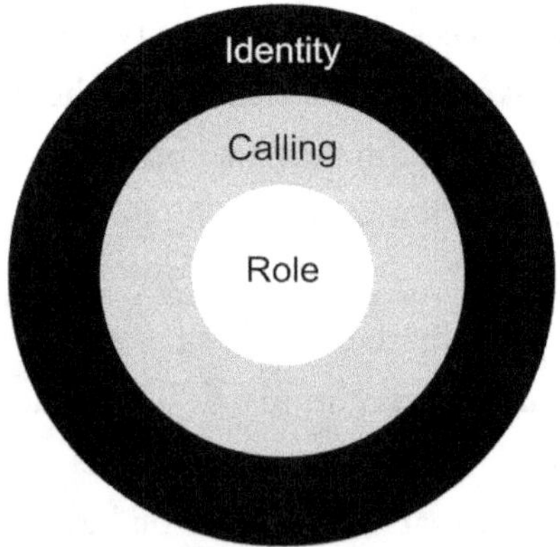

DIAGRAM 8. *Healthy Ministry Model: hierarchy subsets*

This is the healthy realignment that resolves what so many pastors
experience, where their identity and calling are subsumed by the expectations
of the role.

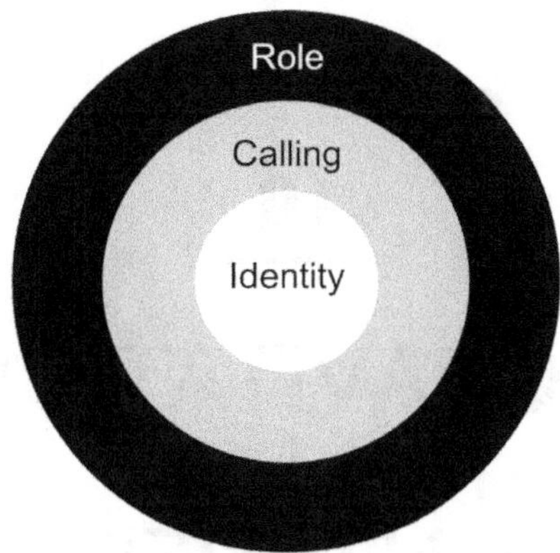

DIAGRAM 9. Unhealthy Ministry Model: hierarchy subsets

Now that we are aware of the importance of operating from this healthy order, how do we shift from knowing it cognitively to experiencing it practically? In other words, how do we realign our rudder so it is pointing in the right direction? To answer this, we first need to understand why we find it so difficult. What is happening within the human heart that draws us away from Christ so easily and makes us so susceptible to counterfeits?

10

THE GRAVITATIONAL PULL OF COUNTERFEITS

Ministry can become consumed with dealing with the latest conflict, organising the next event, breaking through the next growth barrier, and trying to be everything that people are expecting of you. When your identity and sense of self-worth are dependent on how well you achieve any of this, you are increasingly vulnerable. The daily pressures of ministry can seem light years away from Jesus' words that "my yoke is easy and my burden is light" (Matthew 11:30). Ministry can seem anything but.

It is not like Jesus did not know what He was talking about. He did not say these words from some form of idyllic ministry environment. More than being told He preached too long, or people did not like His sermon, He had powerful people publicly challenging Him and conspiring to have Him murdered. As we saw earlier, He even saw His whole 'church' walk out, leaving just the staff behind (John 6:66). If Jesus had fused His identity to numerical growth or the approval of others, He would not have survived. He would have either counted Himself a failure and withdrawn from ministry, or He would have made vastly different leadership decisions to keep people on side and grow His numbers. He demonstrated high levels of differentiation, but how did He do it, and more importantly, how can we?

UNDERSTANDING OUR HUMAN TENDENCIES

To be fair, this issue is not specific to pastors; it is so easy and so common to draw our identity and sense of worth from what we do. When you think about two people meeting for the first time, the conversation can very quickly turn to, "So what do you do?" A person's role can form such a significant part of how they see themselves that when they are made redundant, quit their job, or change focus to have children or be a stay-at-home parent, it can cause an identity crisis.

Henri Nouwen said that we are susceptible to drawing our identity and sense of worth from three counterfeit sources.[1] These are the beliefs that:

- I am what I do
- I am what I have
- I am what others say about me

There is a longing in our hearts to be good enough, and we can often attempt to satisfy this by our success, our popularity, and our power.[2] This was at the heart of the temptation of Christ in Luke 4:1-13; however, Jesus was able to rebuff the devil's attack on His human vulnerabilities and stand strong.

For pastors, these beliefs and temptations can be translated as:

- I am my role and my success in that role
- I am what I have been able to gain and achieve
- I am the approval and acceptance of others

As I reflect on my own ministry, becoming a pastor seemed like a high calling that carried a great deal of dignity and status. Once I stepped into this role, however, I felt pressure to live up to that high standard, and I often felt like a fraud. There was a sense that to prove myself and be a 'real' pastor, I needed to grow the church and grow it remarkably. The role I stepped into was concerned with revitalising a small church, so while it remained small, I doubted if I was good enough and questioned if I had what it took. I believed I would not be taken seriously as a pastor until I proved myself.

The church grew slowly, and it took four years before we saw our first conversion. However, even in a year when we saw twenty per cent growth through conversions, I felt the pressure to achieve the next thing, which was to become a mid-sized church. On and on it went. As I look back, I can see that any sense of satisfaction I hoped to gain from being and doing enough remained elusive.

Our human propensity to draw our identity from counterfeit, external sources is something we see echoed in Jeremiah 2:13. Here God challenges and mourns Israel's preference for useless counterfeits made by their own hands above the satisfying and life-giving nature of what God provides.

> *"My people have committed two sins: They have forsaken me,*
> *the spring of living water, and have dug their own cisterns,*
> *broken cisterns that cannot hold water."*

On one level, we know that we are not our role; it does not define us. However, practically and emotionally, we keep coming back to this well from which we draw our identity. We keep looking into the reflection of our performance to see if we are good enough. No one would consciously choose this, but we do not know how *not* to do it. Even when it is pointed out to pastors, it does not seem to change anything. Simply saying, "Separate who you are from your role" is like saying to someone caught in addiction, "Just stop it." Even if there is a desire to change, the pull to keep doing what you have always done is powerful.

To bring genuine change, we need to address some of the underlying causes and offer a powerful, healthy alternative. We need to find a way to drink from the "spring of living water" that God wants to give us to quench our thirst. We need to rediscover who we are in Him and marinate in this reality. It is only when we are rightly related to God that we can view ourselves and the role in which we serve from the proper perspective.[3]

To understand why we keep coming back to these broken cisterns, we need to better understand how we are constructed and the purpose these broken cisterns may be serving in our lives.

OUR HUMAN DESIGN

The Bible tells us that we are made up of body, soul, and spirit (1 Thessalonians 5:23), so let's take a look at each of these in turn.

We have a body. This is our hardware system, which is composed of bone, blood, sinew, synapses, and neurochemicals, among other things. We use this hardware system to engage with the world. We may be responsible for what we do, achieve or perform with our bodies, but these actions do not ultimately define who we are. Our identity is so much deeper.

What happens in our body can influence our mind, shaping our thoughts and feelings. An experience I am sure you can relate to is coming home late at the end of a long week. Physically, you may be tired and hungry, but emotionally, you are also probably feeling quite 'hangry'. You see, your blood-glucose levels can influence how you feel, what you think, and what you do. Changing your sleep patterns or altering your hormone levels can influence and impact your thoughts and feelings. This can also affect the core of who you are and how you perceive yourself, shaping your sense of identity.

We also have a soul. Interestingly, the word for soul in the Greek text is ψυχή, or *psyche*, where we get the term 'psychology'. In one sense, psychology is the study of the soul. This part of us contains our thoughts, feelings, and emotions. While your thoughts, feelings and emotions come from you, they are not the essence of who you are. They are not your identity. If you are experiencing depression or anxiety, the good news is that this is not the essence of who you are. Equally, if your mind is filled with negative, critical thoughts, what is sometimes described as your 'inner critic', this does not define your identity—it is simply a habit your mind has got caught in.

We are also a spirit. This is the core of who we are. This is the breath God breathed into us. This is what makes us a person. A dead body may be a human, but it is no longer a person. The Bible tells us that there is an intimate connection between our spirit and our soul, just as there is between a bone joint and the marrow in that bone (Hebrews 4:12). Suffice it to say, the core of us, the spirit in us, is somewhat vague and mysterious but also a powerful and essential part of who we are.

Our sense of identity is not only influenced by body, soul, and spirit, but by the unconscious conclusions we have come to or been conditioned to believe about who we are. How you finish these foundational "I am . . ." statements determines how healthy, secure and confident you feel, and how you subsequently behave. If, in the core of your being, you hold a deep sense that you are loved, wanted, significant, accepted, and worthy, you can imagine the healthy and constructive impact this would have on how you feel, think, and act. However, if, in the core of your being, we find beliefs like, "I am rejected, useless, worthless, or a failure," you can imagine the negative impact this would have on your thoughts, feelings, and actions.

In my years of working with people, I have found that most of these "I am" statements are conditional. That is, people will have the sense that:

- I am loved . . . *so long as* I am doing everything that others approve of.
- I am significant . . . *so long as* I am performing at a high level.
- I am good enough . . . *so long as* people are esteeming me.

We are desperate to believe we are all those things. It is this desperation that gives the 'so long as' conditions such power in our lives. They can even become our master and the ultimate definers of our identities.

I have found we all have six essential, deep needs that have a massive psychological impact and, when met, give us a sense of being okay. We will do almost anything to meet those needs, because the idea of not having them met can leave us in various degrees of distress. When we explore these essential deep needs, they provide greater clarity of what is occurring and why we are so captivated by counterfeits.

In my book, *Centred: Knowing Who You Are In An Off-balanced World,*[4] I outline these six essential, deep needs in more detail. They are:

1. Significance: We have worth and value; our lives matter, and we matter.
2. Innocence: We have nothing to prove and are not living under the weight of condemnation and shame.

3. Agency: We have the power to influence our world.
4. Progress: We have purpose and are fulfilling that purpose by growing and achieving.
5. Security: We are safe, and the environment around us is both predictable and manageable.
6. Belonging: We are anchored in a network of relationships in which we are loved and accepted.

Each of these needs is essential to our wellbeing and psychological stability. Perhaps unconsciously, we have formed an "I am . . ." conclusion about each one. Understanding this can help us clarify areas of vulnerability where we need greater reassurance and healing. When people say things like, "I did that as a result of my insecurity," we can understand better what happened and which deep need was lacking security or certainty.

When each deep need feels assured, we are healthy, confident, and act constructively. When we believe they are not assured, or can only be met when we meet the conditional 'so long as' statement, we are left in a vulnerable, exhausting, or painful state. When we find ourselves doing a never-ending dance to fulfil these conditions, we are living insecure, inauthentic, and counterfeit lives.

For pastors, this can look like: "I am significant, so long as my church is growing," or "I am acceptable so long as everyone is happy with me." What is it for you? We end up attaching our identity to some external source. We end up digging cisterns that do not hold any water and can never satisfy us. They just leave us thirsty, yet we keep coming back in the hope that this time it will be different and they will fully satisfy. Of course, they never do, because they are counterfeits. However, as long as we can keep fulfilling the 'so long as' conditions, the counterfeits leave us with the feeling (fleeting though it may be) that we are okay, that we are worthy.

One group of theologians highlighted that our deepest human longing is to be known—to experience ourselves fully uncovered, having the richness of our depth and darkness seen, yet finding we are still loved and accepted.[5] It is our deep desire to be fully exposed and find that we are still completely accepted, loved, and approved of. Nothing more can be found out, discovered, or used against us. We are loved regardless. This is the ache of the human heart. This is the deep desire that echoes back to Eden, where humans lived, "naked, and they felt no shame" (Genesis 2:25). When we feel any sense of uncertainty or insecurity, we tend to desperately find something that compensates, covering ourselves with fig leaves or digging broken cisterns.

Sometimes we do not really see that certain things are counterfeits until we can no longer fulfil the 'so long as' condition attached. This might be when the church starts to experience decline or a plateau in numbers, or when we hear about a fellow pastor's growing ministry or discover they have been invited to speak somewhere 'important'. It might be when someone in the church is upset or offended by something we have done or criticises our sermon, our decisions, or our leadership. It might be when only a few show up to a church prayer meeting or event. Whatever it is for you, it can leave you feeling exposed and vulnerable, causing you to doubt yourself or get angry at others. This is the life so many pastors experience, but it is no way to live. It is not the fullness of life that Jesus came to give us.

When we cannot meet the 'so long as' condition, the prospect of having an unmet deep need can be profoundly distressing and even terrifying. It leaves us with a cavernous sense that we are inadequate, a failure, worthless, not good enough, rejected, excluded, unloved, unwanted, and so on. These feelings can be truly awful and overwhelming, and they are often experienced as 'reactive' or 'trauma' emotions. They are what Sue Johnson calls *raw spots*, and Lori Gordon terms *emotional allergies*.[6] These powerful emotional experiences result in defensive or aggressive behaviour because, consciously or unconsciously, we feel a deep emotional and psychological threat.

As well as a desperation to have our deepest needs met, humans also experience an equally powerful pull to avoid these reactive emotional states. We will do anything to avoid feeling that way. We may not always be aware of the emotions driving us, but the tell-tale signs are apparent in our behaviours, reactions, and over-reactions. This is why we shut down, people-please, pretend, overwork, comfort eat, drink excessively, and so on. In one sense, these feelings are like the terrifying giants preventing us from entering the Promised Land that God has prepared for us—a land of freedom, peace, and confidence in Him.

When a pastor's identity is fused with their role, their deep needs will only feel satisfied when they fulfil the job's external, quantitative-based outcomes. When these role requirements are not met, there is a monstrous feeling waiting for them, even threatening them. This places them in a chronically low or acutely high state of anxiety, stress, and hypervigilance, and has serious repercussions for their mental health. No wonder pastors were found to experience mental health challenges at a higher rate than the general public!

Funnily enough, this place of pain or disease can also be a blessing, because it exposes where we have been dependent on counterfeits. It can become the beginning of our healing. The good news is that God never created us with a 'so long as'. The good news is that He is the only One who has the right to finish our "I am" statements. He loves you and me with an unrelenting, undying love. We discover who we are as we understand *whose* we are and discover how He finishes our "I am . . ." It is important to realise that if we write something more in our "I am" statements than what God would say about us, this is pride. However, if we write something less, this is also pride, because we are unwittingly saying that we know ourselves better than God does. When I share this in groups, there will often be someone who wants to object and correct me, saying, "No. I think less of myself because I want to be humble." Humility, however, is not thinking less of yourself; true humility is simply agreeing with God as to how He sees you.[7] And how does God see you?

It is only when we discover ourselves through Jesus' eyes that we see who we really are. As we allow ourselves to be defined by God, bringing alignment to our sense of identity, we find our deep needs satisfied in Christ and drink freely from "the spring of living water" (Jeremiah 2:13).

11

—

SOURCED IN THE RIGHT MASTER

To realign our identity with Christ, or to put it differently, to re-lay the foundation of our identity so that it is more firmly in Christ, it is helpful to step back and examine how Jesus, the archetype of humanity, differentiated Himself from His ministry. It would be easy to dismiss Jesus' ability to differentiate Himself from His role because He is the Son of God, God incarnate, but He was also human.

Jesus ministered within the limitations and confines of His humanity; He was tempted, tested, weary, exhausted, disappointed, frustrated, distressed, and heartbroken. He modelled what it looks like to be a healthy human and how to minister in a healthy way. Jesus did this by knowing who He was. He did it by knowing *whose* He was. His identity was never fixed to quantitative outcomes but to His relationship with the Father and who He is in God. Jesus' ministry began after an identity-affirming encounter with the Father at His baptism (Mark 1:11), and His ministry concludes with Him declaring, "I and the Father are one" (John 10:30).

As we will explore later, Jesus also directs us to remain in Him and in His love. He is the source from which we are to minister. If we are to resist the pull to have our identity tied to our role and achievements, we need to have it anchored in Jesus. We also discover who we are as we discover *whose* we are, and all that this entails. If this is to be a life-giving and ministry-enhancing reality for us, it needs to be more than something we know at a head level; we need to experience it in our bones.

We know our identity needs to be fixed in Jesus, but how can we experience this practically? This is where it is deeply helpful to know ourselves not only as those made in the image of God *(imago Dei)* but more specifically as those made in the image of Christ *(imago Christi)*. Here we discover who we are because of Him and how we can become more like Him.

POTENTIATING THE TRUTH: AN IMPORTANT ASIDE

We need to pull up here for a second. I am conscious that we are about to dive into some rich theological truths about who we are in Christ and encounter the power that comes from knowing whose we are. My concern is that our tendency as Western Christians is often to engage with this kind of truth with our heads while leaving our hearts (our emotional engagement) disengaged. This tendency limits the potency of God's truth in our lives. As Christians, we can be very good at knowing the *right answer* without experiencing it as a *real answer*. We can receive God's Word at a head level, but it does not always permeate our hearts. As a result, it does not bring the deep change we desire.

To bring about true transformation and realign our sense of identity, we need God's truth about who we are to seep into the very core of our being. We need our identity to marinate in the truth of who we are. When this happens, we move beyond merely knowing what is theologically right and experience the reality of His truth deeply.

Scripture helps guide us in turning a right answer into a real answer by showing the value of mediating on the truth.

> *"Blessed is the one … whose delight is in the law of the Lord, and who meditates on his law day and night. That person is like a tree planted by streams of water, which yields its fruit in season and whose leaf does not wither—whatever they do prospers"*
>
> **Psalm 1:1-3**

Often, the difference between a right answer and a real answer is simply taking time to meditate on the truth it contains. Our culture tends to assume that knowing information leads to transformation when it does not. All it does is layer information upon more information. This is what tends to happen when we attend another conference or listen to another podcast. We gain interesting ideas, but seldom revisit them, reflect deeply, or suck the marrow from the bone, so to speak.

Transformation and change come through the renewing, renovating, and realigning of our minds.

> *"Do not conform to the pattern of this world, but be transformed by the renewing of your mind."*
> **Romans 12:2**

It takes intentionality and time to recondition our minds and turn from our default ways of thinking, feeling, and acting. We need to dwell, meditate and marinate in the truth. By doing this, the right answer can become a real answer as we encounter fresh ways of engaging with the Word so that it captures our hearts. Familiar words can become stale, so reflecting on passages using fresh language can help us grasp the heart and power of the truth once more. I will often suggest to someone wishing to meditate more deeply on the truth to write it out as if they were trying to explain it to a ten-year-old. This forces them to slow down, grasp the essence of what is being said, and find fresh language to bring it alive. You may find a different method that helps your heart truly get it. The goal is to encounter the truth in a way that brings genuine transformation.

I want you to keep this in mind as we look at the truth of who you are and begin to explore the depth of its meaning. I encourage you to take your time with this section and allow your heart and mind to soak in it. As we explore these theological concepts, my hope is that your head may understand it and your heart may fully grasp it.

The truth we are about to encounter speaks directly to our deepest needs and powerfully answers the question of "Who am I?" So let us slow down, explore, soak and meditate on these incredibly rich and life-changing truths.

IMAGO DEI: KNOWING WHO WE ARE BECAUSE OF GOD

Imago Dei means "image of God" and refers to the truth that we have all been made in the image and likeness of God (Genesis 1:26-27). We know ourselves by recognising we are creatures of the Creator, made in His image on purpose and with purpose.[1] Because we come from God and bear His likeness, we have worth and value before we say or do anything. We have it simply by the very nature of being made by Him and being like Him.

More than God acting as some kind of template to make humanity, Scripture tells us that God intentionally and personally created each of us. Even before forming us, He knew each of us and wanted us.

> *"Before I formed you in the womb I knew you."*
>
> **Jeremiah 1:5**

While these words were spoken specifically to Jeremiah, they also reveal a truth that is echoed through the Bible: God is deeply involved in our creation. Before we even had physical form, God knew us. His knowledge of us precedes our physical formation. No one creates what they do not want. God's creation of you was intentional. His creation of you was purposeful. He wanted you. His creation of you was personal. *He* formed you in the womb.

God Himself dreamed you up, knew you, wanted you, formed you, and brought you onto this planet. Think about it for a moment: God, who is Love, wanted you. Unlike the messages we may receive from our culture, I am not saying that love is God, but rather the very essence of God is love (1 John 4:8). So, follow this through. Our God, whose very essence is love, conceived you, shaped you, and made you in His image. You are made by the divine, eternal, loving being that is our God. Your very existence is an *expression* of God's love; that is why you exist. You are more than God's great idea; you are an expression from His very heart.

You are made on purpose with purpose for a purpose. You come from Him. As an image-bearer, therefore, you have worth and value before you ever say or do anything. You are not an accident. You are no mistake. You are not simply tolerated or overlooked. You are intentionally made. God's fingerprints are all over your being. He wanted you, and He deliberately created you.

Your life has meaning, it has purpose, and it has belonging. The opposite cannot be true. Since you are made in His image, you already have value, worth, and significance. These deep needs have never been in question. You are loved. You belong to Him. This is true whether you realise it, feel it, or believe it. It is who you are. It is how you have been made.

IMAGO CHRISTI: KNOWING WHO WE ARE BECAUSE OF CHRIST

As unbelievably spectacular and world-altering as this is, there is more, way more! Our understanding of *imago Dei* deepens and becomes more transformative as we also grasp the significance of *imago Christi*.

To more fully experience the impact of this truth, and the 'therefore' that results from it, we first need to understand the theological substance of *imago Christi*. If we want to understand more fully what it means to be made in God's image, we have to look to Jesus. This is because Jesus is *the image* of God. As the only true and perfect representation of God, we have to look to Him to better understand ourselves. As Marc Cortez, a leading theologian in this area, affirms, "Jesus is central to an adequate understanding of the *imago Dei*."[2] In fact, Jesus is central "for understanding what it means to be human."[3] This is because Jesus is the perfection of humanity. In Him, we see the truth of what human personhood was always meant to be.

Scripture tells us that Jesus is the *imago Dei*. He is "the image of the invisible God" (Colossians 1:15) and "the exact representation of his being" (Hebrews 1:3). In fact, not only is Jesus the perfect image of God, but he is also *fully* God (Colossians 1:19; 2:9). The fullness of the Trinitarian God dwells in Him.[4] To see Him is to see the Father (John 14:9). Jesus is also revealed to be synonymous with the Spirit (2 Corinthians 3:18). Through the incarnation, the eternal Son became human, revealing the *imago Dei*, the exact representation of God, in flesh and blood.

What this means is extraordinary: Jesus is *the* model from which we are made. As one theologian puts it, "We are images of the Image—Jesus Christ."[5] So, while it is true that we are made in the image of God, it is more accurate to say that we are made in the image of Jesus Christ, *imago Christi*. As Paul writes, "For we are God's handiwork, created in Christ Jesus" (Ephesians 2:10).

This is why we find fulfilment in being conformed to the likeness of Christ (Romans 8:29; 2 Corinthians 3:18). Conforming to the likeness of Christ does not make us into something different from who we are, but rather, helps us become more fully who we are meant to be. Jesus is our completion (Hebrews 12:2). He is our Alpha and Omega (Revelation 21:6). Becoming like Christ is not a denial of our identity; it is the fulfilment and perfection of our truest selves.

> *"Imago Christi* becomes the model by which true humanity finds its personhood through its participation in the Spirit being conformed into the image of the Son."[6]

If we want to know who we are, we must look through the lens of Jesus and understand ourselves in the light of *imago Christi*. This truth reveals that not only are we made in the image of Christ, but we are also redeemed and restored by Him, included in Him, and are being conformed to His likeness.

We know that Christ is both fully God and fully human, enabling Him to represent God to humanity and humanity to God. As theologian T.F. Torrance puts it, the outrageously good news for us is that Jesus steps in and becomes "our human response to God. Thus, we appear before God and are accepted by him as those who are inseparably united to Jesus Christ our great High Priest in his eternal self-representation to the Father."[7] Our own condition and efforts could never achieve this. Our acceptance could never be based on our faithfulness alone. It is only through our faith in the perfect faithfulness of Jesus that we can be included in Christ and adopted as God's beloved children.

Our primary calling is to Christ. To appreciate the depth of what this means, and to understand who we are because of it, the Bible uses key terms that offer greater clarity and richness to our identity. Phrases like "in Christ" and "adopted" help us grasp who we are and what we have gained because we decided to receive Jesus and believe in Him. Each of these terms speaks deeply and personally to the question of who we are. They are rich and profound, and it is worth soaking them in one by one.

IN CHRIST: THE LOVE-EMBRACE OF GOD

We are told that we are placed "in Christ" by the Holy Spirit (2 Corinthians 5:17; Ephesians 1:13). The phrase "in Christ" appears repeatedly throughout Scripture and carries with it an astonishingly rich and deep meaning of who we are and what we have been given. The Bible also says that we "have the Son" (1 John 5:12) through whom we become a new creation and receive a new life. This all happens as we are united in Christ (Galatians 3:26-27) and included in Him.

The graciousness of God and the marvel of what He does for us here is profound. In Christ, we are made complete as we are conformed to His likeness. It is through this union with Christ that we discover the true substance of our identity; one that fills the deep need of our humanity and provides the eternal, unshakeable source of our significance and worth.

Take a moment to let this sink in. Jesus, the second Person of the Trinity, not only reveals the true image of God in human form through the incarnation but also conforms us to that image by uniting us with the very mystery and fullness of the divine life (2 Peter 1:4). By being placed in Jesus and united with Him, we gain "a new identity in him, apart from anything we are in and of ourselves," and an identity that comes from something quite separate from anything we ever do or achieve ourselves.[8] Our identity, significance and worth come from Him and are settled in Him. They are not up for negotiation. How insignificant our achievements in any role seem in light of this. We gain such deep significance by being His.

God made us on purpose in the likeness of Jesus, and He places us in Christ by the power of the Holy Spirit. We are created as an *expression* of the triune God's love. What is even more astounding is that we are also made to *experience* the love that exists within the Godhead. Being 'in Christ' takes us into the very heart of the fullness of God. Our baptism into Christ (Romans 6:3; Galatians 3:27) is, in fact, a baptism into God revealed as the Trinity. The words of Jesus are for us to make disciples of all nations, "baptising them in the name of the Father, the Son, and the Holy Spirit" (Matthew 28:19). Because of Christ, we are included in Him to participate in the relationship that exists among the Trinity.[9] God includes us in the relationship He has within Himself and wants us to experience the ongoing, unceasing, deep, affectionate love that exists within Himself.

As theologian Myk Habets puts it:

> "The human person is created with a goal *(telos)* in view, to participate in the triune relationship of the Father for the Son in or by the Holy Spirit. . . . [and with that] living within the overflow of God's boundless love, united by the one Christ through the communion of the Holy Spirit, brings into focus the true dimensions of the Christian life."[10]

God, who is Trinity, exists in a "Communion of Love," the continual and mutual expression of love that the Father, the Son and the Holy Spirit lavish on one another.[11] We are baptised in the name of our triune God (Matthew 28:19), we have fellowship with Him (1 John 1:3), and from His love He makes us His children (1 John 3:1). The depth and ferocity of God's love for us meant He did not withhold the life of His own Son, and even beyond that He wants to "graciously give us all things" (Romans 8:32).

How beautiful and wonderfully overwhelming this is. It makes me want to respond with this paraphrase from Psalm 8:4: Who am I that you even consider me; a frail human that you would even care about me?

Many years ago, when I was leading a small group, we had a person join us who was not a Christian. As we were talking, we got onto the subject of God sending His Son to die for humanity. Our guest asked with understandable incredulity, "How could a loving God do that?" I said to him, "I know what you mean. I am a father myself, and I cannot imagine anything that would be worth risking the life of any of my children, let alone intentionally allowing them to die." I paused, looked at him, and then added, "The only thing that would possibly make me do it would be something I considered more precious than the life of my child. I, personally, could not imagine what that would be, but there was something God valued more than the life of His own Son. Do you know what that was?"

He thought about it for a moment and hesitantly offered, "I don't know. Um, the world?"

I looked him in the eyes and replied passionately, "You! You are the reason! God's desire to have you with Him was worth more than the precious life of His own Son."

This is true for each of us. Not only does God create you on purpose, specifically wanting you and personally shaping you as an *expression* of His love, He also wants you with Him to *experience* the love shared within Himself. You are placed in Christ, and Christ is within the Triune God, "for you died, and your life is now hidden with Christ *in God*" (Colossians 3:3, italics mine). You are wrapped in the love-embrace that is God. You are included in Christ to participate in the divine love that is the Trinity. God wants you to experience the same love that the Father, Jesus, and the Holy Spirit have for one another. He wants this for you, for me, and for everyone. I do not know about you, but I find this truly staggering.

We gain some understanding of the depth of God's love when we explore the very human example of a parent's love for their child. Think of a couple who desire to have a child, whether biologically or through adoption. They have that child because they long to expand their love to another. The child is wanted and welcomed into the love relationship between the wife and husband as an expression of the love between them. The child is wanted for this very purpose: to be loved and experience their love. Similarly, we are wanted by God to share in His love. We are created to be loved and to experience God's love from within Himself.

Now, just so we are clear, when the child enters the love of the parents, the child does not become an equal third party of the marriage. The marriage remains between the husband and wife, but something new is created. The love between them expands to include the child, and a family is born.

In the same way, as we are placed in Christ through the Spirit, we find ourselves wanted, created and included in the loving life of the Trinity.[12] We do not become God or an equal member of the Trinity, but something new is created. The divine love that has always existed expands to include us in the expansive, limitless love of the Trinity. We are welcomed into God's eternal communion of love as dearly loved sons and daughters.

It is here that we begin to discover who we truly are and find our true selves. We have been created to experience this love, and in doing so, we are fulfilled. We "exist to experience the love of God and to reflect this love back to him and all of creation."[13] It is an utterly amazing life-giving reality to discover that we have been created not only as an expression of God's love, not only for the purpose of being with Him, but also to experience the very love that exists within God Himself.

Can you see how this truth speaks directly and powerfully to our deepest needs? How this profoundly answers the core question: "Who am I?" From what we have just explored, how would you begin to answer the question of who you are?

We could rightly respond with something like, "I am a person created by loving Almighty God to be in Christ and receive, experience and enjoy the eternal, unconditional love of God. I am loved with the same love that the Father, the Son and the Holy Spirit lavish on each other." Or perhaps more simply, as Nouwen would put it: "I am God's Beloved."[14]

ADOPTED: TAKING OUR PLACE IN GOD'S HOME

By the power of the Holy Spirit, we are not only placed in Christ, but we also receive "adoption" (Romans 8:15).[15] This second term, 'adopted', is also deeply significant in answering our 'who I am' question. We typically approach a word like this with preconceived ideas and notions, and our understanding is coloured by our associations with modern adoption. To understand the way Paul is using it, however, we need to understand it from *his* cultural context.

In Paul's world, adoption was part of the Roman practice of *coming of age*. Throughout history, each culture has developed its own rituals that mark the transition from childhood to adulthood. These rituals occur at different ages and hold unique significance. In my country of New Zealand, it is not fully clear when children 'come of age'. When I ask people this question, I get a variety of answers, including sixteen, eighteen, twenty-one, or even, "whenever they finally leave home!" Legally, a sixteen-year-old is no longer a minor, but they do not have the full rights and privileges of an adult. That happens when they turn eighteen. Then there is twenty-one, which is really just an arbitrary number and a good excuse for a party.

In Paul's time, Jewish boys would have their Bar Mitzvah around age twelve or thirteen. They would recite the Torah, be tested on it, and then be considered a *son of the law*. In Greek culture, a child took their place as an adult in society at the age of eighteen. The Romans, however, did it differently. We see this reflected in the words Paul uses in Galatians 4:1-7:

> *"What I am saying is that as long as an heir is underage, he is no different from a slave, although he owns the whole estate. The heir is subject to guardians and trustees until the time set by his father. So also, when we were underage, we were in slavery under the elemental spiritual forces of the world. But when the set time had fully come, God sent his Son, born of a woman, born under the law, to redeem those under the law, that we might receive adoption to sonship. Because you are his sons, God sent the Spirit of his Son into our hearts, the Spirit who calls out, 'Abba, Father.' So you are no longer a slave, but God's child; and since you are his child, God has made you also an heir."*

For the Romans, there was no fixed age when a child transitioned to adulthood. It happened whenever the father decided it was time, what Paul refers to as "the time set by the father" (Galatians 4:2). When the father deemed it was the right time, he would formally *adopt* the child as his own. Only then would the boy be considered a legitimate son with full authority and privileges within the household. Only then did he have the rights of an heir. Adoption brought legitimacy, belonging, authority, privilege, and inheritance.

It may seem surprising, but if the father chose *not* to adopt his biological child, then the child had a status "no different from a slave" (Galatians 4:1).[16] Conversely, if the father chose to adopt both his biological son and the son of a slave, they would become equals in status and inheritance. In this system, background, pedigree or lineage meant nothing. The only thing that counted was whether the father chose you and adopted you as his own.

The same is true for you. Your acceptability, your standing before God, has nothing to do with your background, lineage, abilities, or performance. In one sense, that is all meaningless. What matters is that God has chosen and adopted you to be His child alongside His own begotten Son.

Because of this adoption, you are invited to relate to the Father with the same intimacy and closeness as Jesus does, calling Him "Abba, Father" (Romans 8:15). This closeness is yours, not because of anything you have done or deserve. It is a gift that is bestowed on you when the Father adopts you in Christ through the power of the Holy Spirit.

Like the child of the slave in the Roman culture, you have been adopted alongside the Father's own Son. Astonishingly, you have been granted the same benefits Jesus receives, being made "co-heirs with Christ" (Romans 8:17). You have been blessed "in the heavenly realms with every spiritual blessing in Christ" (Ephesians 1:3). There is simply so much contained in this truth.

Your adoption by the Father also means you share in the same right relationship that Christ enjoys with the Father and the Holy Spirit. Being adopted and 'in Christ' means you are welcomed by the Father and treated with equality to Christ.[17] This is not to say that you, or any of us, are Christ's equal, but that through our adoption by God the Father and union with Christ, we are treated with an equality to Christ.

Is this not staggering?! I come back again to the psalmist's words of awe: Who are we that you would even consider us? Such fallible humans that you would even care for us? (Psalm 8:4, paraphrased).

It is through this concept of adoption that Paul helps his readers, and us, grasp how God can bypass our backgrounds, our behaviours, our failures, and our sin. Adoption is also how Paul explains God's ability to transcend previously held divisions between people groups and accept all of us into His family. It no longer matters whether your background is Jew or gentile, slave or free, male or female; the Father has chosen you and adopted you as His own. "You are all children of God through faith" (Galatians 3:26) and are all "one in Christ Jesus" (v.28).

There is another striking expression of God's love, graciousness and kindness that we see in this act of adoption. In Roman culture, you had no say on whether you would be adopted—it was solely the decision of the father. However, what is extraordinary is that God does not force this on us. The eternal Almighty God wants you back with Him to experience His love for you, but nothing is forced. He waits for you to choose Him in return.

> *"Yet to all who did receive him, to those who believed in his name, he gave the right to become children of God."*
>
> **John 1:12**

You have been given the right and power to become a child of God. Nothing is forced. This invitation is *given* to you. The way has been made. The choice is yours. So, the question is, will you allow the Father to adopt you? Will you take your rightful place as His daughter or His son in the household of God? This adoption is based on nothing you bring, do, or achieve. Not on the size of your church or your statistics in the yearbook. Not on how many people like you. It is based solely on the fact that you are His, and He wants to adopt you as His own.

Our adoption in Christ gives us an identity and a life that Henri Nouwen calls our "true self—one no longer dependent on the fragile structures of the world but rather on the eternal love between the Father and the Son, between a loving parent and much-wanted child, a love that is called the Holy Spirit."[18] These "fragile structures" would surely include the tendency to entangle our identity and our self-worth in our role. Yet, our identity in Jesus liberates us from this entanglement and fulfils our deepest human longing. It satisfies our deep human needs.

THEREFORE . . .

Imago Christi helps us to discover the rich truth about who we are, while our understanding of being placed in Christ by the Spirit and being adopted by the Father provides profound clarity. Knowing this, we can now say:

> "I am made as an expression of God's love to experience His love. The Father has chosen me and adopted me as His own, placing me in Christ by the power of the Holy Spirit. I have been made a co-heir with Christ and invited to share in all the benefits and blessings the Father lavishes upon Him. What is Christ's is now mine."

This speaks to our deepest needs and profoundly answers the question of who we are. It gives unshakeable substance to our identity, independent of:

- What we do or achieve
- What others say about us
- What we have

This is both life-giving and psychologically grounding. From this foundation, two essential 'therefores' emerge.

1. We are the Father's beloved
2. We are to remain in Jesus and His love by the Holy Spirit

The first is about who we are to be, or more accurately, who we already are but need to allow ourselves to become. The second is about what we are to do. Both are identity-forming and identity-affirming. Both provide the true soil from which we should live, serve, and minister.

12

CENTRED IN JESUS

When we are placed in Christ and adopted by the Father, we are made co-heirs with Christ. What is Christ's is now equally ours. This includes the limitless love the Father, Jesus and the Holy Spirit have for each other. The astounding truth is that the Father loves us at the same depth and with the same intensity as He loves Jesus. God's desire that we share in the fullness of the love that the Father has for the Son is revealed in Jesus' prayer.

> *"I made known to them your name, and I will continue to make it known, **that the love with which you have loved me may be in them,** and I in them."*
>
> **John 17:26** ESV

This means that the breathtaking love the Father has for the Son is now directed toward us in Christ. We see this profound love on display in the identity-affirming words the Father pours over Jesus at His baptism: "You are my Son, whom I love; with you I am well pleased" (Mark 1:11). These words are equally ours. We are made in Christ's image, we are adopted by the Father, we are placed in Christ, and we are united with Him by the Holy Spirit. These identity-defining words of love are now ours to receive, own, and live from.[1] We are baptised and fully immersed in the same love of the Father.

BEING GOD'S BELOVED

You are God's Beloved. It is easy to skip over these words and miss how powerful they really are. We need to slow down and lean into the words of the Father to Jesus, to dive into the depths of the love that is expressed here, and allow their rich meaning to soak in.

Notice, firstly, that the Father does not call Jesus by name but names Him relationally, "You are my Son." As personal as a name is, calling Jesus "my Son" is an expression of mutual belonging. The Son belongs to the Father, and the Father belongs to the Son. Their identities are inseparable and can only be understood in relation *to* one another. For someone to be a son, the other must be the parent. For someone to be a father, the other must be their child. The one cannot exist without the other. In this moment, Jesus is not just named, He is known. His identity is rooted in relationally belonging to the Father. Jesus is wanted by the Father and belongs to Him. He is the Father's, and the Father is His.

The Father's next words are full of passion and deep affection: "…whom I love." The Greek word here is *agapētos* and has a deep meaning. While the previous words, "You are my Son," define Jesus relationally, *agapētos* reveals the very substance of that relationship. As Henri Nouwen highlights, *agapētos* can be translated as "Beloved."

In this one word, 'Beloved', the Father is saying, "Your identity, Jesus, is the One who is loved by me. Who You are is defined by my love." The Father's love is the subject, the source, and the very genius of who Jesus is. Jesus is the object of the Father's love. The substance of who Jesus is comes relationally from Another. His identity flows from being the One who is loved by the Father. The message packed in here is, "Jesus, You are my Son, my Beloved. You are the object of all of my love." Pause for a moment and let that sink in. Imagine being the object and recipient of all of God's love. Imagine what it would be like to be loved like that. This is beautifully overwhelming.

Finally, the Father expresses not only His love and affection for Jesus, but also the delight He experiences simply because Jesus exists. This is not a one-sided affection; it is a shared and reciprocal joy. The word the Father uses is *eudokēsa,* often translated as "With you I am well pleased." It could equally be translated, "I delight in you" or "You give me great joy."[2] This is the deep pleasure any loving parent experiences as they hold their baby in their arms. I remember holding my children as newborns. They had done nothing nor could they do anything for us, yet their very existence gave us unspeakable delight. Watching their little chests rise and fall as they slept in my arms filled me with such joy that words can barely express.

Before Jesus had done any ministry, performed any miracle, or gathered a single follower, He received this identity-defining affirmation from His Father. This forms the foundation and starting point for His ministry. Jesus begins His ministry with His identity, worth and significance established and rooted in His relationship with the Father. Imagine what it must have been like for Him to carry these words from the Father into every encounter, every trial, and every act of obedience:

> "Jesus, You are My Son. You belong to Me, and I belong to You. You are My Beloved. I love You with every part of My being. I love You with an unquenchable love. Regardless of what You do or what happens to You, I want You to know that You give Me such joy just by being in my life."

Imagine being on the receiving end of so much love. The incomprehensible good news is that you are. You were intentionally created by God in His image, and through faith, you have been placed in Christ by the Holy Spirit and adopted by the Father. You are included in this love and loved at the same level and with the same intensity that the Father loves Jesus. Henri Nouwen longed for us all to understand this truth: *You* are God's Beloved. Before you do any ministry, produce anything, or perform in any way, this is your starting point. It is your unwavering foundation. You are known and defined relationally by God. You are loved passionately by Him. You are wanted by Him, and you give Him pleasure simply by existing.

Take a moment to lower any defences you might have up and allow yourself to receive these words of the Father to you as your own:

"You are mine. You are *My daughter.* You are *My son.* You belong to Me, and I belong to you. You are My Beloved. I love you with every part of My being. I love you with an unquenchable love. You are the delight of My heart. Regardless of what you do or what happens to you, I want you to know that you give Me such pleasure just by being in My life.

The size of your church, who likes or doesn't like you, and the successes or failures you have had don't ultimately mean anything. What matters is that you are His and He is yours. Our identity and our life are in Him alone. This is what Paul is at pains to convey to us in Philippians 3:7-11:

"But whatever were gains to me I now consider loss for the sake of Christ. What is more, I consider everything a loss because of the surpassing worth of knowing Christ Jesus my Lord, for whose sake I have lost all things. I consider them garbage, that I may gain Christ and be found in him, not having a righteousness of my own that comes from the law, but that which is through faith in Christ—the righteousness that comes from God on the basis of faith. I want to know Christ—yes, to know the power of his resurrection and participation in his sufferings, becoming like him in his death, and so, somehow, attaining to the resurrection from the dead."

We truly discover who we are as we discover *whose* we are. This is where our rudder becomes unjammed. Knowing and experiencing ourselves in this way is *the* source of our true identity and worth. It fuels our wellbeing, empowerment and effectiveness in every aspect of life and ministry. This is why I said previously that *imago Christi,* more so than *imago Dei,* is a powerful way to understand ourselves and anchor our identity. The depth of this understanding has the power to unjam our rudder and realign us. It enables us to differentiate ourselves in Jesus, with our identity and worth sourced in Him, not in our role. In Jesus, there is no longer any 'so long as' conditions that we must meet or maintain. In Him, our significance and worth are never in question. Our acceptance, acceptability and beloved-ness are never in question. When we discover who we are by knowing *whose* we are, our deep needs are met and fully satisfied. We begin to drink again from the Living Water God offers us, rather than drawing endlessly from the broken cisterns of our lives.

REMAIN IN ME: MINISTERING FROM JESUS

Being centred and sourced in Jesus is the place from which we minister. This is where any 'doing' begins. The first activity Jesus calls us to is not to lead, preach, or serve, but to remain in Him and His love. You may have read these words from the book of John countless times, heard sermons on it, and nodded in agreement. Yet, it is still so easy to drift from this truth.

The demands of ministry, the expectations of others and the desire to be effective can cause us to root our worth and identity in our performance, achievements, and popularity. We are once again pulled towards pragmatism and driven by outcomes. This is why Jesus calls us—in fact, He commands us—to remain in Him and His love (John 15:1-17). He knows how quickly we forget, and how vital it is that our life and ministry stay rooted in Him:

> *"Remain in me, as I also remain in you. No branch can bear fruit by itself; it must remain in the vine. Neither can you bear fruit unless you remain in me. I am the vine; you are the branches. If you remain in me and I in you, you will bear much fruit; apart from me you can do nothing . . . As the Father has loved me, so I have loved you. Now remain in my love."*
>
> **John 15:4-5,9**

It is not that our achievements are not important to God. His heart is for the whole world to be saved, redeemed, and restored (John 5:17; 2 Peter 3:9). Paul certainly works tirelessly and suffers greatly for the sake of this mission (2 Corinthians 11:23-28). Jesus' desire is also that we would "bear much fruit." Our fruitfulness flows from us being rooted and established in Jesus. Remaining in Him is our refuge and our source. It is here we are rightly aligned, and it is only from here that we can rightly minister. This is our next essential step. After discovering who we are as God's Beloved, we are called to remain in Him.

This is how we maintain our differentiation in Jesus and ensure it is His Spirit that fuels all we produce in ministry. Keeping our identity anchored firmly in Jesus is the remedy against the gravitational pull of other counterfeit sources. Remaining in Jesus is *the* way we are to minister, and it is the only way we can be truly productive.

To help us understand what it means to remain in Him, Jesus uses the imagery of the vine and the branches. He is the vine and we, His followers, are the branches. Just as a branch must stay connected to the vine to live and bear fruit, so we must remain in Jesus. The vine is the creator and sustainer of the branch. When the branch is connected to the vine and remains in the vine, it is both an extension of the vine and an expression of its life. The vine produces the fruit; the branch is simply the conduit for it. When the vine is working through the branch, the branch bears fruit. The branch cannot produce anything by itself. Disconnected from the vine, it withers and dies.

The parallel for us is unmistakable. How are we to live and minister? Only by remaining in Jesus and His love. Jesus is our Creator and Sustainer. Our ministry is supposed to be an expression of Him and an extension of Him. Jesus, through the Holy Spirit, is the One who produces the fruit through us.

He is our Creator. From Him we are to draw our identity. Our purpose, value and worth all come from Him. He is also our Sustainer. We are to remain in Him, walk closely with Him, be filled by Him, and view Him as the source, energiser and carer of our being. From Him we draw the motivation, power and gifts we need to bear the fruit He desires.

Jesus is very clear in this passage: " … apart from me you can do nothing" (John 15:5). This does not mean that we are unable to achieve anything because, of course, we can. People can accomplish many things even if they have nothing to do with Jesus. The word used here for 'nothing' is οὐδέν, which can also be translated "nothing of worth."[3] This is confronting. Jesus is saying that if we do not remain in Him, then anything we do or achieve has no merit in His eyes.

When we apply this to what we produce in our churches, it becomes even more uncomfortable and raises some challenging questions: How much of what we produce does Jesus consider genuine fruit? How much of it has truly come from remaining in Him and from Him working through us?

Jesus' challenge to us regarding the source and substance of our ministry activity does not let up. As the passage continues, His words are increasingly confronting and disturbing: "If you do not remain in me, you are like a branch that is thrown away and withers; such branches are picked up, thrown into the fire and burned" (v.6).

Elsewhere, Jesus gives us words of warning about prioritising production and achievement before intimacy with Him. He delivers the haunting words, "I never knew you" (Matthew 7:23), even to those who called him "Lord." What is sobering here is the defence used by those who were turned away. They pointed to what they had accomplished in His name, seemingly as a result of His power: "Lord, Lord, did we not prophesy in your name and in your name drive out demons and in your name perform many miracles?" (v.22). A contemporary version of this might be, "Lord, did we not grow our Sunday attendance, launch new campuses, or preach to large crowds?"

According to Jesus, the challenge is that not all growth or ministry activity is 'fruit'. Not all growth is healthy growth. Even cancer grows. We will explore the fruit that Jesus desires in a later chapter, but the key difference seems to be the source of the fruit. What produces the fruit and activity? Does it come from remaining in Him, being sourced in Him, and having a relationship with Him in which He knows us, and we know Him?

As we reflect on these passages from John and Matthew, it is clear that *remaining* is deeply relational. Our identity comes from Him, and our ministry needs to flow from an abiding relationship with Him. Issues arise when we begin to create fruit of our own making. We may not realise we are doing it because we can still achieve and produce 'in His name' even while drifting from Jesus. This occurs when our focus on role outcomes takes precedence over our relationship with Him. This is our natural tendency when our identity is rooted in what we accomplish rather than in Jesus alone.

Remaining starts with knowing who you are in Jesus and continues by intentionally drawing close to Him. Which spiritual practices help you remain in Jesus and His love? Before we attempt to lead others, we must first be led by Jesus. This means ordering our lives around the rhythms that keep us abiding in the One who created us, calls us, and claims us as His own. This is the quiet, hidden, and powerful work of formation. Only from this place can we hope to bear fruit that endures, for it is His life, not ours, that brings genuine transformation to the world.

13

THE PASTOR'S CALLING

Our identity in Christ gives rise to our calling. We start with our primary calling, our first love, which is being rooted in Jesus. Once we discover who we truly are, we can discern what Jesus wants to do through and with us. As the psalmist writes, "Take delight in the Lord, and he will give you the desires of your heart" (Psalm 37:4).

We see this modelled in Paul's life. Everything Paul does flows from what he first received from God. When Paul talks about his calling and purpose, it is always grounded in God's initiative. As we have previously noted, in 1 Corinthians 1:11 he writes, "Paul, called to be an apostle of Christ Jesus by the will of God . . ."

In Romans 15:15-16, he adds:

> "*. . . because of the grace God gave me to be a minister of Christ Jesus to the Gentiles. He gave me the priestly duty of proclaiming the gospel of God, so that the Gentiles might become an offering acceptable to God, sanctified by the Holy Spirit.*"

Notice the phrases, "by the will of God" and "because of the grace God gave me." Everything Paul does is a response to who God is and what He has done for Paul.

"For I am the least of the apostles, unfit to be called an apostle, because I persecuted the church of God. But by the grace of God I am what I am, and his grace toward me has not been in vain. On the contrary, I worked harder than any of them—though it was not I, but the grace of God that is with me."

1 Corinthians 15:9-10 NRSV

He goes on:

"Jesus Christ came into the world to save sinners, of whom I am the worst. But for that very reason I was shown mercy so that in me, the worst of sinners, Jesus Christ might display his immense patience as an example for those who would believe in him and receive eternal life."

1 Timothy 1:15-16

Paul's experience of Christ's love compels him (2 Corinthians 5:14). In the same way, Christ's love should compel all of us. For "we are convinced that one died for all, and therefore all died. And he died for all, that those who live should no longer live for themselves but for him who died for them and was raised again" (vv.14-15).

CHRIST IN US CALLS US FORWARD

Our secondary calling is sourced in our primary calling in Christ. When our sense of call is rooted in our relationship with Jesus and the identity we receive from Him, we have greater resilience to face the pressures that emerge.

Since our secondary calling flows from our primary calling to be in Christ, it can often be discerned internally rather than received externally. Philippians 2:13 tells us that "God is at work in you to will and to act to fulfil his good purposes." Our motivations and desires come from Him. This is not about pursuing what we want or our selfish desires, but rather about discerning the gifts God has given us, how He has wired us, and the burden He has placed on our hearts. Paul writes in Ephesians 2:10 that "we are God's handiwork, created in Christ Jesus to do good works, which God prepared in advance for us to do." We need to learn to dream out what God has dreamed into us.

Many years ago, I was praying about what God wanted for my next phase of ministry. I was in pastoral ministry at the time, and I had a sense that God wanted to move me somewhere else. What happened next absolutely floored me. I found myself in a conversation with the Lord, and I felt He said to me:

> "Richard, you said you wanted to go to Australia and learn revitalisation and mission development from key mentors. I made it happen. Did you have fun?

> When you had finished that, you said you would love to work as a church developer, so I made it happen. Did you have fun?

> You then said you wanted to apply what you had learned to help a local church in a smaller community close to a major centre, so I placed you in Upper Hutt, close to Wellington. Did you have fun?"

> "Whoa, whoa, whoa!" I replied. I was kind of in freefall. "Hold on. Each of those times, I was praying about what *You* wanted, Lord, as I wanted to be obedient to Your call on my life. Are you telling me that You were listening to what I wanted and making that happen?!"

> "Yes. Did you have fun?"

This stunned me. I remember thinking, *I had better be careful about what I ask for next!*

What if God has been placing desires in our hearts that He wants to fulfil? Remember, "God is at work in you to will and to act to fulfil his good purposes" (Philippians 2:13). Now, this does not mean that everything we want is a desire He has placed there. This is where discernment comes in. But what if the desire He has placed in our hearts has been buried under layers of traditional understanding, suppressed in servitude to the requirements of the role, and restrained by quantitative markers of success? What if it is confined by our loyalty to a specific denomination or a leader? What if our calling has been immobilised because we are waiting for God to direct us when He has already given us His guidance? Take a moment to reflect on this.

Paul writes in 2 Thessalonians 1:11-12:

> *"With this in mind, we constantly pray for you, that our God may make you worthy of his calling, and that by his power he may bring to fruition your every desire for goodness and your every deed prompted by faith. We pray this so that the name of our Lord Jesus may be glorified in you, and you in him, according to the grace of our God and the Lord Jesus Christ."*

It is God who makes us worthy of His calling. Our worthiness comes from Him. Our part is to remain in Jesus, so that we bear fruit that is truly worthwhile and flows from Him. It is God's power that brings to fruition every deed prompted by our faith in Him. The desire to fulfil His purposes is planted in us; it germinates from the faith He has placed there. When Paul tells us that, "I planted, Apollos watered, but God gave the growth" (1 Corinthians 3:6 ESV), these actions originate from the power of God at work in both of them. This is the power of God at work in the deeds inspired by faith.

God does this so that the name of Jesus will be glorified in us, and we in Him. Far from simply doing what *we* want, this is about releasing what He has already planted in us. When we step into the calling He has prepared for us—carrying out the deeds inspired by our faith, and the works prepared for us in advance to do—the name of Jesus is glorified.

And may it be so. May the name of Jesus be glorified more and more. May the glory of His name be amplified in our churches, communities, and countries forever and ever. Amen.

ENHANCING EFFECTIVENESS

I have sat with countless senior pastors, youth pastors, pastoral carers, denominational leaders, and those in various other roles, and asked them to describe what they are passionate about.

Esmee, a youth pastor, told me:

> "I love hanging out with teens. The non-Christian kids, not the Christian ones. And the messier the better. Spending time with them, giving them hope that their future can be different. I mean, I want them to know Jesus ultimately, but if I can help them see themselves as someone valuable, who can make smart decisions and not get trapped in dumb ways of being, then that's a win for me. I love that I get to do that. My difficulty is that I also need to run the Christian youth group and spend time with their parents."

I responded to her with something like:

> "So, if the church came to you and said, 'We've been thinking. We want to give responsibility for the Christian teens to someone else, and we want you to spend time with the non-Christian teens. You are to build relationships with them, help them to know their worth, make wise choices, construct a meaningful life, and share the gospel with them as you go.' What would that be like for you?"

> "Oh, that would be like a dream come true. But that's not what the job is."

> "Maybe. But we don't start with what a job is, we start with what your calling is. It might be that the job can change to fit your calling. It might be that there is a different role for you."

The first step is to clarify the calling and then explore where it might be best expressed. I would also consider whether expressing that calling in the person's current setting might be a genuine blessing to the church, organisation, or context they are in. So, the conversation with Esmee continued:

> "Tell me, why would your church ever want to invest in you spending time with these non-Christian teens?"

> "Well, I guess because our church has a real heart for evangelism and for raising up the next generation. People seem to admire what I do because they tell me they don't want to do it, or they are not good at it. And I'm like, *seriously?!* They are so easy. These kids are so real, so authentic. They don't pretend."

> "Ok, great. It sounds like your passion in this area may be the very thing your church wants and needs. It is worth praying about this and talking it over with your leadership. Imagine if you were overseeing this ministry to these non-Christian youths and helping others to do the same. Through you, the church would be giving expression to its evangelistic heart and desire to see the next generation raised up. It sounds like this would definitely be worth exploring with the leadership."

> "Totally!"

It is possible that people like Esmee could be the key to unlocking the missional impetus in their churches, but that potential is being limited. It is not being limited intentionally or as a result of anyone's nefarious agenda, but because of common practices around the employment of youth pastors, their role, their job description, and what their wages pay for.

Malcolm was a senior pastor who told me:

> "I've been in ministry now for about forty years. I feel like I have done it all. I'm now sixty and probably looking at retiring when I'm sixty-five. So, what do I do for the next five years? Do I just stay put and coast to the end? I can't see myself going

to another church, I mean, who would want a sixty-year-old heading towards retirement anyway?"

I responded:

"In all that you have done, what do you love. Tell me what brings a deep sense of fulfilment for you. Tell me about what you love doing with Jesus and for Him."

"Oh, I love discipling others. I love seeing people come to faith and spending time with new believers. I think I have a gift in that. Over the years, I have seen many people come to faith, and I have been able to help people in our church share their faith with others, even when they thought that would be something they would never do."

"So, how would you feel if your denominational leader came to you and said, 'We'd like you to step back from leading your church and hand it on to the next generation. Your role would be to help all our churches increase their evangelistic ability. We want you to raise up people in every church to champion this cause and help them train their congregations to share their faith.' What would that be like for you?"

"Like a dream come true. That would get me excited. That feels like what I am made for!"

It may not be true for everyone, but what if a significant portion of our pastors and leaders are limited by ill-fitting roles? Imagine the Kingdom potential and momentum that would be released if they were placed in roles that matched their calling and gifts. The impact would be profound. Not only would pastors thrive with greater effectiveness and increased wellbeing, but the mission of the Church would move forward powerfully. We need to dream out what God has dreamed into us. This determines the extent to which the world we create reflects His Kingdom.

ENHANCED WELLBEING

When a pastor ministers from their sweet spot, they are more likely to minister with resilience and enthusiasm without drifting toward burnout.

At times, people push back and say, "Richard, ministry isn't just about doing what you want. It often involves doing things you don't like doing." This is true. Ministry will always have its challenges. But this kind of response, while sounding spiritual, can be the very mindset that keeps so many pastors unnecessarily limited. Their response comes from a good place. People want to be Jesus-centred rather than self-centred. They want to serve Jesus and not themselves. I wholeheartedly agree with that.

The underlying assumption, however, is that ministry involves suffering, so if we are suffering, then we are being faithful to God. The flip side to this is that if we enjoy what we are doing in ministry, then it must be self-centredness. That assumption, while common, does not reflect the fullness of how God works in and through us "to will and to act."

There will be many challenges in ministry and many things that we find difficult or unpleasant. However, when we are doing what we are called to do, even in these difficult places, there is a "joy set before us" (Hebrews 12:2). Even in the anguish Jesus experienced in the Garden of Gethsemane, there was something deeper the Father had placed within Him that enabled Him to move forward. There was a joy beyond the suffering, a purpose so compelling that it gave Him strength to endure the cross." The same is true for us. This does not mean we enjoy the difficulty, but there is a deeper sense of alignment, purpose, and passion.

This is very different from the sense of 'grinding your gears' that pastors feel when our calling and role are mismatched. It is different from the deeply draining experience of ministry that feels like just another day of pushing jelly up a hill. This is not the type of suffering we are called to; rather, it is an indicator that our calling and role are out of alignment. When our calling fits, even the hard parts carry meaning. When it does not, it wears us down from the inside out.

14

CLARIFYING YOUR MACRO CALL

We can discover the call God has for us in many different ways. It may result from a direct revelation from the Lord or the discernment of trusted leaders, or it may emerge as we engage in ministry through the process of trial, error, and discovery. In this chapter, I will outline some reflective questions I use to help people better understand how God has wired them and to discern their true calling. As they sift through the noise of life and ministry, they begin to see, with greater clarity, what God may have dreamed into them.

Before we get to that, however, we can glean some insights from how Paul describes his own calling in terms of its function, activity, and outcome.

1. Function: To Be An Apostle

"Paul, called to be an apostle of Christ Jesus by the will of God…"

1 Corinthians 1:1

In Ephesians 4:11-12, Paul explains that "Christ himself gave the apostles, the prophets, the evangelists, the pastors and teachers, to equip his people for works of service, so that the body of Christ may be built up." Each one serves a distinct purpose and function to contribute to the overall wellbeing, maturity and effectiveness of the Church. Knowing your distinctiveness is key.

Unfortunately, when someone senses a call to ministry and begins wondering where to serve, their first thought usually tends towards leading a local church as a pastor. The role of pastoring tends to dominate the imagination because ministry has become almost synonymous with church leadership. It offers a clear training pathway, a defined job, and importantly, a secure funding model that makes it a viable full-time vocation. The role of the pastor is established, structured, and resourced, which makes it a clear, obvious choice for anyone sensing a call to ministry.

The emphasis on the pastoral role as *the* role for ministry makes complete sense when you consider that the Western Church operated for centuries from a Christendom mindset. When everyone is presumed to be Christian in some form or other, then the primary need is for pastors to manage and care for those Christians.

The problem is that this has become the entrenched model for facilitating people's calling. As a result, those whose calling has a different shape and function, such as apostolic, prophetic, evangelistic, or educational, have often tried to squeeze themselves into the mould of pastoring a church. This has not only limited their effectiveness and wellbeing but has also negatively affected the people they lead, sometimes with devastating consequences. Much like the Procrustean bed, the unspoken claim is that the pastoral role can be adapted to fit your unique calling and gifts. You can make the role your own. The result is limited and frustrated leaders, distressed churches, or both.

What if denominations and training colleges helped people to identify their function, provided training to excel in that function, and then placed them in roles where they could freely operate out of that function? The Kingdom impact would be huge. To get there, however, requires a whole new way of thinking. It requires us to step out of our current system and structures to re-examine what we are trying to achieve—focusing on our 'hole' rather than our 'drill bit'—and considering how best to achieve it with the resources God has given us. It takes courage to do this. The kind of courage that often only comes from desperation. The question is, are we desperate enough yet?

2. Activity: To Preach the Good News to the Gentiles

> *"He gave me the priestly duty of proclaiming the gospel of God…"*
>
> **Romans 15:16**

Paul loved preaching and proclaiming the Good News. It oozed out of him. He took every opportunity to share it.

> *"Then Agrippa said to Paul, 'Do you think that in such a short time you can persuade me to be a Christian?' Paul replied, 'Short time or long—I pray to God that not only you but all who are listening to me today may become what I am, except for these chains.'"*
>
> **Acts 26:28-29**

In fact, it was his deep desire to preach the gospel where it had not yet been heard:

> *"It has always been my ambition to preach the gospel where Christ was not known, so that I would not be building on someone else's foundation."*
>
> **Romans 15:20**

Proclaiming the gospel was the activity Paul loved doing. It was what he did on behalf of Jesus, and it was the gift he offered to this world. Paul knew firsthand just how good the Good News was. Confronted with his own sin and crimes when Jesus met him on the road to Damascus, Paul's life was radically transformed when he encountered God's grace. Following that experience, the transformative Good News spilt out of him; he wanted everyone to know the profound grace, goodness and kindness contained in the gospel. It compelled him forward (2 Corinthians 5:14).

It is quite common for people to feel called towards an activity or area of ministry that has been influenced by their life experiences, or has been placed in them from God from the moment of conception.

> *"Before I formed you in the womb I knew you, before you were born I set you apart; I appointed you as a prophet to the nations."*
>
> **Jeremiah 1:5**

Within your calling, there will be a grace (charisma) in what you do. This giftedness may be so natural that you do not realise it is anything special. You might say, "Oh, but anyone can do that," and find people look at you strangely. Others may be able to do something similar, but do not let that fool you into thinking it is not a special grace given to you. This is the activity or gift you offer this world for the sake of the Kingdom.

3. Outcome: The Gentiles Becoming an Acceptable Offering to God

> *". . . so that the Gentiles might become an offering acceptable to God, sanctified by the Holy Spirit."*
>
> **Romans 15:16b**

The primary activity or task that Paul feels called to do is "the priestly duty of proclaiming the gospel of God" to a specific group of people—the gentiles. This does not mean he cannot minister in other ways or with other people; it is simply that this is what he is primarily called to do and with whom.

Paul fulfils his calling in various ways. He does it through preaching to people who have never heard of Jesus, discipling gentiles who came to faith, and establishing structures for the newly formed Christian communities. When he was imprisoned, his calling did not change, nor was it limited; he simply changed *how* he fulfilled it. Paul was put in 'lockdown', not due to a pandemic but a miscarriage of justice. Yet he continued to preach the gospel to the soldiers and governors he interacted with and to disciple and guide the gentile Christians through his letters. In one sense, thank God for Paul's imprisonment. We have the New Testament because Paul was put in lockdown.

PAUL'S MODEL TO DISCERN OUR CALLING

Paul's description of his calling gives us a helpful model to follow.

- **Function:** Who has God called me to be?
- **Activity:** What do I love doing for the sake of others?
- **Outcome:** What difference do I long to make in the world?

It would be beneficial, not just for pastors but for all of us, to complete the following:

- **Function:** I believe God has called me to be a . . .
- **Activity:** I love fulfilling this by . . .
- **Outcome:** The outcome I want to achieve is . . .

Another way to approach this is to simply ask yourself what you feel called to be, do, and achieve.

You may need help to complete this, but this framework can ultimately serve as a guide for personal reflection, mentoring conversations, or leadership development. It moves us beyond role-based thinking into calling-based living.

Eventually, you may be able to summarise it into a clear, meaningful, resonating, empowering, provocative statement. The goal is not just to create a pithy statement you can put on the wall, but to give voice to something that captures your heart, stirs your faith, and focuses your action.

Do not worry about finding the perfect wording. The exact phrasing may change over time, but the essence will remain. You may find a more succinct way to clarify your calling. When I was in my early twenties, I was praying about my future. I had walked up a hill to a beautiful spot overlooking the sea. I sensed God wanted to say something, so I paused and asked, "Lord, what do You want me to do?" In response, I felt Him say,

"Richard, you will walk alongside churches and strengthen them to be all I have created them to be."

I was both stunned and excited. I was only just beginning in ministry, yet it resonated deeply. As Mary did in Luke 2:19, I "treasured up all these things and pondered them" in my heart. I did not know if I had heard God correctly, but either way, I held it loosely, trusting that if it was truly from Him, He would bring it about in His way and time.

Those words have remained with me. Over the years, I have expressed the sentiment in various forms: "To empower the local church to thrive so it can change the world for God," or "To equip church leaders to grow healthy churches that make a Kingdom difference." Each phrase reflects the same heartbeat in different ways. In the end, it is not about having the perfect statement. It is about naming what God has placed in you, giving voice to your calling in a way that brings clarity, alignment and momentum to your life and ministry.

DREAMING OUT WHAT GOD HAS DREAMED INTO YOU

I have provided several examples of what this might look like below. Before we get there, though, let me share with you four key questions I ask as part of a process to help people surface what God may have dreamed into them. The aim is to identify what people are passionate about and gifted in as a way of beginning the process of discerning their macro call. Once completed, I encourage people to prayerfully reflect on what has been revealed and share it with trusted people for their insight, discernment, and counsel.

I may take people or churches through this in one sitting, but if you are doing this on your own, it can be helpful to take more time over these questions. This way, you do not rush the process and can spend longer in prayerful reflection.

1. Gifts: What Have You Been Equipped With?

This explores the natural and spiritual gifts you have been given; the abilities, strengths or inclinations that seem to come naturally or have been honed through life's journey. Sometimes they are so embedded in who you are that you barely notice them until someone points them out.

2. Fulfilment: What brings Your Soul Alive?

This is about what you love doing. It is the activity or focus that brings you deep joy and satisfaction; the moments when you feel most alive, present, and at ease in yourself.

3. Impact: What Difference Do You Long to Make?

This focuses on your sense of purpose. What kind of change do you desire to see in the world, in the Church or in others because of your presence or contribution?

4. Energisers: What Gives You Life?

This is about identifying what recharges you. These are the things that fill your cup rather than drain it; the work or focus that gives more than it takes.

Let's look at these one by one.

1. Gifts

There are many things with which we have been gifted. Spiritual gifts are definitely a key part of this, but so too are our experiences, natural abilities, values, resources, qualifications, and even our quirks. God weaves significance into what may seem random at the time. A childhood spent navigating two cultures may open doors for cross-cultural ministry. A painful season might deepen your empathy and call you to walk with others who are hurting. Even practical skills like fixing bikes can become sacred ground when they build trust with local kids and open the door for something deeper. Nothing is wasted. God uses all we have been given as part of His work through us.

I struggled at school in my early years until I was diagnosed with dyslexia and given the learning support I needed. I do not see things as linear as others do. This showed up in my ability with reading and spelling, which were both very difficult for me. Alongside those challenges came a surprising strength—a heightened ability to see connections and patterns others might miss.

I remember as a teenager helping friends who were struggling with their university essays. I knew nothing about their subject, but they would read me the question and tell me a bit about the topic. I would ask a few questions and then say something like: "From what I have heard, is it possible that A, B, and C are combining to cause D, and D is the essential factor in answering this question?" They would often reply, "How do you do that?" For me, it did not seem like anything special; I was simply reflecting what I heard.

This ability to see patterns and make connections has been a gift in my counselling, supervision, leadership coaching, and research. I love helping people make connections that lead to insight or a breakthrough, whether for them personally or for an organisation they serve.

The early struggles I faced, not just academically but also through being bullied, have also grown a deep empathy in me for those who feel sidelined, limited, or dominated. I love seeing people find freedom, believe in themselves, and flourish in who God has made them to be.

What are your abilities, resources, experiences and strengths that could be a gift to others?

2. Fulfilment

What are you passionate about? What stirs something deep within your soul and gives you a quiet sense of joy, a deep satisfaction, or the conviction that you were made for this? For some, it is about helping people discover they are truly loved. For others, it is guiding people to a greater understanding of

Scripture, helping them find healing or come to faith. You might come alive when encouraging people to grow in confidence, find clarity, or overcome wounds that have held them back for years.

Personally, I have noticed my own sense of fulfilment as I work with pastors. When I help leaders find healing, remove obstacles in their lives and ministry, and begin to thrive, something in me resonates deeply. I am passionate about doing anything that helps God's people be who they have been created to be and do what He is calling them to. There is a joy in knowing I have played a small part in making that happen. It is the kind of fulfilment that keeps drawing me forward.

I also find deep fulfilment when I see healing, breakthrough, growth, and flourishing, both in individual lives and in churches collectively. There is something sacred about walking with pastors who feel overwhelmed, stuck, disillusioned, or burned out. As I help them address the underlying issues that are holding them back and see their hope rekindled and energy return, it gives me a profound sense of joy.

Pastors I have journeyed with have shared things like:

> "I feel a weight off my shoulders. I now know what I need to do next."

> "This is the ministry I have always wanted!"

> "I'm more in love with Jesus."

> "I want to get back into ministry. I don't know if it will be full-time church leadership again or not, but I want to get back to ministering with God."

Moments like these remind me why I do what I do. It is not just about encouraging pastors to stay in ministry; it is about helping them rediscover joy, vision, and a renewed sense of calling. That is what makes my soul come alive.

What is it for you? What makes your soul come alive? What brings you a sense of deep fulfilment?

3. Impact

We saw earlier that Esmee wanted to see a generation of teens discover their worth and find faith in Jesus. Malcolm dreamed of seeing more people come to faith and growing in confidence in sharing their faith. Both were outlining the kind of impact they hoped their lives would make.

For me, it is this: I want to see churches transformed so they can transform their communities. I long to see churches and leaders thriving, not just surviving, and making a greater Kingdom impact. That means more people coming to faith, more people finding healing, and more disciples equipped and mobilised to live out their faith in their neighbourhoods. I want to see healthy pastors leading with clarity and energy from their calling and gifts. I want to see Christians raised up and released into their calling and churches shaped not just by tradition or habit, but by a creative, Spirit-led commitment to fulfil God's mission. Ultimately, I want to see people becoming who God made them to be and doing what He is calling them to do.

Leaders like Esmee and Malcolm are often so immersed in what is in front of them or in the expectations they feel that it can be hard for them to imagine anything different. One question I love to offer to help them regain focus and clarity is: "If Jesus came to you and said, 'I know you love Me. Tell Me what you want to do for Me and My Kingdom. You name it, and I'll back you.' What would you ask for? What outcome would you love to see achieved?"

In other words, what difference would you love to make in this world for Jesus if you knew He was backing you, resourcing you, and cheering you on? Often, your calling sits just beneath the surface of that very desire.

I find that many people are stumped by this question. They have never dared to ask it. Many have never permitted themselves to even consider it. Their instinct is to suppress it, thinking it sounds selfish, or dismiss it as being too grandiose or unrealistic. We end up editing out the very things God may have dreamed into us. No one is doing this intentionally. It can be the result of busyness, the way things are normally done, spiritualised passivity mistaken for humility, or simply fear and self-doubt. Unfortunately, there are many reasons we end up burying, suppressing and dismissing the call of God.

How would you answer that question? What would you want to achieve if you knew Jesus was backing you and cheering you on? Your answer to this may be the beginning of discovering what God has dreamed into you.

4. Energisers

What tasks enthuse you, and which ones leave you feeling drained? Often, there are quiet clues to our calling in what we are already doing. There is a deep pull in us to will and to act for His good purposes (Philippians 2:13). We often find ourselves gravitating towards the activities that align with that purpose and feel frustrated or drained when required to do other tasks.

When discerning our calling, describing what energises us and depletes us can be like playing the childhood game of Hot and Cold. As we move closer to the tasks that give us life, there is a gentle whisper that we are getting "warmer, warmer!" This is what we need to tune into hearing.

One simple but powerful exercise I often invite people to do is to make a list of all the tasks they regularly engage in, making it as comprehensive as possible. Next to each task, I ask them to score how much it energises them. Higher scores like seven to ten out of ten usually indicate tasks that are in our sweet-spot, which are life-giving and a natural alignment with how God has wired us. Scores below five usually indicate the opposite. Even if you are highly competent in that area, it can leave you feeling drained.

The aim is not to simply do what we like, but to pay attention to how we are designed. The more we can shape our roles to align with our strengths, gifts, and calling, the more sustainable and fruitful our ministry becomes. Just because it is ministry work does not mean it has to be tedious or difficult. Ministry will always include hard or mundane moments, but they need not be the norm. As we will explore further when we look at what constitutes balanced ministry, sometimes we must operate outside our sweet spot, but long-term health, sustainability, and effectiveness are possible when we learn to minister more often from a place that brings us life.

Sometimes, when we persevere with activities that are not in our sweet spot but are out of a misguided sense of responsibility, we can rob someone else of an opportunity that would energise *them*. I discovered this several years ago when I started running the Pastoral Transformation Course. The course equips people with practical tools for transformation. These tools can be applied in their own lives and can also be used to support others in safe and effective pastoral care.

The course involves designing the content, delivering the training in groups, and providing tutoring and feedback on their assignments. I loved the first two parts, but the last one sucked the life out of me, to the point where I was wondering how long I could continue offering this course. When I mentioned this to one of the counsellors in my team, she replied, "Oh, could I do that?!" She was not only a counsellor but also a qualified teacher who loves written work and helping people grasp new concepts. I jumped at this and handed over that task to her. The result was that I was released to do what I do best, she thrived in her sweet spot, and the participants received even better support. That was ten years ago, and I can report I am still happily delivering this course.

What are the tasks that are life-giving and energising for you? And which ones drain the life out of you? If you had the choice, what would you stop doing immediately? What would you focus on?

Reflection

As you reflect on each of these areas—gifts, fulfilment, impact, and energises—what stands out to you? Try to summarise what you have surfaced using the following prompts:

> What do you feel called to be?

> What do you want to do (your key activity and offering to this world)?

What do you want to achieve (the outcome/impact you want your activity to have)?

This will likely take several prayerful rounds of refinements. Do not feel bound to what you write at first; this is still part of the discernment process. At the same time, try not to minimise what you write because it sounds too bold or beyond you. Be careful not to edit out what the Holy Spirit is trying to write in. Leave any refinement for later. You will have opportunities to bring this before the Lord and trusted others for prayerful sifting. For now, simply focus on writing down what resonates in your spirit.

e.g. I feel called to . . .

Be (function): ____

____

Do (activity): ____

____

____

Achieve (outcome): ____

____

____

CLARIFYING YOUR MACRO CALL

When you discover and clarify what you are called to do, you begin to realise that this macro call is not confined to a single role or context. It can be expressed in a variety of ways across different seasons of life. This understanding brings freedom and resilience. If a job ends or your circumstances shift due to personal changes, leadership transitions, or even something as disruptive as a pandemic, your calling remains. We see this in the life of Paul. Even when imprisoned and unable to travel, preach publicly, or plant churches in person, his calling did not cease. Instead, it found expression through letters, prayer and spiritual influence within his confinement.

Distinguishing our macro calling from a specific role gives us greater clarity and objectivity. This shift is essential for both personal sustainability, faithful stewardship, and enthusiastic engagement. A helpful and ongoing question to ask ourselves, and for our governance board or denomination to reflect on with us, is: *How am I tracking in fulfilling the macro call God has entrusted to me?*

Once we have clarified our macro call, we can start to discern which roles or contexts are best suited to help us live it out. This clarity becomes a compass, helping us to recognise the types of roles that will facilitate rather than frustrate our calling. It allows us to hear more clearly where God may be leading us (in a micro sense) to outwork our calling.

This discernment can save both pastors and a prospective church from the strain of stepping into a role that is a poor fit. It also frees us to assess and adjust our current role when needed, without feeling like we are questioning God's call on our lives. Importantly, it enables us to better discern a change in season, or the need to change a job or ministry setting, without feeling like we are abandoning our call. When we better understand our macro calling, we begin to see that our role serves our calling, not the other way around.

15

——

SLEEPING IN THE RIGHT BED

You may remember the ancient story I shared earlier about Procrustes and his so-called magical bed. It was said to fit anyone, but in truth, unsuspecting sleepers were stretched or cut to size to match its length. This gruesome procedure is a fitting metaphor for pastors. They take a ministry position believing it aligns with their calling, only to discover they are being reshaped to fit the role. Sadly, it is common for pastors to slowly sacrifice parts of themselves to fit a mould they were never designed for.

A ROLE THAT FITS: BEYOND THE PROCRUSTEAN BED

In the famous biblical story of David and Goliath, a young shepherd boy, David, feels a stirring in his spirit and is compelled to fight the giant, Goliath. King Saul is astounded and thrilled that someone is finally willing to oppose Goliath, and in a well-meaning but misguided move, Saul offers to outfit David with his own royal armour and sword. Warriors need armour, and what better way to do this than by generously fitting David with his own? It made perfect sense and would have been a huge honour. The problem was that, despite his good intentions and the apparent wisdom of tradition, they were ill-fitting garments. David could not move freely or swing the sword with ease. If David had submitted to the king's guidance and done things in the expected way, he would have died. The same principle applies to ministry. If the role requires you to shed parts of yourself or suppress what God has uniquely placed in you, something vital is lost. It may seem noble in the short term, but over time, it can leave you spiritually depleted and vocationally misaligned.

There's no doubt David felt called to the role, but he also needed to fulfil that role with the strengths and experiences God had given him, not by conforming to someone else's vision of how it should be done. The role needed to be fitted to him, not the other way round. When you do feel called to a particular context, role, or job (your micro call), the first important question you need to consider is, Does this role genuinely facilitate my macro call? The next question is just as key: Am I free to fulfil this role (and with that, my macro call) using the gifts and priorities God has given me? Or am I being squeezed into an ill-fitting mould, like Saul's armour?

There are so many pastors who need to hand the armour back. It often comes with good intentions, it may have served others well in the past, and it may be just what everyone does, but the bottom line is that it does not fit, and it is limiting you—potentially even killing you. To challenge the usual way of doing things is not an easy feat. It becomes near impossible if you assume that 'success' looks like fighting in the king's armour, and that what the 'king' requires of you is the same as what God requires.

To take the next step, we must not only differentiate our identity from the role but also differentiate our calling from the role. This shift frees us from the unhealthy submission to any 'king' so we can be fully submitted to *the* King. It also frees us from striving towards the wrong markers of role success (fighting in armour that does not fit), and releases us to fulfil what God has uniquely called us to do (defeating specific giants in His strength).

Your role is the specific context in which you sense God inviting you to serve. For most people, this will usually look like leading a specific local church. Your micro call is the concrete expression of your broader dynamic calling, and it has several layers. When someone says they feel called to a role in a micro sense, they may feel called to serve in a specific denomination, a geographical location, an advertised job opportunity, or to a specific set of tasks like preaching or pastorally caring for others. It is vital to realise that all these aspects comprise your micro or tertiary call and need to submit to and align with your macro call. Let me say it again clearly: If you are fully serving Jesus, then the tasks you take on and the roles you step into must serve what He has called you to fulfil.

It is important to distinguish what you are actually feeling called to do. Is it the specific church, the region, the position, the denomination, or simply the tasks described in a job description? Whatever it is, it is essential to realise that all these aspects are part of your micro call, not your macro, and may need to be clarified and refined. To explore this further, let us briefly consider three common aspects of a micro call: denomination, location, and tasks.

1. Denomination

Most churches sit within a denomination, and your micro call may include a sense of call to one in particular. Perhaps you are not especially drawn to a denomination itself, but to a specific local church that happens to belong to it, so part of fulfilling your micro calling in that local church will involve you working within that denomination.

Even in denominations where covenanting relationships are used, it is important to remember that this is still your micro call. You have discerned that the best way to fulfil your macro calling is by covenanting to a specific denomination. In doing so, you willingly come under its authority and seek to adhere to its requirements. In turn, the denomination takes responsibility to support you as you seek to fulfil your macro call. A mutual (but different) submission occurs, and when it is working well, it can be a beautiful partnership.

But what happens when that partnership breaks down? The denomination abdicates its responsibilities to you and uses its authority to fulfil its own organisational needs at the expense of you, your calling, and your wellbeing, which causes you to leave. Does this end your macro call? By no means. A denomination is a means through which you can express and fulfil your macro calling; it is not the call itself. When you think about fulfilling God's macro call on your life, a denomination is a vehicle, not the destination. It is the drill bit, not the hole. The call of God remains.

2. Location

Perhaps you feel called to a specific location or region and find a position available in that area. Just because the position is in that location does not mean it is the right one for you. Likewise, if a position comes to an end, that does not negate your sense of call to that area.

Equally, when you accept a position at a church, you are agreeing to serve that region and outwork your macro calling with the people in that location. Your discernment about accepting a position at a specific church needs to include discerning a call to the people of that region as well. The two are inseparable. Your call to a church is, in part, a call to its neighbourhood.

If, for any reason, you need to leave that region, your calling does not end. God's purposes for your life are not limited to one postcode. The call continues in new places through new people in fresh, new ways.

3. Tasks

Every role involves a range of tasks. Many are regular, some are periodic, and others are exceptional. The difficulty is that people often carry unspoken assumptions about what the role involves. This makes it essential to clarify expectations early on, both your own and those of key stakeholders. Without this, tension can grow. You may find yourself locked in an ongoing tug-of-war over expectations, suppressing your own, or pretending to be in agreement when you are not. The pastoral role carries with it a set of assumed tasks such as preaching, teaching, pastoral care, and discipleship. However, as we saw previously, the reality of a pastor's daily tasks can often be at odds with their macro call.[1]

> Samuel wants to help people "grow in their relationship with Christ," but his role is "ninety per cent administration."

Miriam wants to evangelise and see "souls saved," but she is occupied with the needs of a declining church.

Elijah wants to shepherd people by being actively involved in their pastoral care, but needs to delegate this work to others.

Obadiah wants to preach, teach, and be hands-on in the pastoral care of people, but needs to act like a CEO, strategising and vision-casting.

There is a big difference between clarifying a macro call and giving expression to that call through the tasks you do (calling enactment). It is important to remember that even though you feel called to be a pastor, the tasks involved in a specific position may not be a good match with your macro call.

One researcher illustrates this possible disconnection. Andrew Irvine found that a high percentage of pastors felt a strong calling to their role, yet most also lamented that their position required them to operate more like a CEO than a pastor.[2] This is a sentiment echoed by other pastors.[3] In fact, a research group concluded that "to live one's calling successfully, having sufficient opportunities to enact it is potentially as important as being in the right occupation."[4] Pastors need to be able to engage in daily tasks and achieve overall outcomes that are consistent with their macro calling. In other words, they need to be ministering from their sweet spot. When this occurs, it produces many benefits for the pastor, including significantly reducing the likelihood of burnout.[5] This is such good news and highlights the importance of high levels of role-fit to enhance both the effectiveness and wellbeing of the pastor.

Two vital questions that should be asked before a pastoral position is accepted are:

1. Are all key stakeholders (the church board, the congregation, the denomination, and the applicant) in agreement with the core tasks that will be required of the pastor?

2. Are these core tasks a good fit with the applicant's macro call?

We need to move beyond the notion that the role of pastor is like the Procrustean Bed, limiting the person's calling and effectiveness, and potentially damaging their wellbeing. We need to stop dressing pastors in Saul's ill-fitting armour and then critiquing them when they try to wear it.

SWEET-SPOT MINISTRY

People often ask me, "How do I know whether I am simply doing necessary but unenjoyable parts of the role, or if I am actually in a role that is out of alignment with my calling?" This is a great question. It is a bit like church life, where someone might have a clear ministry or gifting, but everyone still helps stack chairs, vacuum floors, or clean up after events. We all chip in. But if that became our main activity, it would likely become draining.

There will always be parts of any role that are not energising, but when your role aligns with your calling, you will spend the majority of your time in your sweet spot. That is not selfishness; it is good stewardship of the gifts God has given you and the call He has placed on your life.

Below is the Sweet-Spot Matrix, a framework I created to help people refine their roles and better understand what balanced, healthy, and sustainable ministry activity looks like. At the centre of the matrix is your sweet-spot—the place where three key elements converge. This is where you want to spend most of your ministry time. When you do, it is like having the wheels on your car perfectly aligned. You move more smoothly, efficiently, and with less resistance.

When you are not operating in your sweet spot, you can still move forward and get things done, but it creates more wear, burns more fuel, and eventually leads to strain.

The three overlapping elements are:

1. **Ownership:** refers to 'owning' what we do. This has two parts. Firstly, we own it emotionally, or in other words, our heart is in it. We engage in the task willingly and wholeheartedly. Secondly,

we own it in the sense that it is under our jurisdiction. It serves us in the sense that we can do it sustainably.

2. **Service:** refers to serving Jesus and His Kingdom. It is about pursuing His purposes and meeting the needs of others, not simply our own.

3. **Passion:** refers to what we are passionate about and have a strong enthusiasm for. It aligns with our God-given gifts and brings a sense of joy and purpose.

When these three elements overlap, we are operating from a place that is energised, fruitful, and sustainable—our sweet-spot. This will not happen all the time, but the goal is to do so as much as possible and realign ourselves when necessary.

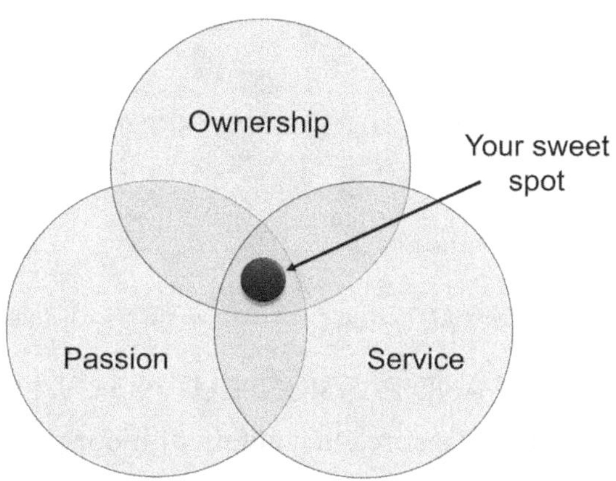

DIAGRAM 10. Balanced Ministry Framework

OWNERSHIP AND SERVICE, BUT NO PASSION

There will, of course, be tasks we can do willingly and wholeheartedly that serve the needs of others, yet they are not areas we are passionate about or particularly gifted in.

When I left pastoring and moved to Christchurch, I went to our local church and offered to serve in any way they needed. They said they needed help in the children's ministry. Now, this is something that I *can* do and was happy to do. I am not passionate or gifted in this area, but I was happy to serve for a year in that role. Every third week, when it was my turn, I served wholeheartedly.

It is possible to minister with both ownership and service in areas that are outside our passion, either by contributing in small ways over a long period of time, or in a significant way over a short period of time. Both approaches are expressions of faithfulness. However, if we stay in this space for an extended period of time, it will dry us up and eventually deplete us.

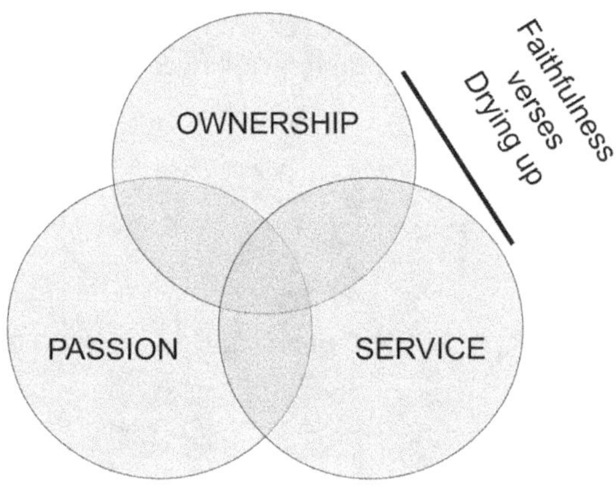

DIAGRAM 11. Balanced Ministry: ownership and service without passion

SERVICE AND PASSION, BUT NO OWNERSHIP

Sometimes we serve in an area that aligns with our passion, but we do not have full ownership over it.

Simon and Lucy were part of a large church and eager to serve. They told the leadership they loved working with youth and wanted to support the church in whatever way they could. Understandably, this was music to the ears of the leadership, who said, "That's so good. We'd love for you to be at all five of our services and attend our mid-week volunteers' meeting as well as your weekly life group." Simon and Lucy responded, "Lock us in!" And they genuinely meant it. The problem was that it was not sustainable. After a while, they became overwhelmed and eventually stepped back entirely.

They eventually left the church, leaving the leadership scratching their heads about what happened.

Serving in an area we are passionate about without adequate ownership can work for a short burst or at a low level over a long time. It can even give life to a ministry for a season. But if it continues at a high level over an extended period, it becomes a recipe for burnout.

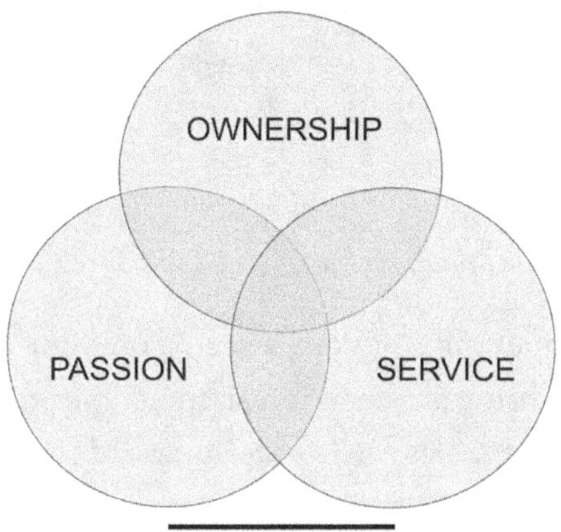

DIAGRAM 12. Balanced Ministry: passion and service without ownership

PASSION AND OWNERSHIP, BUT NO SERVICE

There will also be times when we operate with ownership and passion, but it serves no one else but ourselves. For example, if a church came to me and said, "Richard, we want to send you and your wife to Hawaii to lie on a beach for a week," I would feel a strong sense of ownership over that idea and a lot of passion for it. If I spent a week there, it would likely be quite replenishing. If I spent my life here, this would shift from replenishment to self-indulgence.

Operating with ownership and passion but without service can still be healthy when done in a small way over time or in a concentrated way for a short period. It can bring necessary replenishment and help us sustain our long-term ministry. But if we live here long-term, it becomes selfishness.

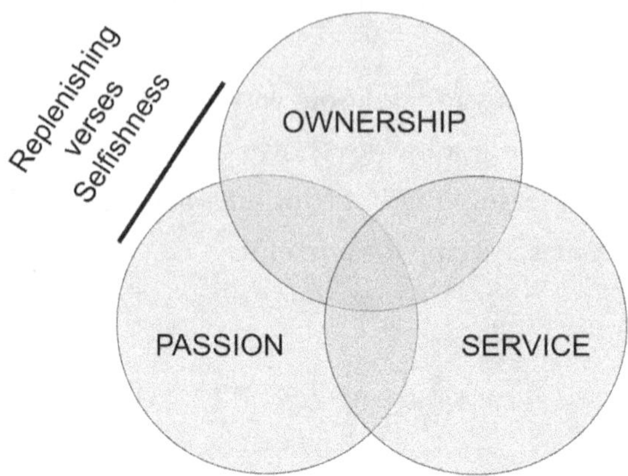

DIAGRAM 13. Balanced Ministry: ownership and passion without service

When you are operating in your sweet spot, your ministry is more sustainable, and you bring greater enthusiasm to your role. There is more petrol in your tank that enables you to keep going and sustainably offer more. There is more oil around your engine, protecting you from the wear and tear that comes from life's demands, the expectations of others, and challenging relationships. By contrast, when you are not in your sweet spot, you are more likely to continually need a break, even when you have just returned from holiday. You are more likely to experience sickness, stress, and emotional fatigue. You are more likely to need time away from work or an intensive self-care plan. This is not a sign of failure, but often a sign of misalignment.

Marcus was a pastor of a large church who would frequently return from holiday and within three months say, "I need a holiday. People don't understand the toll senior leadership takes." If you find yourself needing an extended break every few months, something is not right. There may be a misalignment in your role or some unfinished business in your inner world that needs attention.

Please do not mishear me: Even when you are operating from your sweet spot, you will still need to take holidays, have downtime, look after yourself when you are unwell, and have a replenishing self-care plan. Yet, this will be a part of the normal rhythm of caring for yourself rather than being driven by an extraordinary need for relief. To put it another way:

> "True self-care is not salt baths and chocolate cake; it is making the choice to build a life you don't need to regularly escape from."[6]

When you are in your sweet spot operating from your macro call, life may still be difficult, but you will not feel the need to escape what you are doing. There is a 'joy set before you' (Hebrews 12:2) that energises and sustains you for the purpose to which you are called.

This is the essence of passion. To be passionate about something is to be willing to suffer for it. When we talk about 'the Passion of Christ', we are referring to the suffering He willingly endured. When you are called by God to something, you should experience a deep passion for it and a willingness to endure hardship and difficulties to see His purposes fulfilled.

THE MACRO CALL JOB DESCRIPTION

Anyone in ministry or preparing for ministry may well ask, *How do I know if a role is the right fit for me?* It is an important question.

A desire to faithfully fulfil your calling starts with clarifying what Jesus has actually called you to do. Once this is known, the next step is to ask: *What kind of role would be a wonderful expression of my macro calling?*

A helpful exercise is to write an ideal job description for your macro call. If your role could align perfectly with your calling, what would be its key components? What would you spend most of your time doing?

Sometimes people initially feel uncomfortable doing this because it sounds like you are selfishly choosing to do what *you* want to do. It is essential to remember that our starting point in this process is not you, but Jesus. You are first and foremost called to Him. Only in Him do you discover who you are through discovering whose you are. It is Jesus who gives you your identity. By writing out the ideal job description for your macro call, you are essentially painting a picture of the type of role that would best enable you to do what Jesus has called you to accomplish.

We explored this earlier with Esmee and Malcolm. Esmee wanted to spend significant time with non-Christian teens, building relationships with them, helping them know their worth, guiding them to make wise choices, and sharing the gospel with them. She also wanted someone else to take responsibility for the Christian youth. Malcolm wanted to spend significant time evangelising and shaping a culture of outreach by mentoring others to do the same.

Let us continue this process with Samuel and Miriam, whom we also met previously. Samuel would likely tell us that in his ideal job, a significant portion of his time would be spent helping people to grow in their relationship with Christ through preaching, mentoring, or leading small group studies. He may go on to say that he wants to build a discipleship culture in the church where he disciples a small group of people who then go on to disciple others. For this to happen well, he would need administration support so he could keep the main thing the main thing and not get lost in administrative weeds.

In an interview with a prospective church, Samuel might choose to share his heart and calling. If this aligns with the church's vision, they might agree upon the need for administration support, whether paid or voluntary. Alternatively, if this was not a possibility, they might discuss adjusting expectations or reducing activities to enable greater focus on discipleship.

Miriam would likely tell us that her ideal role would involve spending time with people who are not Christians, building relationships with them, and sharing the amazingly good news about Jesus. She would also want to raise up others to do the same, multiplying the impact of seeing souls saved.

Miriam's best-fit role might not be a traditional pastoral one and certainly does not fit with the pastoral and chaplaincy needs of a declining church. An appropriate fit for her may not even be a paid position in a church. She would thrive in a setting that values evangelism and is willing to release her into that space, while fulfilling pastoral duties through other means.

When you write out the ideal job description for your macro call, remember it is not about locking yourself into one type of job. It is about gaining clarity. It is part of a discovery process to help you better discern where God is leading you and which role might appropriately serve your macro call, as you seek to serve Jesus. It reveals the tasks that are the most meaningful for you and where potential misalignments may lie. Clarifying your sweet spot is a gift to yourself and to the wider Church, as it helps you identify how a role can best serve the calling Jesus has placed on your life.

ROLE-REFINEMENT AND JOB CRAFTING

Sometimes it is not a matter of hunting for the right role, but rather making the role you are in a better fit. This role-refinement is also called job-crafting. You may be in the right position, but the position is not correctly aligned. To continue with our rudder analogy, a lack of alignment can cause drag, making it more tiring to do your role.

Job-crafting is the intentional process of shaping your role so it better reflects your macro calling. It might involve adjusting assigned tasks, increasing focus on tasks that align more closely with your strengths and call, or expanding your work to include new tasks that are a better match. Sometimes it means reframing how you see your current responsibilities in relation to your call, even if they initially seem disconnected. In all cases, the aim is the same: to bring greater alignment between what you currently do and what you are called to.[7]

Realigning your role or refining your tasks might require shifting to a different organisation, denomination, or church within your current denomination. It could mean changing how you are supported, assessed, or partnered in your role. You might adjust your task load, delegating tasks that drain you, seeking support for those that are a poor fit, or reducing your hours to regain alignment. This process is not about escaping responsibility; it is about stewarding your calling well and creating the kind of role that enables you to serve with faithfulness, fruitfulness, and sustainability.

Frederick and Dunbar discuss this further in their book, *Identity, Calling, and Workplace Spirituality*.[8] They describe how a person might have an obvious case of mismatch if, for example, they feel called to be an environmentalist but are working as a receptionist for an organisation involved in fracking. Alternatively, there might be a more subtle mismatch when a person feels called to be a teacher but finds themselves working in a school context that is not a good fit. In such cases, the calling itself remains valid; it is the role that may need to change. As they note,

> "This does not negate the vocational calling. Rather, this individual may elect to pursue the same teaching career at a different school that provides a person environment match with the individual."[9]

Job-crafting has better outcomes when it has the support of the organisation.[10] Ideally, it would be incredibly beneficial if congregations and denominations allowed pastors the flexibility to shape or refine their role to better fit their macro calling. Not only does this bring renewed energy and clarity to the pastor, but it also serves the church more powerfully.

The problem is, many pastors feel they have little or no agency to make changes. They feel locked into inherited expectations or rigid requirements. This is why differentiating identity from role and macro calling from role is so essential. It frees pastors to have greater objectivity and a sense of agency. Without this clarity, pastors tend to internalise limiting narratives and frame their situation in ways that keep them stuck.

We can hear this resignation in the voices of some of the pastors we met earlier. Their words show their sense of powerlessness in changing their role. To survive the tension they feel, they focus instead on changing themselves and lowering their expectations. The idea of job-crafting is not even comprehended, let alone considered. Instead of reshaping the role to better fit their calling, they reshape themselves to better fit the role.

When pastors lack discernment in seeking a healthy calling-role fit or don't have the ability or opportunity to refine their role through job-crafting, they resign themselves to a restrictive or detrimental ministry position. If the assumption is that this is just how things need to be, or this is what God wants, the only option left is to try to survive it. It is common to hear pastors, denominational leaders, educators, and coaches emphasise the need to grow resilience in the role to increase sustainability and decrease mental health challenges. Resilience is certainly needed, but this is only part of the solution.

If our focus is genuinely on a pastor's wellbeing, then it is not enough to simply help someone build resilience within an unhealthy or even harmful context. To put this in more extreme language, this is like helping someone become more resilient in an abusive relationship without addressing the relationship itself. The person needs both resilience *and* a healthy relationship. Pastors also need this. They need to know how to grow their resilience in the role, and they also need roles that align with their calling and an identity that is not tied to organisational role outcomes.

Even if pastors find themselves working in a context and role to which they feel called, role refinement may still be necessary to help them minister from their sweet spot, increasing their overall wellbeing, effectiveness, and fruitfulness.

16

SUCCEEDING IN THE RIGHT JUNGLE

Differentiating and realigning identity, calling, and role will have a profound impact on the effectiveness and wellbeing of most pastors. However, insight alone is not enough to make it stick. We cannot stop at simply making pastors more resilient in an unhealthy system; we also need to make the system healthier.

In chapter six, we explored the powerful system that pressures pastors to keep their rudders jammed. These forces keep pastors stuck in roles and rhythms that are misaligned with their deeper calling. This system is shaped by three key dynamics:

1. **The fusion of a pastor's identity, calling, and role:** A pastor's sense of identity and call is often entangled with their role, leaving them vulnerable to role demands.

2. **The fusion of success with quantitative outcomes:** Success is frequently measured by organisational markers of success rather than Kingdom outcomes.

3. **The reinforcement of quantitative outcomes by the wider church system:** These markers of success are reinforced and perpetuated by the wider church system, including churches,

fellow pastors, denominations, and ministerial training institutions.

Having addressed the first and most central factor, we now need to turn our attention to the other two. Encouragingly, this not only helps pastors but also enhances the wellbeing and effectiveness of churches. Just as a pastor experiences greater freedom and fruitfulness when their identity, calling and role are rightly aligned, the church also flourishes when it embraces and supports that alignment. Thriving pastors and thriving churches are intimately connected.

KINGDOM OUTCOMES: REALIGNING YOUR CHURCH'S MARKERS OF SUCCESS

When a pastor's rudder is unjammed, they gain greater objectivity from which to view the role. From this place of freedom, they can now climb the ladder and assess whether the church is cutting through the right jungle. Untangling their identity from the role outcomes is critical, but we cannot stop there; we also need to assess whether the outcomes we are pursuing are the ones Jesus intends. We need to make sure we are pursuing Kingdom priorities and not just advancing institutional momentum.

It is here that our theological framework of primary, secondary and tertiary calling becomes essential. Our primary calling is to Jesus; it is in Him that we source our identity and discover who we are. From this flows our macro calling (secondary calling), which is derived from who we are in Christ and who He has made us to be. Our micro calling (tertiary calling) is to a specific role or local context. For that role to be fruitful and sustainable, it must align with our macro calling and ultimately derive from our primary call to Jesus. This also means that Jesus is not only the source of who we are but also the One who defines what success looks like in a given role. Any outcomes we pursue in our role must be evaluated in light of His purposes.

As part of our service to Jesus, we need to make sure we are succeeding in the right jungle. For pastors, this includes not only their own ministry focus but also the outcomes being pursued by the church they are leading.

The implicit and explicit markers of success for a church have a powerful influence on the pastor's rudder. If a pastor operates from a healthy alignment of their identity, calling, and role, but the church's markers of success are not also appropriately aligned to Jesus, then they will act like a powerful trim tab, reverting the pastor's rudder to the old, unhealthy patterns. Over time, this misalignment will steer a pastor back into a role-driven identity, a diminished call, and a weary soul.

Watch how this works. Within the Church system, a congregation's markers of success are a critical point of pressure. This pressure can come from many directions and may be explicated or simply assumed. For many pastors, success is equated with numerical growth; for others, it is measured by how frequently they personally visit their members. These expectations are reinforced through feedback loops, such as comments, comparisons, or denominational benchmarks, which create mounting pressure to conform and communicate to a pastor that their success, adequacy or even acceptance depends on meeting those external markers. This puts pressure on the pastor's rudder to revert to unhealthy patterns where role outcomes determine their worth and distort their calling. We need to see clearly how these markers of success, embedded within the system of the Church, unintentionally keep a pastor's rudder jammed.

As we have seen already, the issue is far-reaching and deeply embedded at a systemic level. A focus on quantitative outcomes captivates the attention of pastors, churches, denominations, and ministerial training institutions (MTIs), shaping their structure, priorities, and practice. If we are serious about bringing real and lasting change to pastors' wellbeing and effectiveness, we must establish a clear and shared understanding of what the desired markers of success need to be. We need markers that are Kingdom-aligned expressions of success (the hole), rather than defaulting to familiar quantitative markers (the drill bit). When pastors are no longer tied to familiar methods, they experience greater freedom and flexibility to explore fresh, creative ways of pursuing the same Kingdom outcomes.

I sit with pastors who say to me, "Richard, I totally agree. We need Kingdom-aligned goals and objectives, and we need to reorganise people's roles to fulfil this." Then there is usually a pause and a sigh, followed by, "Can you tell my elders and denomination that? Every meeting, they will put pressure on me, 'How are the numbers doing? How many people did we have on Sunday? How much was the offering this week?' It is relentless."

This is why a shared understanding is essential. Everyone needs to be on the same page, rowing in the same direction. We need pastors to have healthy ministry alignment, and we need churches with healthy Kingdom alignment. When a pastor has a healthy ministry alignment with their identity grounded in Jesus, their macro calling clarified, and their role shaped to serve that calling, they become more Jesus-centric and Jesus-abiding. This alignment not only enhances their wellbeing but also sharpens their focus to become more aligned with the priorities of the Kingdom. Likewise, we need churches to be clear and united around Kingdom-aligned markers of success. When both the pastor and the church are aligned in this way, they are pulling in the same direction with shared priorities and clarity of purpose. This lightens ministry, builds momentum, and positions us to better achieve the outcomes Jesus desires.

Having said that, many churches experience difficulty when both the pastor and the church *are* aligned, but their alignment is built solely on quantitative outcomes. Momentum builds, the church grows, and on the surface, it appears that everything is thriving. Underneath, however, there is often a drivenness at the heart of the leadership culture. Drivenness always has a cost. It wears people down, leading to turnover and burnout in team members. It can create a culture that excuses dysfunctional and inappropriate behaviour because, "God is clearly doing something here, so how can it be wrong?" The church may well be growing, but it is not healthy growth. Remember, the numbers can blind us to dysfunction.

As an aside here, drivenness can often be missed because it is labelled as 'strong leadership' or 'being passionate'. But drivenness is a counterfeit form of passion. True passion is when you are willing to suffer for what matters to you. Drivenness, on the other hand, occurs when you are willing to make everyone else suffer to achieve the results you want. Pressure is applied, sometimes manipulatively and aggressively, to achieve these quantitative outcomes because the pastor's identity, significance, and worth are dependent on those results.

The difference between healthy passion genuinely expressed through strong leadership and the counterfeit of drivenness is found in the fruit. A healthy passion will always leave people feeling encouraged, strengthened, affirmed, and safe. Drivenness, however, will leave people anxious, overworked, weary, and frightened. Frightened of making mistakes, raising a complaint, voicing a concern, or doing anything that will cause them to be labelled as negative or disloyal. This is why healthy alignment of identity, calling, and role is so vital. When a pastor's starting point is in Jesus, the fruit that is produced will be Jesus-infused, and not drivenness-infused.

Returning to our conversation on the importance of having both the pastor and the church aligned around Kingdom outcomes, it is clear that this is not an easy step and can cause disruption or tension, especially if the church is aligned around different expectations. It is essential for the pastor to bring the church on the journey with them, not only for their own wellbeing and sustainability, but so the church flourishes as the people of God.

One of the challenges we have seen throughout this journey is that many of these issues sit below the waterline. When they are difficult to see, they are difficult to address. As we become aware of what is happening, we can start to see, name and address what is really going on. It begins with learning to see our blind spots.

SEEING OUR BLIND SPOTS

"It is impossible for a man to learn what he thinks he already knows." —Epictetus

When I speak about the need to focus on Kingdom outcomes, it can create confusion, and it would be understandable for many of you reading to say:

"Hang on, Richard, aren't we already focused on Kingdom outcomes? We believe Jesus is Lord, and we worship Him collectively on Sundays. We preach from the Bible, want people to grow spiritually and share their faith, and celebrate when people come to faith. How is that not focusing on Kingdom outcomes?"

It is a great question—and a crucial one. Those are all good and important things. Part of the distinction I am making here is the difference between the drill bit and the hole. Our attention can become so captivated by our drill bit—how we 'do' church and how we measure church—that we lose sight of *why* we are doing it. We lose sight of the Kingdom outcomes Jesus desires.

A pastor can have a jammed rudder without realising it because all the right components are present but ordered wrongly. The same is true for churches. They worship, preach from Scripture, talk about discipleship, and celebrate conversions. All the right elements are there, so they assume all is well and do not look any deeper to see if something is wrongly aligned. Their rudder is also jammed, and they do not realise it. There is a disconnect between what they know logically and theologically, and how they are functioning in practice.

When I work with churches or groups of pastors, I try to gently help them see how we are all conditioned to this unhelpful default setting. To help them see their blind spots, I will typically ask a simple question like: "Tell me, what time is your church?"

They will usually respond with something like: "10 a.m. on Sunday," or "We have two services, 9 a.m. and 11 a.m."

I will follow up with a second question, "What address is your church?" The replies are variations of: "123 Church Street, Generic City."

At this point, I tell them, graciously, that I have set them up. If I had asked the pastors a different question like, "What is Church? How would you define it?" most would likely have given me a theological answer like, "The Church is the people of God," or as I prefer to say, "The Church is a community of disciples of Jesus who are empowered by the Holy Spirit to fulfil God's mission of restoring this world under His Kingship."

Do you see the disconnect here? We may say the Church is the people of God, but that is not how we instinctively view it. Our default setting is that church is a place, a time, a building, and an event. It is about what we *do*.

Some denominations speak of the Church as the 'House' and emphasise the importance of "gathering in the House" and being "planted in the House." While this language has spiritual significance, drawing from Old Testament imagery of the temple, it still reinforces the default setting that the Church is a place and an event.

I have heard pastors describe members of their congregation as "worship-night Christians" or "working-bee Christians." These categories are defined by what happens at the building. Conversely, I have not heard leaders talk about "workplace Christians" or "neighbourhood Christians." It is striking how our language centres the church building as the locus of identity and engagement, rather than seeing its people as the dispersed presence of Jesus in the world.

Please do not mishear me; it is a good thing to have a place to gather, to be together, and to worship. Yet those places and events are not the centre. They are not the main thing. They are the tools we use to serve God, rather than being *the* thing we serve and the main thing we measure. They are the drill bit, not the hole. We must distinguish the two. Drill bits are useful, but they are not the goal. The hole is what matters. The Kingdom outcomes Jesus calls us to are the hole. They are the true measure of health and effectiveness. Our structures, buildings, services, programs and events should all serve those outcomes, not the other way around. When we unintentionally invert that, we end up polishing the tool instead of pursuing the Kingdom. We start perfecting methods instead of fulfilling the mission. Our focus must remain on the hole; the fruit that reflects God's reign breaking into the world.

Winston Churchill once said, "We shape our buildings; thereafter they shape us." We design our buildings to serve a purpose and to fulfil a function, and over time, those buildings will shape our lives and priorities. The same is true for the systems we create. We establish them because we want to achieve a purpose, but once they are embedded, they begin to shape the way we think, lead, and measure success. This is not inherently wrong; it is simply how systems work. A problem arises when we stop asking whether the outcomes they are producing are still the ones we actually want. We begin to value, serve and protect the building or system (drill bit) over the primary outcome (hole). When that happens, we end up serving the structure instead of serving the Kingdom.

Gathering on a Sunday around 10 a.m. for about an hour to sing songs and hear a message is not the model Jesus handed down as a definitive template for being the people of God. It is just what we do, and there is nothing inherently wrong with this. As Glenn Packiam helpfully clarifies, "The problem is not with the paradigm; it's with the emphasis we give it."[1] He goes on to make the point:

> "But even the most sacred of interactions can become profane when they are commodified. When church is the site of a religious transaction, when a congregation becomes the consumer of an experience or the seeker of a new high, the encounter paradigm has gone awry."[2]

Equally, there is nothing wrong with a drill bit. It is a useful tool. The issue arises when we elevate it above its purpose of producing the hole. We become fixated on doing what we have always done. We may create narratives to explain why our drill bits are not making the holes they are supposed to. Over time, we may even forget that our goal was to make holes at all. Instead, we begin to measure success by our ability to make, polish and maintain drill bits. We may even hold conferences on refining drill bits and increasing our drill bit-making capacity. (I say this very much tongue-in-cheek.)

This is how our focus subtly shifts towards fulfilling the quantitative outcomes centred around the Sunday gathering. How many attended? How much was given? This is not what we intend, and it is not what we would articulate theologically. It is simply the reality we find ourselves in.

When I ask pastors what their desired outcomes are for the people in their congregation or what outcomes they believe Jesus would desire for their church, their responses are far more qualitative and Kingdom-focused. They share with me their longing to see people being formed into the likeness of Jesus, sharing their faith, and making a tangible difference for the people in their community. The disconnect we see here is the result of the unseen default setting: the rudder is also jammed in most churches. We have shaped our building and systems, and now they are shaping us and blinding us. This does not just affect our structures; it shapes how we disciple and even how we understand discipleship.

I remember sitting with Phillip, who had been a pastor and was now serving as a denominational leader. I asked him how they grow people as disciples, and he enthusiastically shared with me:

> "We have our discipleship pathway all sorted. When someone comes to faith, we put them in a new believers' group and get them connected to a Life Group. We then get them serving somewhere, maybe helping with the youth or being a host on Sunday. If all goes well, we grow them into being a youth leader or team leader. From there, they might lead the whole area, and if they continue to show capability and capacity, we will look to develop them as a department head or an associate pastor. Eventually, we might train them to lead another location."

This all sounds great, and in many ways it is. The difficulty, however, is that this model is primarily about organisational discipleship rather than being a disciple of Jesus. While we hope that people would grow in their relationship with Jesus along the way, the focus and training are centred on growing their leadership and capacity to lead. It is about growing the capacity of the church and its internal structure. It is about growing the size, not the substance, of the church. While this is still very important work, it is not forming people in the ways of Jesus.

Jesus did not say, "Go into all the world and set up Sunday gatherings, teaching people how to serve in those organisations and grow the gathering size." Although we would not say it as bluntly as this, our patterns and emphasis often reveal that this has become our default Great Commission. It is the gravitational pull many churches experience. A jammed rudder will do that.

When we step back and examine the broader system, we can see that this is the logical result of where we started. If the Church is primarily understood as a place and event, then a marker of success will be the number of people attending that event. If attendance becomes the metric, then it makes sense to recruit and train people to enhance that event. We need to assess ministry health through these lenses, so we hire pastors who produce these results, reinforcing the very system we never intended to build.

This is why, if we are serious about releasing pastors into healthier, more sustainable ministry, we must also release the Church. If the wider system does not change its default setting and feedback loops, any internal change for the pastor will eventually revert to the status quo. Such is the power of homeostatic forces; those subtle yet persistent dynamics that pull us back to what is familiar, even if it is unhealthy.

It is not that there is anything wrong with having Sunday gatherings or desiring to see more gathered to worship. The issue is the emphasis we give it and what we prioritise. One pastor gave an insightful challenge at a gathering of pastors, saying, "Tell me how your church is growing without referring to numbers." We need more questions like this. I would add, "Tell me how your church is growing in ways that fulfil the purposes and priorities of Jesus and His Kingdom, without referring to numbers." When we shift the conversation this way, it brings us back to what truly matters: Kingdom outcomes.

When a church is growing because people are genuinely growing as disciples of Jesus, then there will be depth and healthy growth. However, when the focus is simply on growing the Sunday gathering and the structures that support this, then discipleship can be reduced to attending, complying, and contributing. In other words, when quantitative growth flows from qualitative growth, you have healthy growth. The irony is that this is what most pastors would say they want. Yet, the system around them, the unseen forces at work, often drive them in the opposite direction.

Just as pastors can experience misdirected calling, so too can churches. We may be doing many good and faithful things, yet when our emphasis and alignment are out of order, our focus drifts. We end up confusing organisational outcomes with Kingdom outcomes. When the two are synonymous in our minds, it becomes impossible to recognise that anything is wrong or needs to change. The focus of our churches changes, measuring success by the numbers: attendance, budgets, giving levels, staffing, volunteer numbers, and rosters of care. There is nothing wrong with these things; they can be useful indicators, but they are not the whole picture. What do these numbers mean in terms of people coming to faith, growing closer to Jesus, finding healing, or being equipped to be good news in their neighbourhoods, workplaces, and communities?

We need to start by reflecting on what Jesus would consider success to look like for His Church. After all, it is *His* Church. We are simply seeking to fulfil His purposes as an expression of our love for Him. Once this is clear, we are to shape ourselves to fulfil His purposes and objectives. This is what Kingdom outcomes truly are: set by the King, reflecting His rule and reign.

If we examined the hearts of most pastors and Christians, we would find this is exactly what they long for as well. The issue is not desire; it is drift. We assume that what we are building aligns with what Jesus wants, without stopping to check. It might be, but this is too important to leave to assumption. Pastors and churches need to discern together if they are labouring in the right jungle and fulfilling the outcomes the King has called them to.

17

CLARIFYING KINGDOM OUTCOMES

When Jesus had risen from the dead and met His disciples for the last time, He did not hand them a blueprint for how to do Church. He gave them a commission, the Great Commission to "Go . . . and make disciples." It was a commission He had spent the last three years modelling for them.

Jesus does not invite us into a programme or a weekly event but to join Him in God's great mission. To share the good news of the Kingdom of God and to call people into a life-changing relationship with Him, and to be His disciples. We are to extend to others what we ourselves have received: Jesus' invitation to come to Him, take His yoke upon ourselves, and learn His way of life. The tragedy is that, somewhere along the way, we started to treat our frameworks, structures and programmes as if they were Kingdom outcomes themselves, forgetting that they are only tools to help us build what Jesus truly desires. We measure the size of the gathering and assume it tells us the extent of Kingdom impact. We become fixated on the drill bit, forgetting to ask whether we are making the hole the Master Carpenter desires. The result is that we drift from what Jesus originally called us to do.

I remember many years ago a friend said to me, "Sometimes I'm not sure what the Good News really is. If we're honest about what the Christian life is like for most of us, we should probably be upfront and tell people: 'Come to Jesus! Then you too can spend your life in endless church meetings and events.'"

Paul tells us that "the kingdom of God is not a matter of eating and drinking" (Romans 14:17), and equally it is not a matter of meetings, programmes, and due process, although God can work through all of these. He goes on to say that the Kingdom of God is in fact a matter "of righteousness, peace, and joy in the Holy Spirit"—something very different and so much deeper. More pointedly, his words in 1 Corinthians 4 may sit very uncomfortably with many of us, our churches, and our denominations: "For the kingdom of God is not a matter of *talk* but of power" (1 Corinthians 4:20, italics mine). Ouch!

REALIGNING THE CHURCH AND MOBILISING THE PEOPLE

If we are to be the people through whom God's Kingdom breaks in, we need to listen afresh to the voice of the King. Once we discern what He desires, we need to take the courageous steps to realign all that we do in light of that vision. It is not only as individuals that we are called to take his yoke upon us and learn to walk in step with him; it is also something we need to do together as churches.

Every part of our life together, including our teaching, our serving, and our leading, needs to be aligned so that we become the very thing Jesus had in mind all along. This is not simply about tweaking programmes or improving efficiency. It is about rediscovering our purpose and rediscovering our place in God's great redemptive story, then letting that shape the outcomes we pursue and the churches we become.

If we desire to see more of Jesus' Kingdom expressed in and through our lives and churches, making a greater impact in our communities, how do we do that? If we have arrived at a place where we recognise the power of the wider system at work diverting us to shallower versions of the outcomes Jesus desires, how do we resist the pull and take the next step?

Before I share with you the process through which I lead churches, I want to highlight a couple of common objections to be aware of and potentially address. They both revolve around one clear idea: It is just easier not to.

TWO COMMON OBJECTIONS

I was once speaking to one church about the steps that needed to be taken in order to listen afresh to the voice of Jesus and recalibrate the church around His Kingdom outcomes. As I was sharing, Ruth, an elder in the church, let out an audible sigh. "Do we really need to do all of this?" she asked. "Can't we just love and follow Jesus?" It was a fair question, and a revealing one. The reason we need to be so intentional is that we have already been shaped by the wider system in subtle and powerful ways. Without realising it, the system has kept us locked in a default mode of Church that is limiting and restraining, rather than releasing the body of Christ into what it has been called to do and be.

This is why intentionality matters. And it will require effort. To change the power of a system, we must consistently and persistently follow a new pattern until it becomes the new normal. In Matthew 28, Jesus gave us the direction that we are to "go and make disciples of all nations . . . teaching them to obey everything I have commanded you." If we are going to teach others to obey Jesus' commands, we first need to examine ourselves. We reproduce what we are. We need to assess what we are reproducing and realign ourselves where needed, so we do not unintentionally perpetuate a model of church that Jesus never wanted.

Switching metaphors, I am reminded of the old illustration of a pilot who crashed in the desert and had to walk to a city he saw from above. He knew the direction, but his compass was playing up. If he started walking but was one degree off, he could end up missing the city by hundreds of miles. The error may seem tiny at first, but over the course of many miles, that one-degree drift is compounded, until instead of arriving at the city, he finds himself wandering in a barren desert. The same is true in ministry, especially when we are leading others. Ruth's question, "Can't we just love and follow Jesus?" is a bit like saying to the stranded pilot, "Can't you just start walking?" You can—but if you are even one degree off, you will end up miles from your intended destination. In the desert, that is the difference between life and death. In ministry, it can be the difference between faithfully fulfilling Jesus' commission and wandering far from it.

A second common objection people raise is that quantitative markers are easier to measure, whereas qualitative ones are harder to track. That is true; however, when we explore what the qualitative outcomes would look like in practice, we discover they can be translated into concrete indicators, measurable markers, and actionable steps. This is where we learn to quantify the qualitative. The numbers then serve the substance, without replacing or disguising it.

MEASURING WHAT REALLY MATTERS

When the conversation shifts toward qualitative measures, the objection commonly arises: "Measuring the numbers (quantity) is easy. Measuring the mission (quality) is hard." There is some truth in that statement, but it is also an issue of mindset. In reality, we do qualitative measurement all the time.

Take the example of a baby. When a child is born, we measure its weight, length, and head circumference. These numbers allow us to monitor the baby's growth and general health. But when that same child graduates high school, no one says, "Sam Wilson, come on down! Sam, everyone, is six feet two and ninety-five kilograms. Let's give him a round of applause. Your parents must be so proud." Those figures tell us nothing about his academic or personal development. Sam's future will be shaped by other measures, both quantitative and qualitative.

As churches, we measure the qualitative all the time, often without realising it. Even churches that focus exclusively on Sunday attendance will critique the service with questions like:

"Were the welcomers warm and engaging?"
"Was the worship seamless?"

"Was the preaching inspiring with a call to action?"

"Did people respond?"

"Did people remain after the service and connect?"

These questions, though somewhat subjective, are an honest attempt to measure the quality aspects of church life. The problem is not that we cannot measure the qualitative. The problem is that we get stuck in a system that keeps us from intentionally measuring our mission. The real challenge is courage; courage to name the things that truly matter, and courage to measure them, even when they cannot be counted as easily or celebrated as publicly.

When we see clearly and measure wisely, our attention shifts from the numbers to the substance, and we move from good intentions to Kingdom outcomes. With our compass set to true north, we can take the practical steps that will align us with what Jesus desires for His Church.

HEALTHY REALIGNMENT

When a church is ready to take steps toward healthy realignment, two essential questions naturally arise:

1. What are the Kingdom outcomes Jesus desires for our church?
2. How do we align ourselves around those outcomes and mobilise our people to fulfil them?

Over years of walking alongside pastors and churches, I have developed a flexible yet intentional pathway for realignment. It follows a rhythm of discernment and action—not a one-size-fits-all formula, but a set of guiding steps any church can adapt to its own context.

This pathway begins by clarifying the Kingdom outcomes Jesus wants for your church and then moves toward building strategy and embedding change through three key movements:

1. **VIP:** Vision, Indicators, Practices
2. **RPMs:** Reality, Points of Leverage, Measurements & Steps
3. **FIT:** Fulfilling It Together

The first movement focuses on envisioning the future: What would your church look like if it fully embodied those Kingdom outcomes? This is about clarifying the destination.

The second movement focuses on strategy: How to build momentum and sustain the changes that will take you there. This is about constructing the vehicle that will carry you forward. The third movement is about mobilisation: How to help every person find their God-given fit so they can play their part in fulfilling the vision.

Together, these movements create space for prayer, reflection, discernment, creativity, and decisive action, leading to genuine transformation.

FOUNDATION: KINGDOM OUTCOMES

The first step is to clarify the 'hole', in other words, to discover or rediscover the Kingdom outcomes Jesus wants for your church.

This is drawn out by asking two questions:

- If Jesus sat with your congregation, what would He say success looks like for this church?
- What are the outcomes Jesus would love to see occurring in your church and flowing out into the community?

This begins as a simple brainstorming exercise, helping people return to what they already know in their hearts and minds to be true. The answers are rarely surprising. They often include things like: people coming to faith, deepening their relationship with Jesus, sharing their faith in their everyday lives, passionately worshipping God, loving each other deeply, forgiving each other and restoring relationships, caring for the least and marginalised, moving in the power of the Holy Spirit, and seeing others healed and empowered. The list goes on, but notice how all of these are *qualitative Kingdom-focused* outcomes—markers that reflect the heart of Jesus, not just the metrics of activity.

I encourage churches to refine their list into three to six key outcomes to make it more defined, focused, and workable. In my experience, most of these naturally centre around the three loves Jesus commanded, loving the Lord your God, loving one another, and loving your neighbour as yourself, as well as His Great Commission to go and make disciples.

It is not surprising that many churches end up with outcomes that sound similar or fit within the same broad categories. The goal here is not to create something unique, nor to impose a pre-packaged set of answers on a church. What is important is that each church prayerfully discerns and articulates these outcomes for itself. When a church personally discovers and owns its Kingdom outcomes, something shifts. This process helps dismantle the default mindset and rewires the heart and focus of the congregation, so that these outcomes become more than words on paper; they become a shared conviction, shaping every part of church life.

I summarise these outcomes with the phrase M.A.D. Communities. These are churches committed to **Making A Difference** by living as communities of faith who are focused on:

- **Mission:** reaching out to others with the love and message of Jesus.
- **Adoration:** worshipping God through all of life.
- **Discipleship:** growing in Christlikeness by practising His ways and obeying His teachings.
- **Community:** loving and caring for one another deeply.

These four expressions give shape to what it means to be a church aligned with the Kingdom outcomes Jesus desires. They keep the focus on what matters most, ensuring that mission, worship, discipleship, and community remain at the heart of all we do.

FIRST MOVEMENT: VIP

Vision

Once there is clarity around Kingdom outcomes, the next step is to paint a picture of what those outcomes might look like when they are fully expressed in your church. This is a vivid snapshot of a preferred future—a moment in time when Kingdom outcomes are visible in everyday life together. This is the BHAG (Big, Hairy, Audacious Goal) vision or Kingdom vision.

I ask churches to consider:

> "If we jumped forward in time, what would be happening in your congregation that would demonstrate that these outcomes are alive and thriving?"

The core question I use here is the same one I use when helping individuals clarify their calling:

> "If Jesus came to this church and said, 'I know you love Me. Tell Me, what do you want to do for Me and My Kingdom? You name it, I'll back you?' What would you want to achieve?"

What emerges at this point is often a rich and detailed description rather than a short, polished vision statement. That is perfectly fine. It will usually take some time to distil the broader statement down to a clear, captivating statement, but it is important to do this so that it can be owned, actionable, and inform your decision-making. Hidden within the broader description is usually an inspirational picture of what your church could become, and the specific indicators that would confirm you are achieving your goals.

Indicators

Indicators are tangible signs that your church is fulfilling its Kingdom outcomes and moving towards its Kingdom vision. They act like a compass, helping you stay oriented to where God is leading. Some indicators reveal what must be in place to produce your specific Kingdom outcomes (generators). Others give a 'fly on the wall' picture of patterns in your congregation that show the vision is becoming reality (descriptors).

For each key outcome, identify the indicators that would show meaningful progress. These should be recognisable when they occur, even if they are not always easily measurable. They should also highlight the essential elements that generate your vision and make it a lived experience in your church.

Here are some questions to guide you:

- What would your church need to have in place to enable your Kingdom outcomes to be achieved?
- Describe what would be happening in the life of the church that would represent success in these Kingdom outcomes.
- What specific things would you want to see to confirm the church is moving in the right direction and your vision is becoming a reality?

For example, we might see:

- Individuals naturally modelling how to share their faith in ways that suit their personality and context, inspiring others to do likewise.
- People in each Life Group regularly testifying about how they shared their faith in workplaces, neighbourhoods, or community settings.
- People intentionally journeying together in faith.
- A growing hunger for God's presence, expressed through regular prayer and worship gatherings outside of Sunday services.
- Leaders and members demonstrating skill in discipling others, using approaches that align with the church's vision of Christlike maturity.
- Trusted, respectful relationships with people without homes in the community, opening the door to practical care and meaningful engagement.
- Discipleship-based relationships becoming the norm rather than the exception.

Practices

We now turn to anchoring the different elements of your preferred future—this Kingdom-centric, Jesus-honouring vision to which you believe God is calling your church—to practices and principles that would need to be embodied corporately by the church, collectively in small groups, and personally by every individual. These principles and practices become the DNA of the church's culture, expressed, reinforced, and replicated in every aspect of church life. These practices form the spiritual DNA for healthy growth and provide the impetus to become what Jesus desires. They are not simply tasks to complete, but rhythms and ways of living that keep the church aligned to its Kingdom vision and outcomes. Imagine, for example, having *Mission*, *Adoration*, *Discipleship* and *Community*, expressed as specific practices in your church:

- **Corporately:** through official ministries, gatherings, and church-wide initiatives.
- **Collectively:** within groups and teams, such as Life Groups, serving teams, or ministry clusters.
- **Personally:** in the daily practices, disciplines and faith expressions of individuals.

Here are some questions to guide you:

- If every person in your congregation embodied the same few essential practices, what three or four would most powerfully enable your Kingdom vision to become a reality?
- Which practices, when consistently lived out, would naturally generate the indicators you have identified?

In many cases, these will consist of Kingdom outcomes reframed as embodied, repeatable actions and principles in the life of the church.

SECOND MOVEMENT: RPMS

Having discerned what the church is called to do and the direction in which it is heading, we now need to connect its current reality with that future vision. This is where strategy meets discernment—linking today's starting point to tomorrow's destination.

Reality

This step involves conducting a strategic review of the church's present reality. It is not merely about identifying problems, but about gaining a clear-eyed view of the full landscape—celebrating strengths, recognising resources, and naming the challenges. Often, a strategic SWOT review can serve as a simple yet powerful tool to help facilitate this:

- **Strengths:** What are we doing well? What resources do we have? Where are we seeing fruit?
- **Weaknesses:** Where are the gaps, unhealthy patterns, or areas of decline?
- **Opportunities:** What exists around us that we have not yet taken full advantage of? What open doors or emerging possibilities are before us?
- **Threats:** What external or internal factors could hinder our progress?

For example, a church may discover that it has strong relational warmth and community trust (strength), but weak systems for discipling new believers (weakness). It may have a core of capable leaders willing to be trained (opportunity), but face a high turnover in volunteer teams due to burnout (threat).

Points of Leverage

Points of leverage emerge from the 'reality' stage and are the pivotal areas where focused attention, resources and prayer will produce the greatest change and generate significant momentum toward the vision.

To identify these points of leverage, churches need to answer the following questions:

- Which three or four areas would create the greatest improvement for your church? (For example: discipleship pathway, community engagement, leadership development, or prayer culture.)

- Under each point of leverage, pinpoint a strategic objective that would produce the greatest shift.

Let's look at some examples.

Point of Leverage: DISCIPLESHIP ENGAGEMENT
Objective: Develop and implement a clear discipleship pathway that trains and releases leaders to disciple others, aiming to normalise one-to-one and small group discipleship across the church.

Point of Leverage: COMMUNITY IMPACT
Objective: Mobilise members into community-service teams focused on a few high-impact initiatives (e.g., school partnerships, food security, mentoring youth), building on existing relationships.

Point of Leverage: LEADERSHIP DEVELOPMENT
Objective: Create a leadership pipeline that equips and empowers emerging leaders to take responsibility for ministry areas, reducing burnout in current leaders and expanding ministry capacity.

Point of Leverage: PRAYER CULTURE
Objective: Cultivate a culture of prayer by embedding rhythms of personal, small-group, and church-wide prayer, including dedicated seasons of prayer that fuel mission and discipleship.

Quantifying the Qualitative

Objectives are where we qualify the qualitative areas we are prioritising. From here, we can begin to quantify the qualitative. The Measurements form what I call **'Outcome KPIs'.** These are measurable outcomes that we do not directly control but towards which we intentionally work. We cannot control these outcomes directly, but we can observe them, celebrate them, and discern when we need to realign our steps to better achieve them.

The Steps we take to achieve these Measurements—and ultimately fulfil our Objectives—are what I refer to as **'Action KPIs'.** These are specific, concrete, and controllable behaviours that are most likely to produce the desired outcomes. In our personal lives, examples might include daily Scripture reading, engaging in regular prayer, participating in a Life Group, or exercising three times a week. These are actions fully within our control, and they help us achieve the higher objectives we have set.

Some people hear terms like KPIs and worry that we are importing corporate language into the church. But a KPI simply means a *Key Performance Indicator,* which helps us know whether we are heading in the right direction. I am not using this language as a business metric but as a tool to guide discipleship and alignment. If it helps, you can think of these as Kingdom Progress Indicators.

Measurements and Steps

Once the points of leverage are clear, the next step is to translate them into measurable outcomes and the actionable steps needed to achieve them. This involves making qualitative outcomes measurable by identifying tangible behaviours, evidence, or patterns that can be tracked over time.

All measurements should be practical, realistic, and directly connected to your specific Kingdom outcomes. They are most effective when they are SMART:

- **Specific:** Clearly defined and focused
- **Measurable:** Able to be tracked or quantified
- **Achievable:** Realistic within your context
- **Relevant:** Aligned to your Kingdom vision
- **Time-bound:** Set within a clear timeframe

Steps are the practical actions that will ensure measurements are achieved. They bridge the gap between aspiration and implementation, keeping the church moving towards its preferred future.

THIRD MOVEMENT: MOBILISATION

Once the first two movements have been clarified, the next focus is mobilising people to bring them to life and find their FIT (Fulfilling It Together). Mobilisation is the bridge between knowing what needs to be done and releasing the people who will make it happen. The steps identified for each point of leverage reveal clear priorities for the church. These priorities guide the types of leadership and implementation roles that will be required.

I remember sitting with Alistair, an elder in a church, who said, "We have got this vision thing nailed. Pretty much everyone in our church would be able to quote our vision." It was clear that a significant amount of effort had gone into clarifying and communicating those phrases.

"That is so good," I replied, and then asked, "If I were to ask anyone in your church, 'How are you fulfilling that vision? What part are you playing?' what would they say?" He paused, locked eyes with me, and said slowly and thoughtfully, "Ah, yes. That is a good point. I guess there is a bit more work to do."

If your congregation is not personally connected to the vision, you are leaving most of your team on the bench. This is key. Think of an eight-person rowing team.

- If no one rows, the boat drifts. This is where many churches are. They are stuck. Routines happen, but there is no real movement.
- If only one or two row, progress is painfully slow—and this is where many pastors live, carrying the load alone.
- If everyone rows, but in their own way and direction, the result is chaos. There is a lot of activity, but very little progress.
- But if everyone rows in sync, moving together in the same direction, momentum builds, energy multiplies, and the distance travelled far exceeds the effort.

Leaders often know how true this is for a team, so imagine how vital it is for a whole church.

Vision is not fulfilled when everyone can repeat the statement; it is fulfilled when everyone can connect their personal calling with the church's calling and carry the vision forward together.

The best way to mobilise a church is by empowering people in their own calling. Ephesians 4:12 in The Passion Translation captures this beautifully:

> "And their [the fivefold] calling is to nurture and prepare all
> the holy believers to do their own works of ministry, and as
> they do this they will enlarge and build up the body of Christ."

When you equip people in their own calling, you enlarge the church. Think about it: a person's passion is connected to their calling—there is already energy and motivation linked to it. So when you help people clarify their calling, you tap into that God-given energy. Then, by showing them how their calling fits with the church's vision, you connect that passion to the larger mission of the church. This releases incredible power and potential.

Now imagine this is happening not just with a few in your church but with everyone. What difference do you think that would make? What greater Kingdom impact could you have in your community?

Without connecting the congregation to the vision, the impact of a church will always be limited. It is the equivalent of two rowers in an eight-person boat doing all the work. You may be moving, but it is only a fraction of what could be achieved.

When vision stays at the organisational level, a tragic side effect can occur: pastors take a utilitarian approach to their people. They begin to value people primarily for their usefulness in building the church's capacity, rather than for who they are or what God has called them to. The focus becomes positioning people to serve, rather than raising them up and releasing them into their own Kingdom calling.

This approach may strengthen organisational capacity, but it limits exponential impact. You might 'grow' the church, but you are not fully advancing the Kingdom. As strange as it sounds, it needs to be clarified: people's personal callings are not in competition with the church's vision. On the contrary, when individual calling and corporate vision are connected, Kingdom DNA is activated, and the whole body grows stronger. This is what mobilising your people does.

It is one thing to have a vision; it is another to have a church mobilised around that vision. Mobilisation is about releasing the congregation into their callings and helping them find where they fit best in fulfilling the vision. It involves harnessing the gifts, callings and strengths of the congregation so that each person can find their best-fit place of service. Helping individuals to clarify their macro call and ministry strengths enables purposeful deployment, where leaders and members are released into roles that align with both the church's Kingdom outcomes and their God-given design. This type of alignment creates momentum, with everyone contributing their "works of service, so that the body of Christ may be built up" (Ephesians 4:12).

A key part of this alignment starts with the pastor. Having refined the pastor's role so that it reflects their God-given macro call, we now link their leadership to the church's Kingdom-based vision. When the pastor's gifts and calling are in step with the vision, it sets the tone for the whole church to function in alignment.

Mobilisation gains lasting traction when the church connects its vision with people's personal calling, and together you are embodying common principles and practices in the spiritual rhythms as a church corporately, in small groups collectively, and with every individual personally.

Denominational Reinforcement

For mobilisation to be sustained, the new DNA must be reinforced not only within the local church but also by its wider networks and denominational structures. The markers of success for any church serve as a key area of influence and leverage. Securing broad support for this new focus is essential to bring about genuine and lasting change.

When local church mobilisation is matched by denominational reinforcement, the culture shift towards Kingdom outcomes is strengthened at every level. This alignment ensures that what is planted in the local congregation is nurtured and sustained by the wider body, creating the conditions for lasting transformation.

A System-Wide Effort

Denominations and churches working together to align with and achieve Kingdom-focused outcomes would be phenomenal. It takes a concerted effort by all parties to bring genuine change to the default patterns and foci of churches. Yet when these Kingdom outcomes are aligned successfully, they become a significant point of leverage within a church, shaping the focus of the pastor and the nature of disciples produced by the church.

This is such a vital area and represents the second of three strategic areas required to create sustained change towards a healthier model of ministry for pastors and churches. To recap, the three strategic areas of influence within the wider church system, which together produce a reinforced system of healthy ministry, are:

1. **Pastors:** Aligned with a healthy model of ministry, grounded in their identity in Jesus, fulfilling their macro calling, and differentiated from their role.
2. **Markers of success:** Kingdom-focused outcomes that outline what a church believes Jesus specifically wants them to achieve, with people, systems, and leadership mobilised to accomplish them.
3. **Stakeholders' support:** All parties working together to support a healthy model of ministry, including pastors, churches, denominations, and ministerial training institutions.

Having addressed the first two areas, the next focus is the strategic contribution of system-wide stakeholder support. If we are to create real and lasting change, we need everyone to be aligned and moving in the same direction. The challenge is that change in one part of a system alone is rarely sustainable; systems naturally resist disruption. In this context, the system will tend to exert pressure on pastors and churches to revert to familiar patterns. This is why collective, consistent and persistent action from all key stakeholders is essential until the new way of operating becomes the new normal.

18

THE IMPORTANCE OF AARON AND HUR

The previous chapter highlighted the vital role denominational alignment plays in reinforcing Kingdom-focused markers of success. A church may begin to shift towards Kingdom-focused outcomes, but without consistent support from those around it, the gravitational pull of old patterns will soon reassert itself.

The pastor cannot do it alone. He or she needs the support of the wider church ecosystem. They need the help of Aaron and Hur. In Exodus 17:8–13, when Israel faced the Amalekites, Moses went to the top of the hill with Aaron and Hur. As long as Moses held up the staff of God, Israel prevailed; but whenever his hands grew tired and lowered, the battle turned against them. Seeing his fatigue, Aaron and Hur placed a stone under Moses so he could sit, and then stood on either side, holding up his hands and keeping them steady until sunset. Because of their support, Joshua and the Israelite army overcame the Amalekites.

Pastors need the same empowering support. They need denominational backing, the formation and reinforcement provided by ministerial training institutions, and the strength of all stakeholders helping them remain steady in the healthy alignment of identity, calling, and role. True change will not be achieved or sustained unless it is reinforced by the wider system.

Many denominational leaders genuinely desire to focus on Kingdom outcomes but are caught between their convictions and the organisational necessities that drive reporting and accountability. Denominational backing would remove the pressure that many pastors and churches feel to measure success primarily in quantitative terms. I have spoken with pastors from various denominations, and many describe the same tension—everyone wants the focus to shift toward Kingdom outcomes, yet the system keeps pulling them back to the power of the numbers:

> "It's not the denomination that is problematic; it's the system. Our leaders assure us it is not all about 'bums on seats' and that they want us to focus on Kingdom impact. Which sounds great, but then they ask us for our statistics—average attendance, revenue, and other numbers. And when the report comes out, we will all pore through it and assess how each of us is doing in comparison with all the other pastors."

Strong denominational support would not only relieve this pressure but also create a reinforcing feedback loop that normalises and sustains this new way of operating. For this to happen, denominations themselves need to undertake a similarly courageous process of clarifying their overarching purpose (the hole), both collectively and within their individual churches, and to not simply be captivated by the way we've always done things (drill bit). If it is not already happening, it would be immensely beneficial for denominational leaders to engage in prayerful reflection by considering such questions as:

- If Jesus asked us [denominational leaders], "What do you want to do for My Kingdom?" what would our answer be?
- What would Jesus say success looks like for our churches and people?
- If the Kingdom were being expressed more fully in our churches, what would this look like, and how would it differ from what we are seeing now?

- What can we do to facilitate or support this Kingdom vision?
- What would we need to prioritise?
- What would need to stop or be given less attention?
- What would we need to give increased attention to?
- What different leadership qualities would be needed at a denominational level? What different leadership qualities would be needed at a church level?

This process brings denominations and churches into a shared alignment around Kingdom outcomes. It is a significant and strategic step. From here, support can flow more naturally into pastoring their pastors so they remain grounded in their identity, confident in their calling, and rightly aligned in their role. Denominations have a unique opportunity to strengthen their leaders in these three key areas, creating environments where both the church and its pastors can flourish together.

1. Identity

One of the most significant ways denominations can support pastors is by helping them maintain a healthy sense of identity in Christ. When denominational leaders model and embed practices that differentiate identity from role, it strengthens every pastor. This work is essential for healthy ministry.

Denominations can weave this into the fabric of their leadership culture. Training pathways, retreats, formation events, and leadership review will all provide opportunities to help pastors remain grounded in the truth that their worth is not determined by outcomes, performance, or public expectation but by their relationship with Jesus.

Many movements already support this by requiring regular professional supervision and spiritual direction. Where this is not yet the case, adopting such practices will make an enormous difference to the wellbeing and resilience of pastors. Any denominational review of a pastor's ministry should include a supportive reflection on how they are maintaining their identity in Christ and how they are living out their macro calling within their current role.

This creates space for encouragement and healthy differentiation, helping pastors remain anchored in what is true even when ministry is difficult.

2. Calling

Denominations also play a crucial role in helping pastors discern and flourish in their calling. The Church is enriched by a wide variety of gifts and vocational expressions, yet our systems have often centred almost exclusively on the traditional pastoral role. This unintentionally narrows the pathway for many gifted leaders and can force people into roles that do not match the shape of their calling.

A broader vision of calling creates room for leaders to flourish. Denominations that intentionally identify, affirm, and develop diverse calling expressions will release greater Kingdom impact. This may mean widening assessment processes, offering development pathways for different ministry expressions, and prioritising the equipping of leaders according to their calling rather than simply filling vacancies.

When denominations honour the breadth of calling within the body of Christ, more leaders thrive, more ministries grow, and more communities experience the gospel through the full spectrum of God's gifts.

3. Role

Healthy denominational structures not only affirm identity and calling; they also provide clarity and sustainability around ministry roles. When leadership pathways are aligned with Kingdom outcomes rather than institutional maintenance, they become life-giving.

Denominations can strengthen their support of pastors by ensuring their outcomes, structures, and role expectations genuinely reflect the heart of Jesus for His Church. This may include revisiting denominational outcome statements, exploring new and diverse ministry roles (including non-traditional pathways), and ensuring that these roles are financially and structurally sustainable for the long term.

This process of exploring diverse ministry roles creates a system that supports ministry leaders rather than squeezes them, and a pathway that enables Kingdom effectiveness rather than institutional drift.

MINISTERIAL TRAINING INSTITUTIONS (MTIs): PREPARING THE NEXT GENERATION OF LEADERS

Lasting change requires more than denominational support alone. Ministerial Training Institutions (MTIs) also play a crucial role. For Kingdom alignment to take root across the wider system, it must be cultivated not only in churches and denominations but also at the formative training stage where identity, calling, and role are shaped, deepened, and released.

MTIs occupy a unique and influential place in the wider system. They help shape not only the theological understanding of future leaders but also their formation, their expectations, and the inner frameworks that will guide them throughout their ministry life. When MTIs reinforce healthy identity, broaden the understanding of calling, and prepare students for the realities of ministry roles, they help prevent many of the challenges that later emerge in pastors' lives.

1. Identity

One of the greatest contributions MTIs can make is to help future leaders establish a differentiated identity in Christ long before they enter pastoral roles. This formation cannot be merely theoretical. Students need pathways, practices, and experiences that help them internalise the truth that their identity is grounded in Christ rather than in ministry performance.

When an MTI creates space for students to explore and strengthen their identity—through spiritual formation, reflective practice, community processes, and guided discernment—it cultivates graduates who enter ministry with greater authenticity, resilience, and emotional stability. This reduces anxiety around achievement, frees students to serve without self-protection, and lays a foundation for lifelong wellbeing.

2. Calling

MTIs also play an essential role in helping students discern their unique calling. Not every gifted leader is called to serve as a local church pastor, yet this remains the default pathway for many training systems. A broader and more intentional process of vocational discernment enables students to identify their passions, gifts, and macro calling before they step into ministry positions.

When MTIs equip students with tools to understand the diversity of ministry callings—and provide formation pathways that honour these differences—they empower more leaders to flourish. This includes helping students navigate the challenges faced by those whose callings fall outside the traditional congregational model, offering both theological vision and practical support.

3. Role

Alongside identity and calling, MTIs help prepare students for the realities of ministry roles. This involves teaching flexibility, self-awareness, and role-fit discernment so that future leaders understand how to shape roles in ways that align with their gifts and contribute to Kingdom impact. Training in job-crafting skills would be deeply valuable.

By exposing students to the breadth of ministry expressions—traditional and non-traditional—MTIs can broaden imagination and increase adaptability. This equips graduates not only to fill existing roles but also to craft new ones that serve emerging Kingdom needs.

ALIGNED IN VISION

When each stakeholder practically contributes to a shared vision of alignment around Kingdom outcomes, a new way of operating becomes not just possible, but normal. The aim is that as each stakeholder plays their part, we will create a new reinforcing system that sustains this healthier model of ministry. This new system will be marked by:

- Thriving leaders: pastors ministering from a differentiated sense of identity, calling, and role.
- Kingdom-focused churches: churches pursuing and celebrating qualitative, Kingdom-focused outcomes.
- Mobilised disciples: people growing as healthy disciples, mobilised in mission and ministry.
- Releasing denominations: denominations prioritising the support of thriving leaders and Kingdom-focused churches.
- Equipping MTIs: ministerial training institutions preparing pastors to be thriving leaders who lead Kingdom-focused churches.

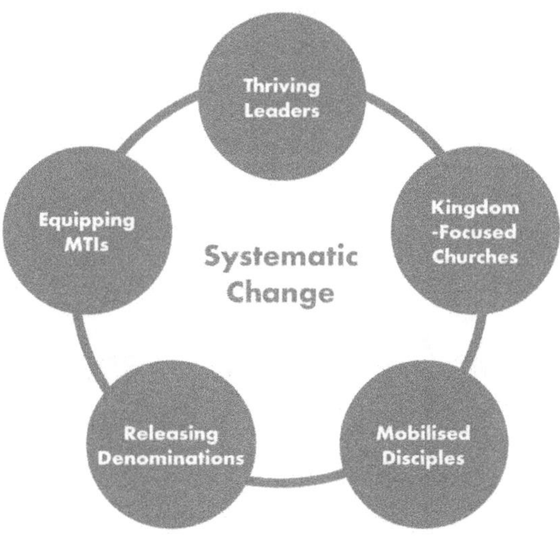

Diagram 14. Systemic change towards a viable and compelling alternative

Each marker carries a unique sphere of influence, and when aligned, they can collectively enable a healthy ordering of *identity, calling, and role* that allows pastors to thrive and churches to flourish.

Ultimately, however, pastors will only truly thrive when they have their own Aaron and Hur; when the wider church stands beside them to create a new, healthier model of ministry. They flourish when supported by denominations that champion Kingdom outcomes, by churches that strengthen their identity and release their calling, and by training institutions that form them well for the road ahead, equipping them with practices for remaining and pathways for diverse calling expressions. When these stakeholders stand together with the pastor, the Church is far better positioned to face the battles before it and to move forward with greater momentum. Success will not come through isolation but through the shared strength of all. This is what healthy ministry looks like. This is the ecosystem we must build. This is the life-giving environment we need for pastors to thrive and churches to flourish.

TO THE PASTOR

A VISION FOR THE FUTURE: GOD'S KINGDOM COME

We began this journey with the good news that change was possible. My hope for every pastor reading this book is that they would not simply survive ministry, but truly thrive. I want you to know that it *is* possible to be healthy, whole, equipped, released and fruitful in the role God has given you—not in some idealised dream world, but in the reality of your current calling.

Our journey has explored the pressures and patterns that make ministry so demanding. We have seen how easily identity becomes entangled with role, how success is too often measured by numbers alone, and how homeostatic forces within church systems resist healthy change. These dynamics are negatively impacting the wellbeing and effectiveness of leaders and, ultimately, the fruitfulness of churches. These challenges cannot be ignored. They require significant, considered and urgent attention to resolve. If we do nothing, pastors will remain limited, stuck, and at risk of burnout. We will continue to see disengaged, consumerist congregations, fewer people stepping forward into leadership, and the mission of the Church being blunted.

We stand at a crossroads. One road is the familiar path of doing what we have always done, perhaps making small adjustments around the edges but leaving the core assumptions and structures untouched. The other is a Kingdom road that calls for deep systemic change in how we understand, train, support, and release our leaders. This road requires humility to admit that some of our ways have been unhealthy, courage to make significant changes, and faith to believe that God can lead us into something far better.

This healthier way requires realignment—the recovery of a biblical, life-giving order for ministry: our identity firmly grounded in Christ, our macro calling flowing from that identity, and our specific role serving our calling, not defining it. This is more than a helpful concept; it is a lifeline. The fusion of identity, calling and role has been normalised to such an extent that its negative effects are often spiritualised, leaving pastors increasingly vulnerable to burnout and at greater risk of developing mental health challenges.

When pastors can differentiate their sense of self in Christ from the role they perform, they gain resilience against the wear and tear of ministry and greater objectivity to serve Jesus first rather than the role. When their role aligns with their God-given calling, they find joy and effectiveness in the work. When the markers of success are Kingdom-centred rather than driven by default numeric metrics, pastors are freed from the tyranny of performance and the fear of comparison, and churches rediscover their purpose in the mission of God.

The responsibility does not rest on pastors alone. Throughout this book, we have seen that lasting change will only come when all four key stakeholders—pastors, churches, denominations, and ministerial training institutions—play their part in creating a reinforcing system for healthy ministry:

- Pastors committed to their own growth and health, building rhythms that keep Christ at the centre, seeking supervision, and ensuring their role reflects their calling.
- Churches defining success in Kingdom terms, supporting their leaders' wellbeing, and helping every member discern and live out their calling.
- Denominations broadening their vision of ministry, releasing leaders into diverse callings, and embedding practices that safeguard identity and calling.
- Ministerial Training Institutions shaping leaders who are spiritually formed, calling-aware, and equipped for a variety of ministry contexts.

My dream is to see pastors and churches empowered to make a greater Kingdom impact in their neighbourhoods, transforming lives and communities. I want to see pastors leading without the crushing weight of unrealistic expectations, churches releasing and celebrating the gifts of all their people, denominations championing healthy leadership instead of merely filling positions, and training institutions sending out leaders who are both theologically deep and spiritually whole.

If we walk this path together, it is not only the wellbeing of pastors that will improve; we will see churches regaining their missional edge, communities touched by the love of Christ, and people turning to Jesus. This is not simply about building healthier leaders; it is about seeing more of God's Kingdom come on earth as it is in Heaven.

Our starting point and our end point is Jesus. All of this begins with unjamming the rudders of pastors' lives, helping them realign their identity, calling, and role in a healthy order. From there, churches, denominations and ministerial training institutions can each make their unique contribution to support the flourishing of the whole body of Christ.

My prayer is that we would choose the Kingdom road. May we collectively work and pray for a Church where leaders and people alike are living out their God-given calling with joy, empowerment, and freedom. May we faithfully and effectively work to see more of:

> *"Your kingdom come, your will be done, on earth as it is in heaven."*
>
> **Matthew 6:10**

And Lord, may it come quickly.

ABOUT THE AUTHOR

Richard Black has spent decades serving the Church. For him, it is a labour of love. He loves her leaders, her people, her mission, and, above all, her God. His life's work has been devoted to helping pastors and churches flourish in both wellbeing and effectiveness.

Richard served for years as a senior pastor, leading a church through revitalisation. It was a stretching and deeply rewarding season. Community engagement grew, people came to faith and were baptised, and the church expanded to the point of seeking a new venue. He expected to remain there for many more years.

Instead, he sensed God calling him into a different expression of ministry: to walk alongside church leaders and strengthen them for the long haul. Stepping into that unknown meant leaving secure employment with a young family and no guarantees, yet it marked the beginning of the work that now defines his vocation.

He completed a master's degree in counselling, researching *Emotional Health in the Role of a Church Leader*. Through this work, he identified five recurring dynamics that undermine many pastors: over identification with the role, misdirected calling, perfectionism, isolation, and misdirected spirituality. These themes have shaped his clinical work, supervision, coaching, and training with leaders across denominational contexts.

For more than fifteen years, Richard has supported pastors in their wellbeing, ministry alignment, and sustainable leadership. Further postgraduate research enabled him to develop a healthy model of ministry designed to strengthen both effectiveness and personal resilience in church leaders.

Richard founded Mind Health™, a counselling and supervision organisation serving the wider Church. He then handed it over to a trusted colleague in order to focus more specifically on supporting the needs of pastors and churches. He now works across the denominational spectrum, concentrating on leadership wellbeing, ministry practice, and the cultivation of healthy church systems that facilitate greater Kingdom impact.

He has shared this journey with Jennifer, his wife of more than thirty years. Together they have three adult children. Richard's enduring desire is to serve Christ faithfully and to see His Kingdom come through healthy leaders and mobilised churches.

ABOUT THRIVING CHURCHES HQ

Thriving Churches HQ exists to see every pastor thriving and every church flourishing. Visit the website for practical resources to support you and your church to thrive. Courses, coaching, leadership development, and pastoral strengthening tools are available online. Personal, tailored support is also available for leaders and churches wanting deeper strengthening of leadership and pastoral care systems.

Scan the QR code or visit the website to begin:

ThrivingChurchesHQ.com

YOUR NEXT STEPS IN

THE THRIVING PASTOR JOURNEY

I wrote this book because I want you to thrive in ministry—not merely survive it. Healthier identity, clearer calling, and better-aligned ministry are possible. I see this transformation in pastors' lives every week.

You have read the book. Now embed the insights into your life and ministry.

Join the Thriving Pastor Pathway

AWARENESS → FORMATION → GROWTH → ACCELERATION

AWARENESS - The Thriving Pastor book

Return to the key frameworks and apply them intentionally to your identity, calling, and role alignment.

FORMATION - The Thriving Pastor Programme

A guided formation journey that helps you embed these principles into daily leadership and ministry life through teaching, reflection exercises, and supported growth.

GROWTH - Leadership Support Sessions

Continue with supervision or leadership coaching to strengthen wellbeing, leadership effectiveness, and long-term resilience.

ACCELERATION - The Thriving Pastor Assessment

A structured ministry review across eight key dimensions of healthy pastoral leadership. The Thriving Pastor Assessment clarifies where to focus next to strengthen both wellbeing and ministry effectiveness.

Start here → thrivingchurcheshq.com

A FINAL WORD

You were never meant to lead with a jammed rudder.
You were never meant to lead on empty or carry the load alone.
Thriving in ministry is possible.
Every pastor thriving. Every church flourishing.
— Richard Black

ENDNOTES

Introduction:

1 Rae Jean Proeschold-Bell and Jason Byassee, *Faithful and Fractured: Responding to the Clergy Health Crisis* (Grand Rapids, MI: Baker Academic, 2018), 37.

2 Christopher R. Gambill, "Emotional Intelligence and Conflict Management Style among Christian Clergy" (PhD diss., Capella University, 2008), 99; Kelvin John Randall, "Emotional Intelligence: What Is It, and Do Anglican Clergy Have It?" *Mental Health, Religion & Culture* 17, no. 3 (2014): 8, 39–40.

3 David Kinnaman, "Signs of Decline and Hope Among Key Metrics of Faith," *Faith and Christianity in State of the Church,* 2020; Daniel Silliman, "Decline of Christianity Shows No Signs of Stopping," *Christianity Today,* 2022; Barna Group, *The State of Pastors: How Today's Church Leaders Are Pursuing Resilience and Stepping into a Hopeful Future,* vol. 2 (Barna Group, 2024), 68; personal communication with New Zealand denominational leaders.

4 Barna Group, *The State of Pastors: How Today's Church Leaders Are Pursuing Resilience and Stepping into a Hopeful Future,* vol. 2 (Barna Group, 2024), 68; personal communication with New Zealand denominational leaders.

5 Barna Group, 2:76.

6 Glenn Packiam, *The Resilient Pastor: Leading Your Church in a Rapidly Changing World,* Kindle edition (Baker Books, 2022), 23–25.

7 Margot Holaday et al., 'Secondary Stress, Burnout, and the Clergy', *American Journal of Pastoral Counseling* 4, no. 1 (2001): 53–72; Andrew J. Weaver et al., 'Mental Health Issues among Clergy and Other Religious Professionals: A Review of Research', Journal of Pastoral Care & Counseling 56, no. 4 (2002): 393–403; Katheryn Rhoads Meek et al., 'Maintaining Personal Resiliency: Lessons Learned from Evangelical Protestant Clergy', *Journal of Psychology and Theology* 31, no. 4 (2003): 339–47.

8 Proeschold-Bell and Byassee, *Faithful and Fractured,* 37; Barna Group, *State of Pastors,* 2:41; Randall, 'Emotional Intelligence', 39–40; Randy Cook, 'Theorizing Identity Harm as a Barrier to Clergy Well-Being' (2021), 7–8; Scott Dunbar et al., 'Calling, Caring, and Connecting: Burnout in Christian Ministry', *Mental Health, Religion & Culture* 23, no. 2 (2020): 173–74; Kathryn Kissell, 'Enhancing Ministry: Exploring the Impact of Bowen Family Systems Coaching on the Work-Related Psychological Health of Church of England Clergy', 2018, 10–11; Gambill, 'Emotional Intelligence', 99; David K Pooler, 'Pastors and Congregations at Risk: Insights from Role Identity Theory', *Pastoral Psychology* 60 (2011): 707–8; Ronald S Beebe, 'Predicting Burnout, Conflict Management Style, and Turnover among Clergy', *Journal of Career Assessment* 15, no. 2 (2007): 257–58; Andrew Irvine, 'Clergy Wellbeing: Seeking Wholeness with Integrity', *Center for Clergy Care and*

Congregational Health, University of Toronto, 2005, 17–18; Holaday et al., 'Secondary Stress, Burnout, and the Clergy'; Weaver et al., 'Mental Health Issues among Clergy and Other Religious Professionals: A Review of Research'; Meek et al., 'Maintaining Personal Resilience'; Mark R. McMinn et al., 'Care for Pastors: Learning from Clergy and Their Spouses', *Pastoral Psychology* 53 (2005): 563–81; Kelvin J. Randall, 'Examining the Relationship between Burnout and Age among Anglican Clergy in England and Wales', *Mental Health, Religion & Culture* 10, no. 1 (2007): 39–46; Maureen H. Miner, Martin Dowson, and Sam Sterland, 'Ministry Orientation and Ministry Outcomes: Evaluation of a New Multidimensional Model of Clergy Burnout and Job Satisfaction', *Journal of Occupational & Organizational Psychology* 83, no. 1 (March 2010): 167–88.

9 Beebe, 'Predicting Burnout', 257.

10 Proeschold-Bell and Byassee, *Faithful and Fractured,* 37.

11 Cook, 'Theorizing Identity Harm', 4.

12 John D. Mayer et al., 'Emotional Development and Emotional Intelligence: Implications for Educators', *What Is Emotional Intelligence,* 2007, 10.

13 Daniel Goleman and Emotional Intelligence, 'Why It Can Matter More than IQ', *Emotional Intelligence,* 1995.

14 Daniel Goleman, *Working with Emotional Intelligence* (Bantam, 1998), 317.

15 Abraham Carmeli, Meyrav Yitzhak-Halevy, and Jacob Weisberg, 'The Relationship between Emotional Intelligence and Psychological Wellbeing', *Journal of Managerial Psychology* 24, no. 1 (2009): 66–78; Gambill, 'Emotional Intelligence'; Moïra Mikolajczak, Clémentine Menil, and Olivier Luminet, 'Explaining the Protective Effect of Trait Emotional Intelligence Regarding Occupational Stress: Exploration of Emotional Labour Processes', *Journal of Research in Personality* 41, no. 5 (2007): 1107–17.

16 Evaluating Emotional Intelligence and D. Goleman, 'What Makes a Leader?', *Harvard Business Review,* 1998; John D. Mayer et al., 'Leading by Feel', *Harvard Business Review* 82, no. 1 (2004): 27–27.

17 Gambill, 'Emotional Intelligence'; Jill Anne Hendron, Pauline Irving, and Brian J. Taylor, 'The Emotionally Intelligent Ministry: Why It Matters', *Mental Health, Religion & Culture* 17, no. 5 (2014): 470–78; Randall, 'Emotional Intelligence'.

18 David Pizarro and Peter Salovey, 'Religious Systems as" Emotionally Intelligent" Organizations', *Psychological Inquiry* 13, no. 3 (2002): 221.

19 Gambill, 'Emotional Intelligence'; Hendron, Irving, and Taylor, 'The Emotionally Intelligent Ministry: Why It Matters'; Randall, 'Emotional Intelligence'.

20 Randall, 'Examining the Relationship between Burnout and Age among Anglican Clergy in England and Wales'; Hendron, Irving, and Taylor, 'The Emotionally Intelligent Ministry: Why It Matters'; Gambill, 'Emotional Intelligence'.

21 Randall, 'Emotional Intelligence', 8.

22 Gambill, 'Emotional Intelligence', 99.

23 Hendron, J., Irving, P., & Taylor, B. (2013). *The Emotionally Intelligent Ministry: why it matters. Mental Health, Religion & Culture,* 17(5), 470–478.

24 Richard Black, *Emotional Health in the Role of a Church Leader: A Critical Literature Review* (unpublished master's research project, Massey University, 2013).

25 Andrea Schlaerth, Nurcan Ensari, and Julie Christian, 'A Meta-Analytical Review of the Relationship between Emotional Intelligence and Leaders' Constructive Conflict Management', *Group Processes & Intergroup Relations* 16, no. 1 (2013): 126–36; Jeanne Morrison, 'The Relationship between Emotional Intelligence Competencies and Preferred Conflict-handling Styles', *Journal of Nursing Management* 16, no. 8 (2008): 974–83.

26 Gambill, 'Emotional Intelligence', 101.

Chapter 1:

1   Kerry Spackman, *The Winner's Bible: Rewire Your Brain for Permanent Change* (Greenleaf book group, 2009), 20–22.

2   Blake E Ashforth and Ronald H Humphrey, 'Emotional Labor in Service Roles: The Influence of Identity', *Academy of Management Review* 18, no. 1 (1993): 98.

3   Thomas V Frederick et al., 'The Effects of Role Differentiation Among Clergy: Impact on Pastoral Burnout and Job Satisfaction', *Pastoral Psychology*, 2023, 5; Céleste M. Brotheridge and Alicia A. Grandey, 'Emotional Labor and Burnout: Comparing Two Perspectives of "People Work"', *Journal of Vocational Behavior* 60, no. 1 (2002): 22.

4   Frederick et al., 'Role Differentiation', 5.

5   Irvine, 'Clergy Wellbeing', 13–14.

6   Glenn Packiam, *The Resilient Pastor: Leading Your Church in a Rapidly Changing World*, Kindle edition (Baker Books, 2022), 51.

7   Glenn Melville, 'Engaging Emotion: Using Critical Realism to Understand the Affective Well-Being of New Zealand Baptist Pastors, and to Design an Affective Well-Being Course' (Thesis, Auckland University of Technology, 2022).

8   Melville, 158–60.

9   Melville, 162.

10   Melville, 162.

11   Melville, 163.

12   Melville, 199–200.

13   Melville, 236.

14   Developing Terms of Call or a Letter of Appointment for a Minister | Presbyterian Church of Aotearoa New Zealand', accessed 26 May 2023, https://www.presbyterian.org.nz/for-parishes/calling-and-working-with-ministers/developing-terms-of-call-or-a-letter-of-appointment.

15   'What Is Calling?', CT Creative Studio, accessed 26 May 2023, https://www.christianitytoday.com/partners/nav-press/what-is-calling.html.

16   Neil Conway et al., 'Using Self-Determination Theory to Understand the Relationship between Calling Enactment and Daily Well-Being', *Journal of Organizational Behavior* 36, no. 8 (1 November 2015): 4–5; Ryan D Duffy et al., 'Work as a Calling: A Theoretical Model', *Journal of Counseling Psychology* 65, no. 4 (July 2018): 425; Meek et al., 'Maintaining Personal Resilience', 343.

17   Cook, 'Theorizing Identity Harm', 33–34.

18   Glen E. Kreiner, Elaine C. Hollensbe, and Mathew L. Sheep, 'Where Is the "Me" among the "We"? Identity Work and the Search for Optimal Balance', *Academy of Management Journal* 49, no. 5 (2006): 1040.

19   Unless otherwise stated, the pastors named in this book are not referring to one specific person but are representative of many pastors who have been experiencing something similar.

20   Peter Scazzero, *Emotionally Healthy Spirituality: Unleash a Revolution in Your Life in Christ* (Thomas Nelson, 2011), 27–28.

21   McMinn et al., 'Care for Pastors'.

22   Irvine, 'Clergy Wellbeing'.

23   Ashforth and Humphrey, 'Emotional Labor in Service Roles: The Influence of Identity', 92–94; Frederick et al., 'Role Differentiation', 6–8.

24   Frederick et al., 'Role Differentiation', 6.

25   Frederick et al., 6.

26 McMinn et al., 'Care for Pastors'.

27 Gambill, 'Emotional Intelligence', 101.

28 Packiam, *The Resilient Pastor*, 86.

29 Pooler, 'Pastors and Congregations'; Irvine, 'Clergy Wellbeing'; McMinn et al., 'Care for Pastors'.

30 Packiam, *The Resilient Pastor*, 87.

31 Melville, 'Engaging Emotion', 164.

32 Jules Badger, personal communication, 30 May 2023.

33 Irvine, 'Clergy Wellbeing', 9.

34 Kissell, 'Enhancing Ministry', 10; Pooler, 'Pastors and Congregations', 709; McMinn et al., 'Care for Pastors', 568.

35 Harold G. Koenig, 'Spirituality and Mental Health', *International Journal of Applied Psychoanalytic Studies* 7, no. 2 (2010): 116–22; Weaver et al., 'Mental Health Issues among Clergy and Other Religious Professionals: A Review of Research'.

36 Ellen Paek, 'Religiosity and Perceived Emotional Intelligence among Christians', *Personality and Individual Differences* 41, no. 3 (2006): 479–90.

37 Sarah Jenay Calvert, 'Attachment to God as a Source of Struggle and Strength: Exploring the Association between Christians' Relationship with God and Their Emotional Wellbeing' (Massey University, 2010); Ruth Harrowfield and Dianne Gardner, 'Faith at Work: Stress and Well-Being Among Workers in Christian Organizations', *Journal of Psychology & Christianity* 29, no. 3 (2010); Paek, 'Religiosity and Perceived Emotional Intelligence among Christians'; Tamara Joanne Williams, 'Vitality and Burnout of Employees in Christian Humanitarian Organisations: The Role of Need Satisfaction at Work and Religious Beliefs: A Thesis Presented in Partial Fulfilment of the Requirements for the Degree of Master of Arts in Psychology at Massey University, Albany, New Zealand' (Massey University, 2012).

Chapter 3:

1 Peter J. Burke and Jan E. Stets, *Identity Theory*, 2nd Edition (New York: Oxford University Press, 2023), 168–70; Pooler, 'Pastors and Congregations', p.707-708; Frederick et al., 'Role Differentiation', 5.

2 Burke and Stets, *Identity Theory*, 179.

3 Burke and Stets, 179–85; Kreiner, Hollensbe, and Sheep, 'Identity Work', 1032.

4 Peter M. Senge, *The Fifth Discipline: The Art and Practice of the Learning Organization* (New York: Doubleday, 2006), 18.

5 Irvine, 'Clergy Wellbeing', 14; McMinn et al., 'Care for Pastors', 564.

6 Meek et al., 'Maintaining Personal Resilience', 342.

7 Kreiner, Hollensbe, and Sheep, 'Identity Work', 1031.

8 Kreiner, Hollensbe, and Sheep, 1039.

9 Melville, 'Engaging Emotion', 202.

10 Melville, 165.

11 Melville, 164.

12 Melville, 159–64.

13 Burke and Stets, *Identity Theory*, 169–70.

14 Nieuwhof, C. (n.d.). *29% of pastors want to quit: How to keep going when you've lost confidence in yourself*. CareyNieuwhof.com. Retrieved November 27, 2025, from https://

careynieuwhof.com/29-of-pastors-want-to-quit-how-to-keep-going-when-youve-lost-confidence-in-yourself/

15 Ashforth and Humphrey, 'Emotional Labor in Service Roles: The Influence of Identity', 106.

16 Allison K. Hamm and David E. Eagle, 'Clergy Who Leave Congregational Ministry: A Review of the Literature', *Journal of Psychology and Theology* 49, no. 4 (2021): 291.

17 Kissell, 'Enhancing Ministry', 10.

18 Carey Nieuwhof, *Leading Healthy Churches,* Conference, Grace Vineyard Church, Christchurch, 15 May, 2018.

19 Irvine, 'Clergy Wellbeing', 14; McMinn et al., 'Care for Pastors', 564.

20 Melville, 'Engaging Emotion', 150.

21 Kreiner, Hollensbe, and Sheep, 'Identity Work', 1031; Pooler, 'Pastors and Congregations', 707–8; Michael E Clinton, Neil Conway, and Jane Sturges, '"It's Tough Hanging-up a Call": The Relationships between Calling and Work Hours, Psychological Detachment, Sleep Quality, and Morning Vigor', *Journal of Occupational Health Psychology* 22, no. 1 (2017): 27.

22 Jan E. Stets and Peter J. Burke, *Identity Theory.* (Oxford University Press, 2009), 136.

23 Melville, 'Engaging Emotion', 151.

24 Pooler, 'Pastors and Congregations', 708.

25 Kreiner, Hollensbe, and Sheep, 'Identity Work', 1031.

26 Pooler, 'Pastors and Congregations', 708.

Chapter 4

1 Alan Hirsch and Mark Nelson, *Reframation: Seeing God, People, and Mission through Reenchanted Frames* (100 Movements Publishing, 2019), 58.

2 Os Guinness, *The Call: Finding and Fulfilling God's Purpose for Your Life* (Thomas Nelson, 2018), 31.

3 Conway et al., 'Using Self-Determination Theory', 1114; Duffy et al., 'Work as a Calling', 423.

4 Duffy et al., 'Work as a Calling', 426.

5 Conway et al., 'Using Self-Determination Theory', 1116; Duffy et al., 'Work as a Calling', 426.

6 DK Chen, 'Pastoral Identity, Calling, Burnout, and Resilience', *ProQuest Dissertations and Theses Global,* 2020, 2; Jeffery A. Thompson and J. Stuart Bunderson, 'Research on Work as a Calling...and How to Make It Matter', *Annual Review of Organizational Psychology & Organizational Behavior* 6 (January 2019): 426.

Chapter 5

1 Stephen R. Covey, *The 7 Habits of Highly Effective People* (Simon & Schuster, 2020), 101.

2 Melville, 'Engaging Emotion', 164.

3 Melville, 164.

4 Melville, 164.

5 Melville, 164.

6 Melville, 164.

Chapter 6

1 Tak Bhana, New Zealand and Beyond Conference, 2023.

Chapter 7

1 Senge, *The Fifth Discipline,* 84–85; Michael P. Nichols and Richard C. Schwartz, *The Essentials of Family Therapy* (Pearson/Allyn and Bacon Publishers, 2009), 55–57; John McLeod, *An Introduction to Counselling* (McGraw Hill education (UK), 2013), 210; David L. Fenell, *Counseling Families: An Introduction to Marriage and Family Therapy,* 3rd ed (Denver: Love Pub, 2002), 156.
2 Melville, 'Engaging Emotion', 164.
3 Melville, 164.
4 New Zealand ministerial training institutions also have the influencing factor of having to provide training for pastoral roles that meet the New Zealand Qualifications Authority's (NZQA) requirements. It is not clear to what degree this is, or is not, a factor contributing to unhelpful homeostatic forces.

Chapter 8

1 Senge, *The Fifth Discipline,* 64.

Interlude

1 W. E. Vine, Merrill F. Unger, and William White Jr., *Vine's Complete Expository Dictionary of Old and New Testament Words* (Nashville, TN: T. Nelson, 1996), 58.

Chapter 9

1 Kissell, 'Enhancing Ministry', 162.
2 Thomas Frederick, Susan Purrington, and Scott Dunbar, 'Differentiation of Self, Religious Coping, and Subjective Well-Being', *Mental Health, Religion & Culture* 19, no. 6 (2016): 555; Gregory D Wasberg, 'Differentiation of Self and Leadership Effectiveness in Christian Clergy: A Mixed Methods Study', 2013, 3; Simon Hardesty Stokes, 'Learning to Sail in the Storm: Integrating Murray Bowen's Concept of Differentiation of Self with Pastoral Theology and Leadership' (PhD diss., Duke University, 2020), 21; Sarah A. Crabtree et al., 'Humility, Differentiation of Self, and Clinical Training in Spiritual and Religious Competence', *Journal of Spirituality in Mental Health* 23, no. 4 (2021): 346.
3 Frederick, Purrington, and Dunbar, 'Differentiation of Self', 22; Kissell, 'Enhancing Ministry', 22.
4 Daniel Goleman, 'Emotional Intelligence. Why It Can Matter More than IQ', *Learning* 24, no. 6 (1996): 49–50; Peter Salovey and John D. Mayer, 'Emotional Intelligence: Imagination, Cognition and Personality', *Imagination, Cognition and Personality* 9, no. 3 (1990): 1989–90.
5 Frederick et al., 'Role Differentiation', 18.
6 Beebe, 'Predicting Burnout'; Frederick, Purrington, and Dunbar, 'Differentiation of Self'; Frederick, Dunbar, and Thai, 'Burnout in Christian Perspective'; Frederick and Dunbar, *Work and Family Burnout;* Dunbar et al., 'Calling, Caring, and Connecting'; Frederick and Dunbar, *Identity, Calling, and Workplace Spirituality;* Frederick et al., 'Role Differentiation'.
7 Beebe, 'Predicting Burnout', p.266-268; Dunbar et al., 'Calling, Caring, and Connecting', p.176-178; Frederick et al., 'Role Differentiation', p.17-18; Kissell, 'Enhancing Ministry', 36; Wasberg, 'Differentiation of Self', 68–69; Crabtree et al., 'Humility, Differentiation of Self, and Clinical Training in Spiritual and Religious Competence', 346; Çiğdem Yavuz Güler and Tuğba Karaca, 'The Role of Differentiation of Self in Predicting Rumination and

Emotion Regulation Difficulties', *Contemporary Family Therapy* 43, no. 2 (2021): 118–21.

8   Beebe, 'Predicting Burnout', p.266-271; Frederick, Purrington, and Dunbar, 'Differentiation of Self', p.5-8; Frederick et al., 'Role Differentiation', p.17-18.

9   Frederick and Dunbar, *Work and Family Burnout*, p.49-51; Frederick et al., 'Role Differentiation', p.9-16; Kissell, 'Enhancing Ministry', p.40-47; Wasberg, 'Differentiation of Self', p.110-113.

10   Wasberg, 'Differentiation of Self', 68–69.

11   Frederick et al., 'Role Differentiation', p.15.

12   Kissell, 'Enhancing Ministry', 34; Elijah Lee, 'An Examination of Attachment to God, Individualism, Collectivism, and Differentiation of Self in Second-Generation Christian Korean Americans' (Regent University, 2020), 68; Peter J. Jankowski and Steven J. Sandage, 'Attachment to God and Humility: Indirect Effect and Conditional Effects Models', *Journal of Psychology and Theology* 42, no. 1 (2014): 78; Wasberg, 'Differentiation of Self', 36.

13   Paek, 'Religiosity and Perceived Emotional Intelligence among Christians'.

14   Beebe, 'Predicting Burnout', 269.

15   Gambill, 'Emotional Intelligence', 101.

16   Gambill, 101.

17   Beebe, 'Predicting Burnout', 260–62; Cook, 'Theorizing Identity Harm', 33–34; *Samuel Park, Pastoral Identity as Social Construction: An Exploration of Pastoral Identity in Postmodern, Intercultural, and Multifaith Contexts* (Texas Christian University, 2010), 93–94.

18   Senge, *The Fifth Discipline*, 84–88; Fenell, *Counseling Families*, 156.

19   Kissell, 'Enhancing Ministry', 162.

20   Melville, 167.

21   Melville, 167.

22   Melville, 167.

23   Melville, 168.

24   Dunbar et al., 'Calling, Caring, and Connecting', 178.

25   Dunbar et al., 179.

26   Frederick and Dunbar, *Identity, Calling, and Workplace Spirituality*, 25.

27   Guinness, *The Call*, 31.

28   Guinness, 31.

29   Christopher J. Cocksworth and Rosalind Brown, *Being a Priest Today* (Canterbury Press, 2006), 5.

30   Packiam, *The Resilient Pastor*, 59.

31   Frederick et al., 'Role Differentiation', p.17-18.

32   Frederick and Dunbar, *Identity, Calling, and Workplace Spirituality*, 48–49.

Chapter 10

1   Samuel Seung Yeop Lee, 'Central Role of Spiritual Identity in Youth Ministry: Integrating Henri Nouwen's" Life of the Beloved."' (Thesis, Acadia University, 2022), 22.

2   Henri Nouwen, *Life of the Beloved: Spiritual Living in a Secular World* (London: Great Britain: Hodder and Stoughton, 1992), 27.

3   Myk Habets, 'Spirit, Selfhood, and Salvation', in *Being Saved: Explorations in Soteriology and Human Persons*, ed. M. Cortez, J. R. Farris, and S. M. Hamilton (London: SCM Press, 2018), 147.

4   R. Black, *Centred: Knowing Who You Are in an Off-Balanced World* (Mainly Music International Trust, 2019).

5   Jack O. Balswick, Pamela Ebstyne King, and Kevin S. Reimer, *The Reciprocating Self:*

Human Development in Theological Perspective (Illinois: InterVarsity Press, 2016). Chpt 2.
6 Sue Johnson, *Hold Me Tight: Your Guide to the Most Successful Approach to Building Loving Relationships* (Hachette UK, 2011), 129; Lori Heyman Gordon and Virginia M. Satir, *Passage to Intimacy: A Practical Guide to Repairing and Rekindling Your Most Important Relationship* (Simon and Schuster, 1993), 33.
7 This definition has been attributed to different people over the years, most recently to Danielle Strickland.

Chapter 11

1 Myk Habets, 'Spirit, Selfhood, and Salvation', 147.
2 Marc Cortez, *Christological Anthropology in Historical Perspective: Ancient and Contemporary Approaches to Theological Anthropology* (Grand Rapids: Zondervan Academic, 2016), 21.
3 Marc Cortez, *ReSourcing Theological Anthropology: A Constructive Account of Humanity in the Light of Christ* (Grand Rapids: Zondervan Academic, 2018), 259.
4 Cortez, *ReSourcing Theological Anthropology, 186–87; Cortez, Christological Anthropology, 27–28.*
5 Myk Habets, 'Spirit, Selfhood, and Salvation', 147.
6 Andy Thrasher, 'Substantial Persons in Trinitarian Relationality: Trinitarian Theology, Imago Dei, and Personhood', in *Eastern Regional Conference, Evangelical Theological Society,* 2017, 15.
7 Torrance, Thomas F., *The Mediation of Christ,* Revised edition (Edinburgh: T&T Clark, n.d.), 80.
8 Kathryn Tanner, *Christ the Key* (Cambridge: Cambridge University Press, 2010), 57.
9 Myk Habets, 'On Getting First Things First: Assessing Claims for the Primacy of Christ', New Blackfriars 90, no. 1027 (2009): 358.
10 Habets, 'Spirit, Selfhood, and Salvation', 150.
11 Habets, 150. Quoting Torrance.
12 Stokes, 'Sail in the Storm', 40.
13 Habets, 'Spirit, Selfhood, and Salvation', 150.
14 Henri Nouwen, *Life of the Beloved,* 26.
15 Stanley J. Grenz, 'The Social God and the Relational Self: Toward a Theology of the "Imago Dei" in the Postmodern Context', *Personal Identity in Theological Perspective,* 2006, 92.
16 Kenneth L. Barker and John R. Kohlenberger, eds., *Zondervan NIV Bible Commentary* (Grand Rapids: Zondervan Pub. House, 1994), 728.
17 Stanley J. Grenz, *The Social God and the Relational Self: A Trinitarian Theology of the Imago Dei,* vol. 1 (London: Westminster John Knox Press, 2001), 325.
18 Henri J. M. Nouwen, Rebecca Laird, and Michael J Christensen, *Discernment: Reading the Signs of Daily Life* (HarperOne, 2013), 136.

Chapter 12

1 Dunbar et al., 'Calling, Caring, and Connecting', 180; Lee, 'Life of the Beloved', 31.
2 Timothy Friberg, Barbara Friberg, and Neva F. Miller, *Analytical Lexicon of the Greek New Testament,* Baker's Greek New Testament Library 4 (Grand Rapids: Baker Books, 2000), 178.
3 Friberg, Friberg, and Miller, 287.

Chapter 15

1 Melville, 'Engaging Emotion', 159–60.
2 Irvine, 'Clergy Wellbeing', 13–14.
3 Lynne Taylor, 'Pastors in Transition - 2023 Insights' (Baptist Union of New Zealand, 2023), 4.
4 Conway et al., 'Using Self-Determination Theory', 1126.
5 Chen, 'Pastoral Identity', 2; Thompson and Bunderson, 'Work as a Calling', 426.
6 Brianna Wiest, 'This Is What Self-Care Really Means, Because It's Not All Salt Baths And Chocolate Cake', n.d., https://thoughtcatalog.com/brianna-wiest/2024/04/this-is-what-self-care-really-means-because-its-not-all-salt-baths-and-chocolate-cake-2/.
7 Duffy et al., 'Work as a Calling', 429.
8 Frederick and Dunbar, *Identity, Calling, and Workplace Spirituality*, 67–88.
9 Frederick and Dunbar, 79.
10 Duffy et al., 'Work as a Calling', 429–30.

Chapter 16

1 Packiam, *The Resilient Pastor*, 130.
2 Packiam, 132.